For You

TABLE OF CONTENTS

I. Introduction
II. Highlighted Biographies
Edward Albee: Pulitzer-Prize winning Playwright 11
Sir Alexander Bustamante: Prime Minister of Jamaica 14
George Washington Carver: Scientist 18
Jacqueline Cochran: Aviator 23
William Lloyd Garrison: Abolitionist 29
Evonne Goolagong: World Tennis Champion 37
Alexander Hamilton: First U.S. Secretary of the Treasury 42
Scott Hamilton: Olympic Skater 51
John Lennon: Singer/Songwriter 56
Hugh Leonard: Irish Author 67
Gregory Louganis: Olympic Diver 70
Lue Gim Gong: The Orange Wizard 74
Catherine McCauley: Founder of the Sisters of Mercy 79
James Albert Michener: Bestselling Novelist 87
Carlos Montezuma: Indian Doctor 89
Moses: Receiver of the Ten Commandments 94
Jim Palmer: Baseball Player 96
Edgar Allan Poe: American Author 98
Eleanor Roosevelt: First Lady of the World 106
Sir Henry Morton Stanley: Explorer 112
R. David Thomas: Founder of Wendy's International 120
Maria von Trapp: Singer and Refugee from Nazi Germany 124
Edgar Wallace: Novelist 129
Phillis Wheatley: Black Poet of the American Revolution 131
Daniel Hale Williams: History-Making Surgeon 140
III. Brief Biographies
George Hamilton-Gordon Aberdeen: British Prime Minister 147
Jean Le Rond d'Alembert: Mathematician and Philosopher 147
Josephine Antoine: Opera Singer 148
Aristotle: Greek Philosopher 149

Relative Origins

Ingrid Bergman: Actress 149
John Green Brady: Governor of Alaska 150
Angie Elizabeth Brooks: Government official, diplomat, lawyer . . 150
Rosie Casals: Tennis Star 151
Catherine I: Empress of Russia 152
Nicolas Sebastien-Roche Chamfort: Playwright, Conversationalist 153
Jean Baptiste Charbonneau: Mountainman, guide 153
Edward Day Collins: Educator 154
Countée Porter Cullen: American Poet 154
Dalai Lama: Spiritual and Temporal Ruler of Tibet 155
Alexandra Danilova: Ballerina 156
Peter Duchin: Pianist 156
Peter Francisco: Revolutionary War Hero 157
Sir Matthew Hale: Lord Chief Justice of England 158
John Hancock: Signer of the U.S. Declaration of Independence . . 158
Deborah Ann Harry, "Blondie" Singer 159
Joseph Haydn: Austrian Composer 160
Lemuel Haynes: Minuteman/Clergyman 161
Herbert Hoover: 31st U.S. President 162
Langston Hughes: Poet 163
Stonewall Jackson: Confederate General 164
Steven Paul Jobs: Cofounder, Apple Computer 165
Frederick Mckinley Jones: Inventor 166
Benito Juárez: National Hero and President of Mexico 167
Edmund Kean: English Actor 168
Rudyard Kipling: English Author 168
John Mercer Langston: Black leader, Educator, Diplomat 169
Robert Laurent: Sculptor 170
Malcolm X: Militant Black Leader 171
Nelson Mandela: South African Political Leader 171
Harry Martinson: Nobel Prize for Literature 172
Stan Mikita: Hockey Player 173
Marilyn Monroe: Actress 174
Anthony Newley: Actor, Director, Writer, Singer, Composer . . . 175
Gabriel Pascal: Film Director 176
Pierre Esprit Radisson: French Explorer and Fur Trader 177
Harold Robbins: Bestselling Novelist 178
John Baptist Rossi: Saint 179
Jean Jacques Rousseau: French writer and Philosopher 179
William Tecumseh Sherman: Civil War General 180
Vishwanath Pratap Singh: Prime Minister of India 181
Robyn Smith: Jockey 182
Dame Kiri (Janette) Te Kanawa: Opera Singer 182

Table of Contents

Giovanni Battista Tiepolo: Italian Painter 183
Leo Tolstoy: Russian Novelist 183
Francois Truffaut: French Film Critic and Director 184
Maxime Weygand: Commander-in-chief of Allied Armies 185
Flip Wilson: Comedian 185

IV. Foster and Adopted Children in Fiction

Louisa May Alcott: Little Men 187
Mildred Ames: Foster Home 187
Frank Baum: The Wizard of Oz 187
Anne Bernays: Growing Up Rich 188
Rose Blue: Seven Years From Home 188
David Budbill: Bones on Black Spruce Mountain 188
Frances Hodgson Burnett: The Secret Garden 189
Betsy Cromer Byars: The Pinballs 189
Helen Fern Daringer: Adopted Jane 189
Charles Dickens: David Copperfield 189
Judith Guest: Second Heaven 190
Nan Hayden: Joe Bean 190
Roberta Hughey: Radio City 190
Louis L'Amour: Reilly's Luck 190
Rutgers van der Loeff: Children on the Oregon Trail 191
George Eliot: Silas Marner 191
Lucy Maud Montgomery: Anne of Green Gables 191
Thomas Meehan: Annie 191
Eleanor Porter: Pollyanna 192
Jim Razzi (adapter): Pinoccio 192
Ovida Sebestyen: Far From Home 192
Roberta Silman: Somebody Else's Child 192
Mark Twain: Tom Sawyer 193
Jean Webster: Daddy Long Legs 193
T. H. White: The Once and Future King, ... 193

V Afterword
VI Bibliography

INTRODUCTION

We share as human beings the uncertainty of our past. No one has been able to answer satisfactorily those eternal, compelling questions: Where do we come from? How did we get here? Where are we going to?

The early Greeks became famous for their myths that tried to answer these haunting questions. Although the myth of *Orpheus and Eurydice* does not attempt to unlock the mystery of our past, it raises the even more pertinent issue of what attitude to take toward our past. It is the story of a handsome young musician named Orpheus and a beautiful girl named Eurydice. Orpheus played on his lyre . . . music so enchanting that animals, trees, and even stones followed him, and rivers, too, stopped their constant rushing to listen in wonder. Orpheus soon fell deeply in love with Eurydice. One day, Aristaeus, the beekeeper, saw Eurydice and he, too, fell in love with the charming girl. Loyal to Orpheus, Eurydice tried to escape from Aristaeus, but as she ran away a snake bit her foot and she died. Beside himself with grief, Orpheus could not contemplate living without her. He decided to venture into the Lower World and bring her back to earth. Hades, god of the dead, was so impressed by his music that he agreed to grant Orpheus his dearest wish — but only on one condition: that he not look back at Eurydice as they climbed the steep, narrow path on the way up to earth. But Orpheus loved Eurydice so much, and he had been without her for so long that, unable to help himself, he glanced back too soon and Eurydice vanished. The remainder of Orpheus' life on earth became sheer misery as he pined away for his missing love.

The story of *Orpheus and Eurydice* encloses a powerful message. It is natural for people tow ant to look back at the past. But if, as in the case of Orpheus, we look back too much . . . we cannot go on with the process of living.

The famous people contained in this book are real people who lived and breathed and dreamed. Some are still living today. They share in common the fact that they were raised — for part or the entirety of their childhood — by people other than their biological parents. There were times when many were unsure of themselves and felt keenly the missing link in their past. Most learned that life is not always easy and there are times when we feel empty or filled with unhappiness. But they came to see life as a precious gift which they chose to live in benefit of others, changing the world for better. We admire them today and hold them up as heroes. They understood that the hope for the continuation of the human race begins anew with each individual. They dared to write their own history. But above all, they share in common the ability, the courage, the determination to look forward to the future with optimism.

HIGHLIGHTED BIOGRAPHIES

Edward Albee   (1928-)
Pulitzer-Prize Winning Playwright

Who's Afraid of Virginia Woolf? Not Edward Albee! This play describing the rocky
marriage of a college professor and his wife is considered by many critics to be
Albee's finest work. Abandoned by his natural parents after his birth on March 12,
1928 in Washington D.C., the baby was speedily adopted by millionaire Reed A.
Albee and his wife Frances of New York. After much thought, they decided to
name their new son Edward Franklin Albee III for his adoptive grandfather, who
was part-owner of over two-hundred very successful vaudeville theaters. These
theaters extended from coast to coast and were known as the Keith-Albee Theater
Circuit.

Edward Albee does not know his natural parents. In fact, in the plays that have
skyrocketed him to fame there often appears an abandoned child. Many of his plays
deal with the topic of rejection. His well-known play *The Death of Bessie Smith,*
for example, is about a southern hospital's refusal to admit a black singer.

As a child Edward lived in a huge Tudor house filled with servants. He took riding
lessons, often spent his winters in Miami or Palm Beach and his summers sailing
on Long Island Sound. He had a number of pets, including a St. Bernard who would
pull him around the snow-blanketed grounds on his sleigh and an assortment of
guinea pigs. Little Edward was especially close to his maternal grandmother. Later,
he would dedicate his popular play *The Sandbox* to her. Growing up, Edward came
into contact with such writers as Thornton Wilder and W.H. Auden. Wilder would
later encourage Edward to try his hand at writing plays.

From an early age Edward loved transforming the world around him into words.
He began writing poetry at age six. At twelve, Edward composed his first play,
three acts long, entitled *Aliqueen*. A couple of years later, he decided to scratch out

11

a novel and ended up with 1,800 pages. At sixteen, he wrote another novel, this time a mere 900 pages.

Although Edward loved to write, he could barely stomach school. With all his heart he hated sitting in straight rows, in stuffy rooms, his lungs filling with chalk dust, only to move, with the other students, like a herd of cattle, at the sound of the bell. Part of the problem came from the fact that Edward was constantly being uprooted. Frequently his parents spent their winters in Florida and Arizona and Edward would have to change schools.

After attending the Rye Country Day School, he went to the Lawrenceville preparatory school in New Jersey hut was expelled for cutting classes. Next he was thrown out of the Valley Forge Military Academy in Pennsylvania. Edward was sent then to Choate, a preparatory school in Connecticut. Here, at last, Edward seemed to find a school where he was happy. His English teacher at Choate says he remembers the day that Edward came into his classroom, the flush of inspiration still on his cheeks, and proudly handed him fifty big, hand-written pages.

The director of Admissions at Choate predicted that Edward would be a successful writer. Yet no one can foretell the future and by most people's standards, Edward, so far, was a disaster. After all, he had been expelled not only from preparatory schools, but even from a military academy! But his two years at Choate, Albee says, fueled his dream of becoming a writer. At Choate he received what he most needed: encouragement. His poems, short stories, essays, and one play were published in the Choate Literary Magazine. In 1945, he even succeeded in having his poem entitled *Eighteen* published in *Kaleidoscope*, a Texas magazine.

After graduating from Choate, Albee went to Trinity College in Connecticut. There he learned about some of the practical aspects of writing and producing plays as the Emperor Franz Joseph in Maxwell Anderson's *The Masque of Kings*. Albee was asked to leave Trinity, though, after only a year and a half for — again — cutting classes and not attending Chapel. This same student — some years, many plays and prizes later — would be awarded an honorary Doctorate of Literature from Emerson College in Boston, and from Trinity itself in 1974, as well as becoming a distinguished lecturer in universities in the United States and in other countries.

After leaving Trinity, Edward wrote music programs for radio station WNYC. Then Edward decided it was time for him to gain new experiences. In his heart he was determined to become a writer. Albee's parents were saddened when he left home in 1950. They even tried to stop him. But with a pen in his pocket he left to try life on his own and to unravel onto paper the lines that would crease his brow.

His adoptive grandmother had set him up in 1949 with a $100,000 trust fund. According to the terms of the trust fund, Albee was to receive approximately $250 a month from age twenty-one until his thirtieth birthday, after which he would come into full possession of the money. Even so, life in Manhattan was expensive and Albee shared an apartment in Greenwich Village, taking on odd jobs. During these years Albee moved to several different places. But through it all, says Albee's friend, William Flanagan, Albee remained firm in his resolve to become a writer.

In 1958, just before Albee's thirtieth birthday, when it was beginning to look as if Albee's dream was merely a dream and nothing more, he plunked himself down at his wobbly kitchen table, and, using some poor quality yellow paper, banged out *The Zoo Story* on an old typewriter.

Three weeks later, when he typed out the last letter of the last line of the play, Albee jumped up from the table — the play was good and he knew it! But even then it was not easy for Albee; the play was rejected. Shoulders sagging he walked back to his apartment.

It was then that William Flanagan decided to take matters in his own hands. He put the play in a large envelope, licked a stamp and sent it to David Diamond in Florence, Italy, who sent it to Pinkas Braun, an actor in Zurich, who, in his turn, sent it to Mrs. Stefani Hunzinger, director of the dramatic department of S. Fischer, a big German publishing house in Frankfurt. It was in this roundabout fashion that the play was finally produced by Boleslaw Barlos at the Schiller Theater Werkstatt on September 28, 1959 in Berlin. Excited, Albee booked a flight to Germany to see his play on stage. But as Albee sat among the audience, he was more in the dark than anyone. Albee could not understand a single word of the German translation! The play was produced in twelve other German cities. Then, this same play that had not so long before been rejected in New York was rapidly produced at the off-Broadway Provincetown Playhouse in Greenwich Village on January 14, 1960.

In 1962 Albee directed the production of his play *The Sandbox* at the Cherry Lane Theater. Like Jerry in *The Zoo Story,* Grandma in *The Sandbox* also feels abandoned. She is eighty-six years old and her daughter and son-in-law are waiting for her to die. Also in 1962 Albee's *Who's Afraid of Virginia Woolf?* was produced on Broadway, winning the Drama Critic's Award, five Antoinette Perry Awards for directing and acting, the Foreign Press Association Award, and other prizes.

It was fast becoming clear that in America Albee was a leader in the "theater of the absurd" which is a form of theater that uses fantasy and surrealism (dreamlike distortions of real life) to point out how absurd human life can be in an irrational world. The Foreign Press Association Award of 1960-61 went to Albee for his plays *The Death of Bessie Smith* and *The American Dream.* He won this prize again in 1963, to become the first two-time winner in the history of this award. Along with Richard Barr and Clinton Wilder, the producers of *The Zoo Story,* Albee, in 1964, continued his work in the theater of the absurd, with a group called "Theater 1964."

In the 1963-64 theater season, four of Albee's plays ran more or less simultaneously. The play *Who's Afraid of Virginia Woolf?* ended after an incredible 663 performances, *The Ballad of the Sad Cafe* after 124, *The American Dream* and *The Zoo Story,* which ran on the same bill, after 143 performances. Albee sold the movie rights to *Who's Afraid of Virginia Woolf?* to Warner Brothers for approximately $500,000 which would become an Oscar-winning movie in 1966.

Albee has become well known for helping young playwrights. In 1963, with Barr and Clinton Wilder, Albee created the Playwrights Unit, whose purpose was specifically to aid new and inexperienced playwrights. For nine years the Playwrights Unit was kept in operation.

Albee's interests range from taking long walks to bowling, reading, modern painting, listening to music, and a preference for Pekingese dogs. Albee is quick to criticize the lazy attitude among some Americans who see no point in doing anything besides sitting and watching television.

There was no way, of course, that Reed or Frances Albee could have known on the happy trip home from Washington D.C. so many years before that their son would one day become one of America's most enduring playwrights. During the 1960s Edward Albee ruled the American stage, frequently directing his own plays. In 1967 and 1975 he won Pulitzer prizes for, respectively, *A Delicate Balance* and *Seascape.* In 1985 Edward Albee was inducted into the Theater Hall of Fame.

Sir Alexander Bustamante (1884 - 1977)
Prime Minister of Jamaica

The island of Jamaica — a paradise of sandy beaches, clear streams, brilliant flowers and birds, cool mountains, and blue lagoons. Slightly smaller than the state of Connecticut, Jamaica is part of the Greater Antilles, and is located four hundred eighty miles south of Florida. The trade winds blow through Jamaica and the temperature is fairly constant between seventy-six and eighty-one degrees Fahrenheit. The motto on Jamaica's coat of arms says "Out of Many, One" and refers to the Africans, Asians, and Europeans that inhabit the island, forming a beautiful kaleidoscope of cultures.

When Columbus sighted Jamaica in 1494 the island was inhabited by the Arawak Indians who had come from South America hundreds of years before. The Spaniards, more interested in other, richer colonies, neglected the island. In 1655 Britain took Jamaica for itself. Throughout the years in which Britain ruled the island, the government suffered many attacks from the Maroons, who were descendants of slaves that escaped the cruelty of their Spanish and English masters in the 17th and 18th centuries, and who retreated to inaccessible hideouts in the hills.

On this island where the imagination conjures up pirate ships and buried treasure, William Alexander Clarke was born in the year 1884. His father was a planter from Ireland and his mother was an Arawak Indian. The Clarkes had thirteen children and were very poor. Tragically, in this tropical world of plenty, the Clarke children often went hungry, and day after day there was work to be done. It was not a happy time in the life of little Alexander and one that he did not want to remember.

But when Alexander was fifteen a most extraordinary occurrence took place that was going to change the course of his whole life. An officer from the Spanish army, Colonel Arnulfo Bustamante — attracted by what he had read of the famous island — came to Jamaica on vacation. It is not clear how this officer met young Alexander but he took an immediate liking to the boy that soon turned to affection. Colonel Bustamante soon realized Alexander's great potential had not so far been tapped, and legally adopted the boy. When his vacation ended he took Alexander back to Spain with him.

Colonel Bustamante was wealthy and moved in the best circles. At first Alexander found the new country and customs very strange and he could not understand the language. But his father engaged tutors for him and Alexander — an excellent pupil eager to please his father — learned quickly, his sharp mind absorbing all subjects he was taught. Soon his knowledge of Spanish enabled him to attend the Royal Academy of Spain, and a few years later he graduated, making his father a very proud man.

It was natural that Alexander should follow his adoptive father's footsteps by enlisting in the Spanish Army. At that time Spain was engaged in a bloody battle against the Riff tribes in Spanish Morocco, a long and bitter war in which many lives were lost. The discipline required to survive fighting in hot, uncomfortable, harsh and arid North Africa contributed to form young Bustamante's character. Fighting took on a guerrilla quality, resembling the warfare of the Maroons in his native Jamaica and the battles of the American army against the Indians in the American West. Bustamante fought with courage, but ambushes were common and during one such skirmish the Riffs captured Bustamante. Using all his cunning and knowledge of the tribesmen and of the terrain, he managed to escape, running for his life through desert country, without food, water or weapons. Managing to reach a village he escaped dressed as a nun, not an easy feat for a broad-shouldered man over six feet four inches tall.

When Bustamante left Morocco, he left his military career behind but continued his adventures in far-away places. "Busta" — as he was called years later by the Jamaicans — wanted to continue learning and wished to see the world. He became an inspector of police in Havana, a traffic manager for a streetcar in Panama, and even worked as a dietician in New York's Hospital for Joint Diseases. But in every job he undertook he performed his duties well.

While Bustamante was in New York City, in the year 1929, the stock market crashed. People panicked all across the country, as entire fortunes were lost. Bustamante, however, did not panic, seeing instead his opportunity to become wealthy. He invested his few savings and the money he obtained he loaned at an interest, and his profits soared. In a short time he was so well off that his entire future was assured.

Then, with no financial worries, Bustamante decided to visit the island he had left as a poor youth. As he had no children, and he wanted to return to others the kindness he had received from his adoptive father, he began to ask himself where his efforts would be most useful. Looking around him at the condition of his lovely island, he decided to devote his talents to improve the plight of the worker. His tool: the pen he had learned to use so well. He wrote letters to Jamaican and English newspapers to make the public aware of the injustices committed by the government against the workers.

When in 1938 there were strikes, riots, and other clashes between employers and workers, Bustamante saw that the time had come to act. He called the workers to organize and to demand better housing and better pay. Bustamante knew the risks he was taking and, indeed, he was arrested and jailed as an agitator. The charges had to be withdrawn, much to the chagrin of the government, and no sooner was he out of jail than "Busta" formed the Bustamante Industrial Trade Union, soon the largest on the island. Bustamante spared no effort in his crusade: in 1939 he called for an island-wide strike. Invoking emergency defense regulations, the government succeeded in stopping the strike. And although the government also interned him, hoping to put an end to what they considered his troublemaking, nothing could stop Bustamante.

A man of high principles, Bustamante did not let intimidation affect his actions. The workers needed help and he was going to provide that help. As soon as he was released from his internment, Bustamante reorganized the Bustamante Industrial Trade Union, forming the Labour Party of Jamaica.

Bustamante had accomplished his objective. He had stirred the government in London to action; a commission was sent to investigate the conditions on the island. The investigation was thorough and resulted, in 1944, in a new constitution for Jamaica. Now all Jamaican adults could vote, and the local government was given freedom to make more decisions. A House of Representatives with thirty-two members was created and elections were held. As was expected, Bustamante's party won and he himself became Minister of Communications. This was only the first in a long series of government positions. Among others "Busta" was the mayor of Kingston, the capital of the island, and Chief Minister of Jamaica.

Bustamante kept his party in power for ten long years. In 1955 — in the colorful, ages-old ceremony of chivalry — Bustamante was knighted for his services to Jamaica by Queen Elizabeth II of Great Britain. No greater honor could be wished or conveyed upon a British subject, and was an unparalleled recognition for the once poor little boy who did not even have enough to eat.

Now a new issue confronted Jamaica: Should the island become independent? A majority of Jamaicans chose to become independent, and in 1962 Bustamante once more became their leader. He knew that his little island could not defend itself if attacked, and he made a treaty with the United States for protection should invasion occur. With his country secure, Bustamante lent his efforts to preparing the needed new constitution as Jamaica was now an independent nation with dominion status within the British Commonwealth.

Under the intelligent leadership of "Busta" Jamaica joined the United Nations, and the International Monetary Fund. Bustamante initiated programs to establish new schools, hospitals, build new houses, plan new roads and land reforms and to deal with unemployment. In 1962 Bustamante supported President Kennedy's blockade of Cuba during the missile crisis.

In his personal life Bustamante suffered the loss of a wife he dearly loved, and he had no children. After many years of living alone, he married again in 1962 to the woman who had been his indefatigable private secretary for twenty-seven years.

Sir Alexander's record is impressive. He spoke with a conviction that aroused crowds to action, possessed great courage, and was a friend of the underprivileged whose cause he always defended. Born a poor boy, given no schooling, he was adopted by a loving father and rose to the highest possible position in the country of his birth. Sir Alexander Bustamante died in 1977, but his memory lives on in the hearts and minds of all Jamaicans.

George Washington Carver

(1859?-1943)

Scientist

"Four score and seven years ago our fathers brought forth, upon this continent, a new nation, conceived in Liberty, and dedicated to the proposition that all men are created equal."

These were the words of Abraham Lincoln in his famous Gettysburg Address. But in 1863, the Civil War was raging and not everyone believed what Lincoln said. They thought that white skin color made a person superior. Today we see how very primitive it was to think that anyone could judge what a person's mind and heart were like by glancing at the person's skin.

Sometime around 1859, a little boy was born to a black slave named Mary. His father, from a neighboring plantation, had been killed hauling heavy logs shortly before he was born. Mary named him George and she would have been shocked to learn that this frail child would one day have kings, millionaires, and inventors from all over the world come to seek his advice.

George's mother had been bought by Moses Carver when she was thirteen years old for seven hundred dollars. The Carvers lived on a one hundred forty acre farm outside of Diamond Grove, Missouri. Moses Carver did not believe in slavery but as his wife grew older, she needed help with all the farm work. There were no servants for hire so, guiltily, Carver bought the only slave he ever owned. Soon Mary became almost a part of the family and Carver even believed his wife when she said that Mary was better off with them than with another family who might not treat her as well.

One night very late, as a cold wind howled outside Mary's cabin under the star-buttoned sky, she rocked and hummed quietly to George while a fire crackled. Her three year old son Jim slept peacefully. But George was ill with whooping cough. Closing her eyes she prayed that her little boy would soon grow strong. Suddenly Mary heard the pounding of hoofbeats on the cold, hard, wintry ground accompanied by loud gunfire and shouting. Moments later her door was thrust ajar and her owner, Mr. Carver, stood there panting.

"It's Night Raiders, Mary! Quick! Run!" he wheezed. Grabbing the sleeping Jim he dashed in the direction of the woods. Frightened, Mary rose to her feet. Night Raiders were men who used the war as an excuse to steal slaves and sell them again for profit. Mary had little time to react before her door was flung open again, this time with such violence that it crashed against the wall. Bending his large frame, a man with a bandanna covering his mouth and nose stepped inside. His eyes laughed into evil slits when he spotted Mary. Crouching in a corner, trembling, she clutched George, her terrified face starkly illuminated by the red-orange flames of the fire. Roughly, the man jerked Mary to her feet and dragged her screaming from the cabin to throw her on his horse.

The Carvers did everything in their power to recover Mary, but her whereabouts were skillfully hidden by the Night Raiders. The sickly, one year old George, torn from his mother and abandoned by the Raiders, was eventually found. Mr. Carver bought him back, exchanging a three hundred dollar racehorse for him. But the whooping cough had damaged George's throat; all his life he spoke in a thin, high-pitched voice.

The Carvers had no children. George helped Mrs. Carver whom he called Aunt Sue while his stronger older brother Jim helped Mr. Carver with the heavier farm work. George was a quiet little boy who was always at Aunt Sue's elbow. Mrs. Carver soon discovered how intelligent George was; he could learn things just by watching. One day she gave George a Webster's speller and taught him to read and write.

But George especially loved plants and growing things. Standing in the open wound of bright red roses on the Carver lawn, the little black boy could often be found, tending to the beautiful flowers. George was happy in the Carver household. Mary's children held a special place in Moses and Sue Carver's hearts.

Like most children born as slaves, George took Mr. Carver's last name. But if George had one driving desire, it was for knowledge and the Carvers did not stand in his way. At age ten, all alone, George left the Carver farm and walked eight miles to the Lincoln School in Neosho, one of the very few schools for black children. This was the Reconstruction period in the south following the Civil War and times were tough. They were especially tough, however, for a small black boy with no money.

When George arrived in Neosho he spent the night in a barn. Bright and early the next morning he sat on the school steps, hands folded in his lap, waiting for the school to open. A kind-looking black lady stopped and asked him what he was doing there. When he told her, she smiled and said that he would be waiting a long time. It was Sunday.

The lady's name was Mariah Watkins and she and her husband were childless. She asked George if he would like to stay at her house while he went to school. The lady told him to call her Aunt Mariah and her husband, Uncle Andy. The Watkins were very happy that George was going to live with them. They were glad, too, that George was eager to learn. Aunt Mariah told him that before the Civil War there had been a law making it a crime for anyone to teach slaves to read and write. Now, at the Lincoln School, Seventy-five black children, eager to learn, gathered in the one-room cabin.

By age thirteen, when George had learned all there was to learn at Lincoln, he knew it was time to find another school somewhere else. This realization made George very sad; he would miss Aunt Mariah and Uncle Andy. When the Watkins learned of George's plan they were very sad too. But they understood. If blacks were ever going to get ahead, they would have to become educated. Before George left, Uncle Andy asked George to write him out a will. He wanted to leave everything he had to George, who had become a son to him.

George hitched a wagon ride to Ft. Scott, Kansas. There he did odd jobs and whenever he got enough money together he would go to school for a few months. One day in Ft. Scott, quiet, good-natured George was beaten up by whites. They stole his schoolbooks and left him bruised and bleeding. A few days later George saw a black man burned to death. Desperately he wanted to help other blacks like himself. But what could he do?

Mrs. Lucy Seymour, who had been a slave in Virginia, taught George all she knew about laundering. Mrs. Seymour and her husband, like the Carvers and the Watkins, had no children. When they moved to Minneapolis, they took George with them. Here George opened up a laundry business while he attended high school. At this time, George was informed that his older brother James had died of smallpox. Filled with grief George busied himself even more with his studies.

When he finished high school George applied to Highland University. One day a letter came back saying that the university would be happy to have him. Clicking his heels and dancing a little jig, George read the letter over and over.

When opening day at Highland arrived, George stood smiling broadly in front of the director's desk. The director, however, did not return his smile. He stared at George in disbelief. Then he shook his head and told George sharply that the university did not accept Negroes. A dozen words all trying to come out at once choked in George's throat. He started to protest but the director waved him impatiently away. Numbly George stumbled out the door. He had been denied entrance simply because he was black. This was a blow that would be repeated throughout George's life.

On a day in September in 1890 George Carver trudged along an Iowa road leading to the town of Indianola. Determined, George was going to try again to get into a college. If they admitted him, he wanted to study painting. Many times as a child he had gone into the woods near the Carver home and painted on the rocks with mashed berries and leaves. Dr. Holmes, president of Simpson College, listened to George and his respect grew. He decided to give George a chance. George counted out twelve dollars for tuition. He had ten cents left in his pocket.

Because he had not had the preparation of the other students, George had to work twice as hard as they did. He also had to fight the prejudices of the teachers who could not understand why a black student wanted to study art. A trade was fine, but art? Only after brilliantly finishing a painting for another student was he allowed to continue his studies.

Although George encountered cruelty, unkindness, and prejudice, he also found admiration and friendship. On one occasion, when George had no money and was trying to support himself while going to school by operating a laundry, several of his college friends learned that he had no furniture whatsoever. While George was out they completely furnished his cottage. They all claimed ignorance of the incident. They knew that if George were ever sure of who had given the gifts, his pride would make him return the articles he so badly needed.

Graduating from Simpson College in three years, George went to Iowa State College of Agriculture. It was 1893, many years after President Lincoln's proclamation freeing the slaves, but still people were convinced that blacks were inferior and George was made to eat in the kitchen with the field hands. But soon George distinguished himself both academically and in the National Guard, where he became a captain. It was not long before he was sitting at those same tables, eating with the other students. And that was not all — George was the first black to graduate from the Iowa State College of Agriculture. Four of his paintings were selected to be shown at the World's Columbian Exposition in Chicago. After graduating George was offered, and he accepted, a teaching position at the college.

But George still dreamed of helping other blacks. Two years later, in 1898, George accepted the offer by black leader and educator, Booker T. Washington, to be the head of the new Agricultural Department at the Tuskegee Institute in Alabama which Washington had just opened for blacks.

When George arrived at Tuskegee there was only one brick building and a few old cabins. George had thirteen students. He taught them how to use old leaves and pond mud for fertilizer and to grow crops besides cotton.

Soon George started a school for farm families called the Farmer's Institute. On weekends he took his wagon, farm tools, seeds, and other demonstration materials out to surrounding farms. He looked at gardens and answered questions. He encouraged blacks to buy land. Never did he deny his help to anyone, black or white.

When farmers throughout the south ran into an emergency, they turned to George. A small insect called a boll weevil was damaging all the cotton plants. George told them to burn the infected cotton and in its place to grow sweet potatoes, cowpeas, and peanut vines. But cotton was a money-making crop. Who, the farmers demanded, was going to buy all the peanuts George was telling them to grow? Immediately George went to work in his laboratory at Tuskegee. Experimenting, George found three *hundred* useful products that could be made from peanuts, including peanut butter, instant coffee, milk, cheese, pickles, linoleum, shampoo, wood stains, soap, dyes, and tan remover. Because of George's experiments, peanuts became just as important a crop as cotton in the south. By 1938, millions of acres were used for growing peanuts which were bringing in $200,000,000 dollars worth of business and trade a year.

When World War I broke out, the United States appealed to Dr. Carver for help — the same country that had told him he was inferior and had treated him cruelly so many times, now expected him to snap to attention and help in the war effort. George decided he would. At the beginning of the war, the United States was dependent on Germany for chemicals, fertilizers, and dyes. But Dr. Carver found vegetable dyes that neither faded in washing, nor in the light. Another of Dr. Carver's products that became extremely important during the war was his sweet potato flour. From sweet potatoes George had found over a hundred uses, from vinegar, starch, molasses, to ink, rubber and library paste.

Dr. Carver soon became known as the "Wizard of Tuskegee." Often, Henry Ford, inventor of the Ford car, consulted with him. In 1928 the Crown Prince of Sweden stayed for several weeks with George to learn about the possibilities of using agricultural waste for industrial raw materials. The Duke of Windsor, the Prince of Wales when he visited George, passed, as did the scientist Julian Huxley, several hours spellbound in his laboratory.

George continued to decline opportunities to make himself rich. Thomas Edison once offered him $50,000 a year for five years to do research for him. Another offer George received is said to have been at a salary of $100,000 a year. A synthetic marble company from Mississippi asked him to join their company earning any salary he named. When George politely said no, the company itself moved to Tuskegee in order to benefit from George's advice, which he always gave free of charge. When peanut growers sent him a check for eliminating a disease of the plant, he returned it! George insisted that what he did, he did because of his profound love of science and humankind, not for money.

George Washington Carver was not only a scientist but an artist at heart. Producing brilliant-hued paints in his test tubes from the rich Alabama soils, George created astounding works of art and even rediscovered the ancient Egyptians' secret of lasting colors. One of George's paintings, in particular, caught the attention of the Luxembourg Gallery in Paris and they wanted to purchase it. The painting is of a rose and represents the "Infinite Mind." George, although he did not wish to sell the painting, arranged to make it a gift to the gallery upon his death.

Dr. Carver never sought fame, but his brilliance could not go unnoticed and it promoted racial understanding and proved to people of all races that accomplishments are not due to the color of the skin but to the quality of the mind. He was made a fellow in the Royal Society of Arts in London, awarded the Singarn Medal by the NAACP (the National Association for the Advancement of Colored People), and appointed collaborator in the Bureau of Plant Industry, United States Department of Agriculture.

In 1940 Dr. Carver donated thirty thousand dollars — his life savings — to create the George Washington Carver Foundation to continue research in agricultural chemistry.

President Theodore Roosevelt attended Dr. Carver's funeral when he died in 1943 at the age of eighty-two. At the time of his death he was still earning one hundred twenty-five dollars a month — the same salary as when he first came to Tuskegee so many years before.

George Carver never forgot the kind people who took him in and cared for him as a child so that he could obtain an education. Eighteen schools have been named after George Carver, B.S., M.S., D.Sc., Ph.D. Perhaps this honor would have meant the most to Dr. Carver who cherished learning.

(For more information about this individual, see *Black Scientists of America*, National Book, 1990.)

Jacqueline Cochran (1910? - 1980)
Aviator

A hungry chicken struts hurriedly over to eat a grain of corn. What the chicken does not know is that the corn is attached to a string and once it swallows the innocent-looking morsel, an even hungrier little girl will slowly pull the string and gather up the unsuspecting chicken.

Little Jackie lived in Florida. It was hard for her to understand why she was different from her family, in so many ways. Her mother was lazy, unkempt, and mean, beating her children without mercy. Finally, one day, Jackie overheard her mother talking with another woman and learned that she, Jackie, had been orphaned as a baby and that her "mother" had promised never to tell the little girl. Had Jackie lived in a happy family she might have been heartbroken, but as her life was one of constant mistreatment, hunger, dirt, and loneliness, she was overjoyed. This newly gained knowledge made it easier for Jackie to understand her differences and to take refuge in her dreams when life was especially difficult.

Jackie had no toys. She did not go to school and — until she was working full time and bought them herself at the age of eight — she did not have a pair of shoes. Her dresses were made from discarded flour sacks.

The family lived by working — when work was available — in the sawmills. Here people received "chips" instead of money and these "chips" could be exchanged for food and clothing at the company stores. But even in such a poverty-stricken environment there were the "rich" people — the doctor, the paymaster, the foreman — and the "poor" people, to which Jackie's family always belonged. It had not always been so. Whoever had left Jackie with the Cochrans had also provided for her keep with a tract of land near Muscogee and some oxen. However, the legacy had been quickly sold and the money squandered by Jackie's foster parents.

The family had no beds; they slept on pallets on the dirt floor, the children crying themselves to sleep while hunger pains gnawed at their insides. Yet even this meager existence was not to be taken for granted. When a sawmill closed down, the family had to go in search of another where the father and the two older boys could work. On these journeys the family rode in the train's caboose and had to gather fuel for the engine at certain stops.

One of Jacqueline's most painful childhood recollections occurred during such a journey. A man came on board the train selling food. As usual the family had no money, but Jackie was accustomed to going hungry. Then, with a twinkle in his eye, the man suddenly produced some glass pistols full of candy for sale. Jackie had never seen anything so pretty. Her eyes followed the man's every move as she watched those glass pistols disappear into the eager hands of other children. Never before had Jackie wanted anything so badly. Her eyes moist with unshed tears, she had to sit silently watching the other children enjoy their treats. Jackie knew that all she had to look forward to at the end of her long journey was to lie down hungry in a broken-down shack.

Food became even scarcer. On occasion Jackie helped herself to some sweet potatoes that a farmer was boiling for his pigs. Needless to say, electricity was out of the question; the family made do with a mojo lamp — a hollow corn stalk with a wick placed in a bottle with some oil at the bottom.

Jackie was growing up like a wild little girl, fishing when she could, running free in the woods the rest of the time. Because she had such a fertile imagination, she could always lose herself in her dreams. Often her imagination was fired by an old man who used to gather children around him and tell them stories. He once explained to Jackie that when she was a little girl an Indian had shot her in the stomach and that was why she had a belly button.

Jackie's foster parents never went to church but the little girl was urged to go to Mass whenever there was a priest in town. This was possibly as a result of a promise made to her birth parents that she would be raised as a Catholic. Jackie liked the big priest who became the first positive influence in her young life.

Jackie's existence was continually full of hardships. When she was six years old she got lost in the woods. Knowing no one would come searching for her, she had to conquer her fear of the dark woods, with its creepy noises, and make her way home a day later. On several occasions Jackie was so unhappy that she decided to run away. She tried to persuade a travelling circus to take her along with them and was sorely disappointed when, having fallen asleep, she discovered that they had left her behind.

One morning, after thinking about it for a while, Jackie decided to try school. On the third day, when the teacher slapped her, Jackie's hot temper flared and she slapped the teacher back, quickly running away. But a year later, knowing a new teacher was now in school, Jackie thought she would give school another try. This time her experience was much better. The new teacher, who owned the most beautiful dresses Jackie had ever seen, never slapped her. In fact, the teacher gave Jackie her first real dress to wear so her flour sack dresses would not be laughed at by the other schoolchildren. The teacher even made a deal with Jackie. The little girl would keep her room supplied with firewood and the teacher would pay her ten cents a week. What riches! Jackie loved to spend time with her teacher, in what seemed to her an elegant and cozy room. Now she was learning to read and the teacher taught her also to keep clean. Later on, as an adult, Jackie tried for a long time to find this marvelous person who had first instilled her with ambition, but try as she did, she was unsuccessful.

Jackie was not a shirker when it came to work. She helped new mothers and cooked and cleaned for them although it meant rising before sun-up. She was paid ten cents a day for this work but often money was so scarce that the women could not pay her the money they owed. However, no matter how small, Jackie's earnings were a help to the family.

One Christmas Jackie saw a little stove and a doll in the company store. The doll was to be raffled among the people who were given tickets whenever they bought toys. To a little girl who had only played with rocks and tin cans, the doll was the most beautiful thing in the world. Every day Jackie spent all her free time gazing at the doll. She tried to earn as much money as she could so that her tickets, too, would go into the raffle. She drew water for the women to do the laundry until her hands bled and, after working for two weeks, she had collected fifty cents. Rushing to the store, clutching the coins in a tight fist for fear of losing them, she quickly spent the money and was given two tickets for the raffle. Miraculously, on Christmas eve Jackie won the doll! Ecstatic with happiness and hugging her precious possession, she ran all the way home, her eyes shining. Showing the family her treasure, her foster parents snatched it from her arms and gave it to their two-year-old grandchild. Jackie cried and cried that night.

By the time Jackie was eight she was working a full time job — the twelve to fourteen hour night shift in a cotton mill, earning about six cents an hour. Her foster mother took all her earnings the first week, but after that Jackie decided it was only fair that she keep half. Her first purchase was a pair of high-heeled shoes. She paid for them in installments and — with some clothing that she had bought from the same peddler — Jackie felt very elegant indeed. However, she soon found that she could not walk through the cotton mill in high heels, so her second purchase was, by necessity, a pair of sneakers!

Through all the hard times, Jackie kept dreaming: One day she was going to travel and she was going to have pretty clothes. Many obstacles stood between the little girl and her dreams. After three months of working in the cotton mill, a strike at the mill left Jackie without a job. Undaunted, she found a job in a beauty shop and lived with the family of the owner, rising every morning at five to help with the household chores. Because she was intelligent and industrious she soon began shampooing hair and helping to give permanents, which were new at that time. She was given free room and board, worked between twelve and fourteen hours a day and was paid $1.50 a week. But Jackie increased her income by eight to twelve dollars weekly by helping the hairdressers so that they could tend to more customers. Although independent now, Jackie never abandoned her foster family, to whom she faithfully gave exactly one half of what she earned each week.

When Jackie was thirteen, the beauty shop, along with many others, was checked for child labor. The owner, Mrs. Richler, not wanting to be fined, stated that the girl was sixteen and her pupil. Jackie seized the opportunity and demanded full pay as the trade she was bringing in averaged to more than two hundred dollars a week. Now Jackie was really earning money. In a year she had several hundred dollars — quite a small fortune in those days for a girl so young. Then Jackie moved again, this time to Montgomery, where she met the first woman to hold public office in the state of Alabama and a judge in the Juvenile Court. Mrs. Lerton introduced Jackie to young people and she soon had a wide circle of friends. Next Jackie bought a car — a model T Ford — learned to dance and went to college parties. Jackie's world was quickly changing and she was changing with it.

Mrs. Lerton taught Jackie cooking, crocheting, and needlework, and continued to supervise her reading. She also talked Jackie into training as a nurse. Although Jackie had no formal schooling, Mrs. Lerton was able to get her admitted into the training program. Although she passed all her subjects, Jackie did not do well in academics. And although Jackie disliked the sight of blood, she was remarkable in the operating room. After finishing her training she went to work for a country doctor. Once again she encountered the poverty, dirt, and lack of education she had known as a child and it made her even more determined to help these people. But before she could help others she had to help herself. She must get away and make money. So Jackie became a partner in a beauty shop for a while, selling patterns and materials in her car. Then she went to Philadelphia to learn all the new hairstyles. As it turned out, Jackie knew more than the teachers . . . and she was hired as an instructor. Yet even when things were going well Jackie's life was not easy. Her purse was stolen and for a week all she ate was cheese and crackers.

Jackie's next destination was New York where she went to work for another salon — Antoine's. She made good money, worked extremely hard and was so well liked that in the winter she went to Antoine's shop in Miami Beach. This was lucky because at a party there she met a handsome, intelligent banker and industrialist named Floyd Odlum who would become her husband. And while talking with Floyd, Jackie first got the idea of . . . flying. Never one to delay when she had an idea, Jackie took a three-week holiday that was due her, marched onto Roosevelt Field in Long Island and took her first flying lesson. On the third day she was flying alone. Jackie studied Morse code and flew as many hours as she could. Always practical, however, she began developing her own cosmetic business. She started a beauty salon in Chicago and set up a chemist in a laboratory in New Jersey. During World War II Jackie did not have much time to devote to her business but she kept an eye on it. Realizing that men bought enormous amounts of cosmetics — hair lotions, after shaves, mustache wax — she developed that line of the cosmetic industry as well. It was a great success.

While she lived in New York, Jackie remembered her foster parents' grandchild — the one who had been given her Christmas doll. Jackie brought her to New York to give her a better start in life. Jackie only stipulated that the doll be returned. She cleaned up the doll, dressed her in new clothes and kept her with other dolls she had since collected. Only then did Jackie put behind her that sad childhood episode and once more experience the joy she had felt so long ago, when she had first hugged her beautiful doll!

Now that Jackie could fly her own airplane, she wanted to be a test pilot. But all test pilots were men. Her only option was to buy her own equipment and test it herself. Why not? Sometimes Jackie tested speed, other times altitude, always bringing in new information. Jackie flew to 33,000 feet in a non-pressurized airplane, without an oxygen mask, and on one occasion a blood vessel in her sinus ruptured. Jackie's data proved invaluable in creating pressurized airplanes.

In 1938 the little girl who "borrowed" a chicken when she could, was awarded the General "Billy" Mitchell Award given to the American pilot who has made the greatest individual contribution to aviation.

In 1939 Jackie tested a new fuel. Three years later, when she had forgotten the incident, she received a letter from the White House stating that her reports had contributed heavily to the decision to utilize this fuel during World War II.

Like all pilots Jackie had to learn to cope with emergencies. When the nose of her plane caught fire she had to land, and escape quickly, but not before an entire field of hay caught fire. She also had to do a belly landing while carrying two nervous passengers!

Before the United States lost its neutrality during World War II, U.S. pilots were recruited in England as civilians to be part of a transport system. Of course, Jacqueline Cochran was one of the obvious choices to fly these planes. No one, certainly not Cochran, was prepared for what happened next. Male pilots called a mass meeting and threatened to strike. All sorts of allegations were made. Because she was a woman, they said, the Germans were sure to shoot her down more easily. The male pilots also insisted that their jobs would seem less important and dangerous if a woman were allowed to fly with them. After these heated protests died down, Cochran was only allowed to be First Officer. The navigator, a pilot in his own right, and, more importantly, a man, would be in charge of taking off and landing the plane. Jacqueline Cochran was forced to either accept the position of First Officer or leave altogether. Cochran decided to comply, although she new, as did the male pilots, that she could fly as well as any of them. On her first flight to London as part of the transport group, the main fuse for the lights blew out, an aurora borealis made its appearance, and the Germans sent tracer bullets aimed at her plane. Cochran kept right on going.

Mostly through Cochran's efforts, the WASPs (Women's Airforce Service Pilots) were accepted as part of the Air Force Reserve. Cochran and her group proved that women pilots could be trained at no higher cost than men and that they could fly all types of aircraft as safely and as efficiently as men.

Cochran personally witnessed many glorious moments for the United States. She was in Manila for the surrendering of the Japanese troops under General Yamashita. She was the first American woman to land in Japan after the war. She also travelled to many other parts of the world and met many people including the Shah of Iran and the Pope. She attended the trials at Nuremberg of the Nazi officials who had been accused of war crimes, had an audience with General Franco of Spain, met President Syngman Rhee of Korea, ate with General Chiang Kai-shek in Formosa, and travelled in President Peron's private plane.

Flying in a Sabre jet, in 1953 Cochran broke the world speed records for both men and women. That same year she also became the first woman to break the sound barrier. In 1954 she was awarded the Gold Medal of the International Aeronautical Federation. A few years later she would fly at Mach 2 (twice the speed of sound). Retired from the Air Force Reserve in 1970 as a colonel, Cochran became a special consultant to NASA. In 1971 she was elected to the Aviation Hall of Fame.

When Jacqueline Cochran died in 1980 she had lived her life to the fullest, proving that where a person comes from is not as important as where that person is determined to go. Between the starving little girl who lured chickens for the family pot and the brilliant aviator had been many years and as many trials. But she never let those trials deter her from pursuing the dreams of success that had settled in the heart of that little barefooted girl from the sawmills of Florida so many years before.

William Lloyd Garrison   (1805-1879)
Abolitionist

In the year 1807 the Congress of the United States, in a momentous decision, prohibited the slave trade. But cotton production in the South had increased after Eli Whitney invented the cotton gin. With increased production came a greater demand for slave labor, and thus slavery continued. Besides, although the importation of new slaves into the United States was prohibited, the buying and selling of those already in the country was not, and slaves and their children could be traded among plantation owners. Many slave owners were compassionate and did not break up families; others did not care, and husbands, wives and children were scattered throughout the South without hope of ever seeing each other again.

Not all were indifferent to the plight of the slaves; some actively sought to free them. But the majority, then as now, was indifferent to what did not affect them directly. In the South, however, most were pro-slavery. Northern businessmen who traded with the South also hesitated to offend their associates by defending the cause of emancipation. One man, however, did all he could do to break the chain of slavery, using pen and words as his only weapon.

William Lloyd Garrison, called Lloyd by his mother, was born on a cold December day in the year 1805 in Newburyport, Massachusetts, the fourth child of Abijah and Frances Maria Garrison. His father was a sailor who had lost his job due to President Jefferson's Embargo Act of 1808, which prohibited merchant ships from carrying goods to other countries. This frustration, coupled with the death of a daughter who died after eating poisonous berries, proved unendurable for Mr. Garrison. Already drinking heavily, he left Newburyport never to return.

Bleak were the family's prospects. Their one staunch friend and landlady, Mrs. Farnham, allowed them to stay on in the one room they had occupied, knowing all the time that she would never collect the rent. Yet food was also needed, so Mrs. Garrison became a nurse. But as the embargo continued, even the wealthy had to cut expenses and jobs were hard to find. In desperation, Mrs. Garrison made molasses candy, which little Lloyd sold at the town square. In later years he remembered the pitiful glances of people who passed by. Others, less kind, mocked him openly. If sales were not successful and there was no food for the family, the little boy had to beg for food at the entrances of well-to-do homes. He usually collected enough scraps for a meager meal, but often bigger boys grabbed his pail and on these nights the family went hungry. Lloyd wept tears of frustration and anger but he was too little to oppose the big bullies alone.

"I want to go to sea," said Lloyd's older brother James, as both boys discussed plans for the future. "I want to learn and be famous one day," responded Lloyd. But in school Lloyd had a problem: he was left-handed at a time when being left-handed was not acceptable — when boys were rapped on the knuckles for lesser faults. Little Lloyd desired to please and learned to write impeccably with his right hand, practicing for hours. His desire for learning was such that he cried bitterly when his mother took him out of school because he was needed at home to care for his small sister.

About that time Mrs. Garrison found an opening for herself in the town of Lynn, a short distance away. There were several shoemaking factories in the town as well, and that gave Mrs. Garrison the idea that James, if apprenticed in one of these factories, would learn a profitable trade. So both mother and son prepared to leave the town of Newburyport. Maria, the baby, was too little to take along and she was left with kind Mrs. Farnham.

Among the inhabitants of Newburyport was the Bartlett family. The father was a Deacon, a kind man who, after consulting with his wife, offered to take Lloyd into his family. He had more than once been impressed by Lloyd's independence, courtesy and willingness to work. He would house and feed the boy if he helped around the house.

The Bartletts treated Lloyd as a member of the family, the first true one he had known, sharing his joys and sorrows and giving him the best advice they could. But all the members of the family had much work to do and Lloyd was no exception. In the freezing winter, shivering, Lloyd went out to fetch water for cooking and then ran to school. Lloyd was prepared to work: indeed all children had chores, and those who were poor were expected to be self-sufficient. He didn't have much time to study, but the family was a warm and happy one and Lloyd felt wanted; he was content and he was secure.

Mrs. Garrison, however, was not happy. She wanted Lloyd to have a trade. What better than for the boy to become a shoemaker as his brother James was doing? So away went the boy to Lynn, sadly leaving the Bartletts whom he thought of as his family.

The work in the shoe factory was overwhelming, but Lloyd always tried to do his best. At night his body ached and he could not sleep. The treatment of the children in the factories was very harsh and Lloyd cried silently at night not understanding why he should be treated so when he worked as hard as he could. Of course, with the exertion, lack of fresh air and sunshine, and poor food, Lloyd fell ill. He wanted his mother by his side but Mrs. Garrison had her own job and could not leave it to care for her son; they needed, now more than ever, the money she earned.

One day Mr. and Mrs. Bartlett, who had missed the boy sorely, said that they wished to take him back into their home. They would care for him, they assured Mrs. Garrison, and care for him they did. His illness was long but slowly he improved. When he was stronger he was given light work selling apples from the family orchard while sitting in the Bartlett's front yard. During these hours spent in the fresh air, Lloyd read and he thought. Happy and relaxed again with his family, Lloyd discovered new talents in himself. He began singing in the choir at church as Mr. Bartlett proudly watched from the altar.

All too soon, it seemed to Lloyd, his mother recalled him again. She and James were going to travel to Maryland where a shoe factory owner had promised them employment. Lloyd was seasick the whole time. He kept thinking about the Bartletts and how he wished he were back with them.

In those days, workers did not spend eight hours at their jobs as they do now, rather they worked from can-see to can't-see (dawn to dusk) and they worked on Saturdays as well! His brother James, who detested the job as much as Lloyd did, ran away to sea, perhaps in the hope of meeting his long-lost father and realizing his dreams of visiting far-away lands. Lloyd begged his mother to allow him to return to the Bartletts. His mother consented at last. but Mrs. Garrison could not help worrying about her son's future. One day, without consulting anyone, she signed the documents that legally apprenticed Lloyd to a carpenter. As always, Lloyd tried to be a dutiful son. When he informed Uncle Bartlett of what his mother had done, the Deacon expressed his sadness at losing the boy but reminded him of his obligation to obey his mother, and consoled him by saying that the distance between the two houses was not great.

In those days apprentices lived with their masters and Lloyd felt strange in the new household but he applied himself to his job with all his might. However, he soon knew that carpentry was not for him. Never would he make a good carpenter — try as he may. He asked himself in desperation many a night — after futile attempts to learn his trade — if there was anything at all that he could do well. One day he could not take it any more and in desperation stole away in the night. He didn't want to hurt his master's feelings, for he was a good and kind man. Neither did he want to disappoint Mr. Bartlett or his mother. But he did not know what else he could do as the contract his mother had signed bound him legally to the carpenter for seven long years. His master, who suspected the motives behind Lloyd's flight, followed and caught up with the boy. Being an understanding man, he released Lloyd from all obligations.

Naturally Lloyd turned once more to Uncle Bartlett. The family atmosphere and the contentment and security he felt in their home gave Lloyd the time he needed to prepare himself for the years to come. He still did not know what he wanted to do, but he was sure there was a mission waiting for him. Then one day, the world seemed to open before him. In her incessant quest for a trade for her son, Mrs. Garrison once more apprenticed him, this time to the editor of the Newbury Herald. This time Mr. Bartlett, too, approved; the job was splendidly suited to the boy. Lloyd was hesitant, for he would have to leave the Bartletts again, but this time his heart felt lighter. He trusted Uncle Bartlett's judgement and believed this time he might be able to do the job.

The first day he went to the printing office with a feeling of apprehension, but no sooner had he spent a few hours on the job than he knew without a doubt what he wanted to be. He had found his vocation and someday he would run a newspaper and become famous as he had promised his brother James years before! Lloyd found he had many ideas and discovered too, the power of the written word. He decided he was going to use that power to defend those who could not defend themselves: the poor, the underprivileged, the uneducated. Injustices made him want to cry out and now he could do it at last, he thought, remembering the times he had lost his scant food to the big bullies.

While Lloyd set type and did the chores that his master gave him, he thought and mentally composed his own writings. Yet he was too unsure of himself — too shy — to come forth openly with his ideas, so his first attempt at writing, was a letter addressed to the newspaper where he worked. Protesting the decision of a judge to fine a man who had left his fiance, it was signed "An Old Bachelor." Lloyd had his own ideas about everything and he expressed them. So successful was he that Mr. Allen put a notice in his paper asking the "Old Bachelor" to come to his office that he may shake his hand. Lloyd was forced to confess, not sure how Mr. Allen was going to react. With great relief he saw that Mr. Allen was delighted, although quite astonished at the surprising admission on the part of his young apprentice.

Although by law Lloyd was not entitled to any vacation during the seven years of his apprenticeship, Mr. Allen gave him a month off to encourage him in his writing. Lloyd went straight to his foster family, the Bartletts. They were overjoyed to hear of his success. For the first time in seven years Lloyd also had time to visit his mother and console her in her recent sorrow. Finally able to support her daughter Maria, she had brought the girl to live with her . . . but Maria died in an epidemic of yellow fever shortly after her arrival. Mrs. Garrison was also ill with the disease and was never completely well afterwards. Lloyd saw that his mother needed care but his hands were tied until he fulfilled the terms of his apprenticeship. It grieved him very much that his mother, who had cared and helped so many, was alone and helpless now herself.

The only person who took pity on her was Henny, a slave of Mrs. Garrison's former employer who had obtained permission from her mistress to care for Mrs. Garrison in her short moments of leisure. This unselfishness and true neighborliness so impressed Lloyd that he dedicated himself to the cause of the emancipation of all slaves.

At age twenty Lloyd finished his apprenticeship and was his own master, beholden to no one. His first idea was to open his own newspaper which he called *Free Press*. This enterprise failed, for Lloyd had not yet acquired the experience and objectivity to deal with all points of view. He was ready to express his own opinions but not so ready to listen to the opinions of others.

Hard times followed. Lloyd had alienated his former master and true friend by publicly criticizing his political views in his own newspaper. This was done out of rashness and inexperience, not from a desire to offend, but by the time Lloyd realized what he had done it was too late to make amends. Perhaps, Lloyd thought, he should make a new start. With this in mind he traveled to Boston where he often went hungry and slept outdoors. Finally, after a year of privations, he found a job as editor of the *National Philanthropist*. He was happy to be working for such a newspaper, dedicated to show the evils of drinking. Lloyd himself abhorred drinking, no doubt because the father he had never really known had doomed the family to poverty when he abandoned them.

Unfortunately, Lloyd was, as always, ready to express his own opinions, the strongest of which was to denounce the evils of slavery. His singlemindedness showed too frequently in the pages of their newspaper, the owners thought, and he was fired.

But this setback did not daunt Lloyd and he was ready to launch his campaign. The first step was to stir Americans to end the indifference that many felt towards slavery. Then Lloyd met a Quaker who had already founded many anti-slavery societies. The name of his new friend was Benjamin Lundy. Their ideals united them and they started a newspaper called the *Genius of Universal Emancipation*. Lloyd Garrison recommended that slavery be forbidden by law, but the year was 1829 and most Americans did not think of slavery at all. Nor did they read anti-slavery publications. How then, Lloyd asked himself, could he spread the message to all citizens, break down their indifference, and make them realize that slavery was not just something that went on in the South that could be ignored by Northerners?

Lloyd Garrison's first years in his self-imposed campaign were far from easy. He wrote an article accusing a wealthy ship owner who transported slaves of murder. He was sued by the ship owner, lost the case, and was sentenced to pay one hundred dollars. As he could not raise the money, Lloyd spent four weeks in jail. Of course, he put his time to good use — writing articles and protesting that in his person the freedom of the press had been attacked — the latter a stroke of genius as it interested the editors and the public alike.

While in prison Lloyd Garrison had time to formulate his plans. He wished to start his anti-slavery campaign where the laws were made, in Washington D.C., but he was not able to generate enough interest and support. Therefore he began speaking in New York and Philadelphia. This was necessary, for although the institution of slavery had not taken hold in the North, discrimination against blacks did exist. Hired only to do the most menial jobs, schools refused to take their children for fear whites would not attend. It was among this poor community of blacks that Garrison naturally found his greatest support. They had little money to give, but the little they had they were happy to share with Garrison to support his campaign.

Back in Boston, Garrison resumed publication of his newspaper. However, this alone did not satisfy him any more. He should be addressing crowds; surely the ministers who followed the teaching of Christ would open their hearts and doors to him and would let him use their churches for his speeches. But none did. Lloyd made his plight known in his paper and a society of free thinkers was the only one to respond. Of course Garrison accepted the offer. He spoke sincerely, telling of the horrors and cruelty endured by the slaves. He made them come alive as people, not as objects without feelings whose families could be separated and children sold without creating pain or sorrow. Among the people who had come to listen and — moved by his speech — offered their help . . . were some of those ministers who so recently had not wished to allow him the use of their temples.

Because Garrison was determined to make slavery the one issue of his life, he changed the name of his newspaper to *The Liberator* — precisely what he himself hoped to be! Slowly, money began to come in from sympathizers. With the added publicity, however, he became a focal point for intensified feelings about an increasingly emotional issue. Letters arrived from the South threatening him, and a reward was even offered in South Carolina for the arrest of any white man caught sharing *The Liberator* with others.

Now that the groundwork was laid, Garrison directed his campaign to congressmen and senators — after all, the ones who could legally end slavery. All members of his anti-slavery society had two responsibilities: to recruit more members and to collect money. Garrison was busy doing the same. He also encouraged many of the schools organized for free blacks, and he even went to England to talk about slavery and gain support. This was a mistake, however: whether America was right or wrong, the War of Independence fought against England was too fresh in the minds of Americans to allow any Englishman to tell them how to run their country.

And now other groups in American society were angered too — traders and businessmen felt their dealings with the South would suffer if Garrison continued his critical attitude. To express their disapproval, they broke up meetings and threw stones at Garrison and other abolitionists. When an English friend of Garrison's came to speak, tempers in Boston reached boiling point. Nevertheless Garrison decided to attend the meeting of the Boston Female Anti-Slavery Society at which he was to speak. He felt that, as only ladies were involved, the chance of any violence was minimal. In this he was wrong; only the opportune presence of the Mayor of Boston and the policemen he had brought along saved Garrison.

During this period, to his great surprise, Garrison — the "old bachelor" — had fallen in love and married. Now that his life was threatened, his wife convinced him to visit her family's home in Connecticut for a little while and escape public notoriety. This he did, but nothing could prevent Garrison from writing letters to his newspaper.

William Lloyd Garrison always stood for what he believed, even if by doing so he made enemies. Since he believed in women's intellectual equality, he gave women important positions in his abolitionist society. This also angered many who thought that women should be concerned solely with domestic affairs and occupy their hours in womanly pursuits.

One brilliant stroke of his campaign against slavery was to present to his audience a most unexpected and startling speaker — the escaped slave Frederick Douglass. Garrison let Douglass speak for his own people for after all nobody could do it better.

And then a momentous historical happening took place before Garrison's very eyes: the Civil War, which brought with it in 1863 the Emancipation Proclamation. Garrison could not contain his joy. The approval by Congress of the 13th Amendment was greeted by *The Liberator* with the headline "Praise be to God." Long were the lines of people who came to shake Garrison's hand, and proud was the committee of distinguished citizens that was sent to honor him from Newburyport.

Often Garrison thought of those long-ago conversations with his brother. Well, he at least had tried to make his dream a reality. Garrison felt that, at last, he had paid the debt to that kind slave Henny who had cared for his mother in her last days, and who years later he tried in vain to find. Somehow fame was not as important as it had seemed to the little boy, but abolition was. Happy for Garrison was the moment when he travelled to Charleston and saw, among the throngs of black men and women there, his son George leading a unit of free black soldiers.

But Garrison's struggles on behalf of others had left him tired. He made a painful decision: *The Liberator,* his beloved newspaper, would end its life with the edition published on December 29, 1865. After all, it was no longer needed.

Too involved with his crusade, making money had never seemed a priority and Garrison had very little in worldly goods. Unknown to him, however — for Garrison was a proud man — his friends collected over $25,000 to be used for his retirement. Now the last cloud was removed from his horizon. Garrison had the satisfaction of giving all comforts to his wife in her last years. After her death, he lived in the house of his only daughter — now married to a wealthy New Yorker — content in the midst of his family, finding comfort in the thought that he had, as he had promised himself as a little child, used his life in a worthy cause.

Evonne Goolagong (1951-)
World Tennis Champion

Spinning back the clock to 1971, Margaret Court — age twenty-seven, the three-time winner and defending Wimbledon champion — and the little-known Evonne Goolagong, age nineteen, walk onto the tennis court. Suddenly the band strikes up "Waltzing Matilda," the Australian national anthem. Moments later, under an angry sun, Evonne is facing Margaret across the net. In ready position, Evonne watches, measuring the ball. She returns a slice backhand for a cross-court winner. Powerfully Margaret winds up for the serve and aggressively Evonne moves forward to chip and charge. Then she leaps up high, beautifully smashing Court's defensive lob. Shading their eyes, the spectators watch, open-mouthed, as Evonne Goolagong crushes the defending champion, 6-4, 6-1 in just over an hour to take the women's singles crown.

She was called a freak; it was said she had no killer instinct and that she had a low I.Q. They said she didn't have what it took to be a champion. They were wrong.

Evonne Fay Goolagong was born on July 31, 1951 in a small town called Barellan in the state of New South Wales in Australia's Outback. Evonne, who has seven brothers and sisters, is the third oldest. Evonne's family is part-Aborigine and, according to her father, who was a sheep-shearer and fruit-picker, the name "Goolagong" means "nose of kangaroo." The Goolagongs lived in a tin shack at the end of a bumpy dirt road. Packs of kangaroos could often be seen roaming the countryside. Growing up, Evonne's favorite meal was rabbit stew.

As a very little girl Evonne would play with some dead tennis balls her father found in a used car he had bought. One day her father borrowed a racket that belonged to his employer's wife and Evonne started hitting balls against the side of a butcher shop. She loved running after the ball and hearing the 'ping' of her racket strings as the ball made contact.

When Evonne was five years old she became a ball girl at the Barellan Tennis Club. A year later her aunt gave her a racket of her own, which she even took to bed with her. After hours, when all the club members had left, Evonne would practice hitting tennis balls on the empty court. A couple of shaggy dogs were her only audience. But then, one day, Evonne's younger sister burned her precious racket for firewood. Evonne cried and cried.

However, the little girl's skill and enthusiasm for tennis had already impressed Bill Kurtzmann, the president of the Barellan Tennis Club. Smiling, he handed the red-eyed youngster a brand new racket. He even gave her an old net to take home, telling her to practice whenever she could. Evonne secured the net to both sides of a large fenced-in area next to her house. True, the area was choked by weeds and scattered with broken furniture but it became Evonne's very own tennis court.

When Evonne was ten years old, a tennis tournament was being held in Narrandera, a neighboring town. Bill Kurtzmann entered Evonne in the competition. On the day of the tournament he insisted that the entire Goolagong family come along to watch. But when they arrived they were disappointed. Kurtzmann found that the tournament was for adult players. No matter, Kurtzmann pressured — Evonne was a match for anyone. Reluctantly the officials agreed to let Evonne play and then watched, flabbergasted, as she brilliantly won the championship.

During the summer, a tennis camp — headed by Vic Edwards — came to Barellan. Eagerly, Evonne signed up for lessons. Standing on the sidelines, one of Edwards' talent scouts, Colin Swan, became increasingly astounded by Evonne's ability. In fact, one day, he excitedly telephoned his boss.

"You *have* to come and see Evonne Goolagong," he told Vic Edwards all in a rush, "She's a natural!"

Vic Edwards did come. He was very impressed with Evonne's ability. It was evident that she had great promise. But he was cautious. "Practice as much as you can with your older brother," he told Evonne, "and when I come back next year I might enter you in a few tournaments."

Edwards' real reason for coming back a whole year later was to determine whether tennis was merely a passing fancy with Evonne or whether she was serious about the sport. Every day, even when she did not feel like it, Evonne practiced. When Edwards returned, he nodded approvingly.

But Bill Kurtzmann felt Evonne had little chance to really improve in the Outback. She needed stiffer competition. Colin Swan had mentioned once that Vic Edwards and his family had taken in a country girl, Jan Lehane, in the 1950s to live with them. Jan had grown up with the Edwards' older daughters and become, under Edwards' tutelage, a high-ranking Australian player. Why couldn't they do the same for Evonne? It was true that Lehane's parents had been able to pay for Jan's upkeep while Evonne's parents were poor and would never be able to afford such expenses. Also, Jan was white. She had fit right into the Edwards' family. Evonne was an Aborigine. Still, Kurtzmann spoke to Edwards. He was told that, first of all, Mrs. Edwards would have to agree to the idea. Secondly, they would have to see if Evonne got along with his younger daughters, Patricia and Jenifer, who were roughly the same age as Evonne. And, of course, there was the very important matter of how Evonne herself would feel about living in a strange house. A few days later Edwards spoke to the Goolagongs and it was agreed that Evonne would stay in Sydney for three weeks with the Edwards' family. When Patricia and Jenifer Edwards learned that a little Aboriginal girl was coming to stay with them, they imagined her getting off the plane wearing a loincloth and carrying a spear. Instead, a girl with a shy smile greeted them, dressed in new clothes and clutching a tennis racket.

Evonne spent the next two summers with the Edwards family. But Mr. Edwards realized that Bill Kurtzmann was right: if Evonne was ever to become a champion she needed year-round training. So Vic Edwards approached the Goolagongs and asked them if Evonne could stay on a more permanent basis with him and his family in Sydney. The Goolagongs trusted Mr. Edwards and felt he could offer their daughter opportunities they could never give her, so they agreed. Vic Edwards became Evonne's legal guardian as well as a dedicated coach and friend.

At first, as she thought of her family in the Outback, Evonne was very homesick. The Edwards let Evonne choose whether she wanted to attend a co-ed school or a private girl's school. Evonne chose the Willoughby Girl's School, where Patricia Edwards went. Evonne and "Trisha," who was also an excellent tennis player, became very good friends, and soon Evonne felt comfortable in the Edwards' household. With Mr. Edwards' help she was also winning every junior tournament she entered. In her spare time Evonne liked to listen to music turned up very loud in her room. She was always buying records and cassettes and knew the words to almost every Top Forty hit.

Although Evonne was extremely shy with adults and strangers, she was perfectly at home on a tennis court. Over and over again the newspapers hailed the ability of Evonne, "the colored girl" or Evonne "the Aborigine." Evonne made a good story because she was the first Aborigine in tennis. One day, when Evonne was sixteen she and Trisha Edwards were playing two older women in an interclub league. Evonne and Trisha won the match and went to the net to shake their opponents' hands. "That's the first time I ever lost to a nigger," one of the women said disgustedly.

Trisha immediately started to cry believing the woman had hurt her sister's feelings. Then Evonne started to cry, not because of what the woman had said but because Trisha was crying. Mr. Edwards was furious when he heard what had happened. Immediately the club president telephoned and apologized, assuring that the woman would never again play for their team.

The Aborigines in Australia have suffered a fate similar to that of the American Indians. When the white settlers came to Australia, they seized the natives' land

and destroyed their culture. On equal turf in tennis, Evonne realized that she could make a powerful statement for all Aborigines.

In 1970 Evonne captured the under-eighteen Australian championship and Edwards felt it was time to take Evonne overseas. She played in Holland, France, and Germany. In England Evonne beat five of the world's top-ranked women players. After winning three consecutive major tournaments in England, Evonne qualified for Wimbledon. But nervousness kept her from playing her best and Evonne's hopes were quickly dashed by American Peaches Bartkowicz. However, at nineteen, in her first year of international competition, Evonne had won seven tournaments including the Bavarian and Welsh titles. And despite Evonne's giftedness in tennis, Mr. Edwards insisted that she attend a business college when she graduated from high school. He wanted her to be able to earn a good living, always.

In Australia it became clear that there was only one player who could top Evonne Goolagong. Her name was Margaret Court — and she was Evonne's childhood idol. When Evonne was eleven years old, she had her picture taken with Margaret. The picture — one of Evonne's most treasured possessions — shows Evonne staring adoringly up at the tennis superstar who had won the Wimbledon, French, United States, and Australian women's championships. How, Evonne wondered, could she ever face Margaret Court as an equal?

In 1971, Evonne entered in the Victorian Championships in Melbourne, finally confronting Margaret Court, who had won the championship seven times before. But it was Evonne who won 7-6, 7-6. When they played again a few weeks later, however, a cramp in a calf muscle cost Evonne, leading 5-2, the Australian Championship. Margaret commented after the game that she had naturally taken advantage of Evonne's cramp by making her run all over the court.

In June, 1971, Goolagong won the French championships. Edwards was extremely happy but he was particularly pleased at *how* Evonne had won. Edwards had always felt that Evonne's only shortcomings were a tendency to let her mind wander during a game and not enough of the killer instinct. But Edwards knew Evonne possessed determination in large doses and he felt that was enough to make her a champion. Edwards had planned to wait until 1974 to enter Evonne in Wimbledon. But after seeing her perform in Paris, he decided it was time . . . and in a chauffeur-driven Rolls Royce, Mr. and Mrs. Edwards and Evonne were taken to the tournament.

Very few people believed Goolagong had a chance of winning even a match, much less the Wimbledon Championship, the most prestigious championship in tennis. Goolagong, however, made short work of her first opponents: Julie Heldman and Nancy Richey Gunter, beating each in less than an hour. The next day, Goolagong stunned the audience winning 6-4, 6-4 against Billie Jean King, the two-time

Wimbledon champ. There was only one more person to face. And that was none other than her fellow Australian Margaret Court.

As a hush fell over the crowd, Court spun a racket to see who would serve first. Winning the spin, Court served up the ball. But it was Goolagong who emerged the victor, defeating not only Court but her skeptics. Searching the stands amid thunderous applause, Evonne found Mr. Edwards who was beaming with pride. Triumphantly she held her racket in the air.

A month later, Evonne travelled back to Barellan. The entire town, with Bill Kurtzmann and her family at the head of the welcoming procession, turned out to cheer her through the streets and wave their banners. After all, Evonne had put their little town on the map!

But being famous had its drawbacks and sometimes hindered Goolagong's social life. When a man asked her for a date, she wondered if he wanted to go out with Evonne Goolagong, the person, or Evonne Goolagong, the tennis champion. Her doubts were laid to rest, however, when she met Roger Cawley, a kind, handsome Englishman whom she married in 1975.

Goolagong missed the 1977 season to have her first child. By 1980 she was almost twenty-nine years old and it was generally believed that her champion days were over. But Goolagong shocked the world by winning the women's singles finals that year against Chris Evert Lloyd (now Evert Mills), 6-1, 7-6, becoming the first mother since Dorothea Lambert Chambers in 1914 to win Wimbledon.

Throughout the seventies and the start of the eighties, Evonne Goolagong was considered one of the five best players in the world. With a racket in her hand and Vic Edwards as her coach she dazzled audiences. In the dedication of a book she co-authored with Bud Collins, a sportswriter for the Boston Globe, she calls Vic Edwards her second father.

In July, 1988, Goolagong entered the International Tennis Hall of Fame. But even in competition, where she loved to use her great skill she never allowed winning or losing to overshadow the reason she began playing tennis as a little girl in the Outback.

Alexander Hamilton (1755 - 1804)
First U.S. Secretary of the Treasury

Sometimes Alexander Hamilton, with dark-blue eyes almost violet in color, would stare intently through the window at the puckering sea, his quill pen momentarily stilled between his fingers. Watching the mixture of expressions the other clerk wondered curiously what the boy was thinking as he gazed beyond the harbor. He would have hooted in derision had he known that fourteen-year-old Alexander Hamilton, clerk in the dusty counting house of St. Croix, dreamt of *fame* and *glory*. But always, Alexander's daydreaming was broken with a worried frown. He was unusually aware of time. People said a clock gave the hour, but to him a clock's teasing face showed with every glance how it took precious time away. And there was so much he wanted to do!

Alexander Hamilton, the future Secretary of the Treasury of the United States, was broke at the age of eleven. His mother Rachel Faucett had married John Lavien, a sugar planter, who imprisoned her for unwifely conduct. But not long after the birth of their son Peter in 1746, Rachel left her husband and child. She had fallen in love with James Hamilton, a handsome Scotsman who had come to the West Indies to make money. Together they sailed to the island of Nevis where, still unable to get a divorce from Lavien, Rachel had two sons. The older son was named James after his father and the younger one, born on January 11, 1755, was named Alexander. A very bright child, at age four he memorized the Ten Commandments — in Hebrew.

James Hamilton moved his family back to St. Croix in 1765. Most people knew that Alexander's mother had left her legal husband for his father and even that she had spent time in jail. Walking down the streets, eight-year old Alexander had to endure unkind looks and words from the "better" people of St. Croix. In those days, illegitimate children were labeled "obscene." Anger burning in his heart, Alexander marched on, telling himself that one day — one day! — he would show them all who was "better." He did. Had Alexander Hamilton not contributed his talent and energy to the War of Independence and to the founding of the United States of America, there is a good chance that the new nation would have remained just a dream in the hearts of a few Patriots.

On August 1, 1765, probably with her family's help, Alexander's mother again left a husband; James Hamilton had failed to make money. As if it scorched her tongue, Rachel never again used the Hamilton name, except when forced to refer to her sons. This unforgiving attitude hurt Alexander and, it seems, when he grew older he never remembered his mother with much affection.

Set up in a small store by her relatives in St. Croix, there is evidence that the success of Rachel's store was owed in great part to young Alexander's intelligence and hard work. But after some years, in February 1768, Rachel and Alexander were stricken with a tropical fever. Alexander eventually recovered but Rachel died.

Immediately upon Rachel's death, her former husband, John Lavien, swooped down on her possessions. Everything — including what Alexander had worked so hard to achieve in the store — Lavien made sure went to his own son Peter, Rachel's only legitimate child who had not seen his mother in eighteen years. Not a single thing went to Alexander or his brother James. In the meantime, Alexander's father had sailed to St. Kitts alone, never to return for his sons.

Peter Lytton, Rachel's nephew, was made guardian of the boys, but died tragically and again the Hamilton boys were left on their own. Soon James was apprenticed to a carpenter and moved into the carpenter's home. Alexander went to live with his best friend's family. The two brothers, who had always been very different, saw little of each other after their mother's death.

For the first time in his life, Alexander found himself part of an orderly household. He had grown so used to the shouting matches between his parents about how they were going to pay the bills that here, in the Stevens' house, everything seemed strangely calm. About a year later, Alexander's friend Neddie Stevens sailed to the colony of New York to continue his education. Saddened that he could not afford to go with his friend, Alexander entered the world of work.

In the city of Christiansted, St. Croix, Alexander was employed by a firm of merchants called Nicholas Cruger and Company. In a few short months, he was promoted from apprentice to regular clerk. Nicholas Cruger's respect for his young employee's intelligence and judgement grew daily. When in the fall of 1771 Cruger became seriously ill, he called Alexander to his side. Deciding to go to New York to seek medical treatment, Cruger was putting Alexander in charge of his company. When other people — including rival businesses — heard that the prosperous, level-headed Cruger was leaving his company in the hands of a fourteen-year-old boy for several months, they told him — to his face — that he had gone positively mad. He would be thrown into financial ruin! Cruger only smiled and shook his head. None of them, obviously, knew Alexander Hamilton.

On October 15, 1771 Cruger confidently set sail for the English colonies. Alexander, not so confident, swallowed hard. It was not going to be easy giving orders to much older men and being the last responsible for all major decisions. Alexander was faced with one particularly ticklish dilemma. The company attorney was quite clearly wasting company time and money. After many hours of thinking it over, Alexander fired him. When Cruger returned in March, 1772 he found his business thriving and congratulated a rather uneasy Alexander for replacing attorney Hassell with someone much more conscientious.

There were three people on St. Croix who greatly influenced Alexander Hamilton. One was Ann Venton, a cousin who came to live on St. Croix about two years after Alexander's mother died. She was the only person who gave Alexander the motherly love he so desperately craved. Another major influence was a Presbyterian minister named Hugh Knox who immediately recognized Alexander's brilliance and persistently tried to convince Alexander's relatives that the boy must be sent to college. Knox himself had little money but he taught Alexander everything he could and generously opened his modest library to the young boy. Nicholas Cruger, for his part, solidified a quality that all leaders must have: self-confidence. Later, too, Cruger would give Alexander considerable monetary aid.

Cruger soon began hinting to Alexander that he would like to make him a junior partner. Alexander gratefully thanked Mr. Cruger but inwardly he was panicstricken. True, a partnership in Cruger and Company would earn the townspeople's respect, something he had always wanted. But it would also mean being chained forever to St. Croix, never to perform the heroic feats he dreamed. Yet, Alexander was practical by nature and he just might have remained on St. Croix had it not been for the hurricane.

On August 31, 1772 St. Croix was struck by the most severe hurricane in a hundred years. Alexander was at Cruger's when he first heard the whistling winds from the southeast. Quickly, Alexander saddled a horse and set off, determined to help Ann secure the distant Lytton plantation. Heavy rain slashed at Alexander as he rode his horse at a feverish gallop, keeping his head low with the horse's neck. Powerful, roaring winds sent thick trees a-curtseying, their heads sweeping the ground in a freakish, terrifying dance. Odd pieces of furniture whipped through the air sometimes inches from Alexander's head. It was a horrific, nightmarish ride and yet, Alexander found it exhilarating. Forcing his way through the unmovable screen of wind that tried to hold him and his horse back, Alexander reached the Lytton house. For two days he battled the hurricane to keep the house from certain destruction.

When Alexander road back to Christiansted, he saw all the terrible destruction the hurricane had wrought, made more vividly horrible by a brilliant sun. Alexander went straight to Hugh Knox who listened, spellbound, to Alexander's account of his unforgettable journey at breakneck speed. When Alexander finished, Knox insisted he write down what he had told him. Alexander did, in the form of a letter to the father he had not seen in six years. Hugh Knox was so impressed by the descriptions that he asked Alexander for a copy of the letter telling him his account was worthy of publication. Two weeks later, Knox strode into Cruger and Company and wordlessly spread open the *Royal Danish-American Gazette* on Alexander's desk. There, published in black and white, was Alexander's letter. Alexander stared in astonishment while Hugh Knox, his eyes twinkling, simply smiled.

Alexander's hurricane letter caused quite a sensation on St. Croix. Even Governor Walterstorff wanted to know more about the boy who had authored such a moving account of the terrible storm. Amid all the hoopla, Alexander seized the opportunity to ask his relatives for help so he could study in the English colonies. Finally, with a sigh of relief, Hugh Knox gave Alexander any money he could spare as did Ann Venton. Cruger's contribution was so generous that not only was Alexander's passage to the colonies paid but his expenses at college too.

As Alexander watched the island grow small against the horizon, he felt sad — but excited too. Hugh Knox wanted him to go to The College of New Jersey, today Princeton University, where he himself had gone. However, a few weeks into the journey, a terrible fire broke out on the ship. For twenty-four hours, the passengers and crew were drawing water from the ocean with buckets, feverishly trying to extinguish the greedy flames. Black smoke wafted upwards, hovering on the deck. Choking passengers and crew alike stared hollow-eyed into one another's faces, masking the intensity of their struggle to remain alive. In October of 1772, amid cheering, the blackened ship and crew floated into Boston harbor.

Yet no sooner had Alexander set foot on land, than he was on a stagecoach to New York to see his friend Neddie Stevens. But Alexander was also anxious to start his own studies. After being tutored for a year, Alexander was admitted to the College of New Jersey but was told that he would have to wait until the start of the new school year to begin. Alexander went directly to President Witherspoon and explained that time was very important to him. He wanted to take and finish classes at his own pace. Bluntly he was told that he would have to follow the same schedule as any other first year student. Instead of bemoaning his fate or accepting blindly what the trustees of one college told him, Alexander headed up to King's College in New York, now Columbia University, and tried his luck there. He was accepted and informed that he could indeed complete courses at his own pace. Alexander entered King's College in the fall of 1773.

Exchanging isolated New Jersey for New York, the third largest city in the colonies, Alexander found himself in the heart of the political hullabaloo. Unknowingly, the trustees at the College of New Jersey had done Alexander — and their future country — a great favor. Here in New York, Loyalists (who remained loyal to King George III of England, also called Tories), and Patriots (to the English, Rebels) who wanted to free themselves of the king's rule, heatedly argued in every tavern. At college Alexander joined a debating club and found he enjoyed speaking in front of others. But as the spirit of rebellion deepened, Alexander found himself wishing he could become more actively involved. Many of the restrictions put on the merchants of New York, Philadelphia, and Boston by the English Parliament had also been put on the merchants in St. Croix. Dipping his quill determinedly in ink, Alexander set to work. His first article "Defense of the Destruction of the Tea" met with tremendous success and Alexander continued to produce passionate arguments defending the Patriot cause. Some of the most important Patriots in the city, among them thirty-year old John Jay began commenting on the logic and force with which "Mr. Hamilton" wrote. Not knowing this new writer, Jay pictured him as a snowy-haired, pot-bellied, clever old gentleman. He would later be astonished to learn that "Mr. Hamilton" was still in his teens.

In the fall of 1774, as Alexander enthusiastically continued to write pamphlets defending the radical Patriots, the First Continental Congress met and decided to boycott all British goods in the colonies. One of Alexander's professors at college, Dr. Cooper, was a very outspoken Tory. One night, Alexander learned that an angry Patriot mob was planning to tar and feather Dr. Cooper. As a Patriot, Alexander did not share Dr. Cooper's political views, but he respected his teacher. Bravely Alexander stood alone on the professor's doorstep trying to persuade the angry mob not to carry out their plan. But just as Alexander had almost won the crowd over, Dr. Cooper, red-faced and shaking a fist in the air, suddenly popped his head out a window and pleaded with the mob *not* to listen to Alexander Hamilton. Dr. Cooper knew Alexander was a Patriot and believed, when he saw the scene, that Alexander had brought the screaming mob to his door. Turning to face his teacher, Alexander tried to explain but Dr. Cooper shouted over him, addressing the mob,

"He's a rabble-rouser! He's a lunatic! Don't listen to a word this man tells you!"

The crowd burst out laughing. But in spite of Dr. Cooper's and Alexander's cross-purposes, Alexander managed to take Dr. Cooper to safety.

On the sixth of January 1776, the New York Provincial Congress decided to form an artillery company to aid in the defense of the colony. Hamilton applied for a command position with the artillery and received, a week later, his orders as captain. Tirelessly, Alexander drilled his men until he made valuable soldiers out of untrained civilians. He soon gained the notice of high-ranking officers.

In 1776 General William Howe, the English commander-in-chief, landed on the New York shores with a well disciplined army of thirty-four thousand men. His orders were simple: crush the colonist rebellion. General George Washington, the American commander-in-chief distributed one half of his small, undisciplined army to Manhattan and the other to Brooklyn Heights. Against Washington's ill-equipped forces Howe launched his attack on the 27th of August. There are some historians who believe that if Howe had moved decisively that day and destroyed the American army in Brooklyn, he would have convinced most colonists that their fledgling nation did not stand a chance against the superiority of British troops and weaponry. But General Howe decided to withhold further attack until the following morning, which gave the Americans — even in their desperate situation — a loophole through which they escaped to Manhattan and safety.

Against the British and the awful Hessians, who were German mercenaries that England used during much of the war, Alexander, nicknamed the "Little Lion," battled bravely. Slowly but surely, victories were won. Alexander's bravery came to the attention of General Washington who made him his special aide-de-camp with the rank of lieutenant colonel. Alexander missed the excitement of fighting on the front line. But as Washington's secretary, he was corresponding with the most important men in the colonies.

One day Alexander received a request to keep the New York Convention informed about everything that was happening on the battlefields by writing them daily letters. Officially this was not part of his duties as Washington's secretary, nevertheless, Alexander agreed. As it turned out, Alexander's influence with the New York Convention became extremely important to Washington; New York and other colonies were growing impatient with Washington's continual retreats. As many colonists sat in front of their cozy fires at home, they became convinced that they could do a much better job than Washington. Why, they asked each other, didn't Washington just face the British and battle it out, finishing the war? It was Alexander Hamilton who came to Washington's defense and convinced the colonists that Washington, with insufficient troops, weapons, and other supplies was doing all that was humanly possible on the battlefields. Wasn't American freedom, Alexander reasoned, worth any amount of time it took to ensure victory? The colonists agreed.

One day, American soldiers were forced to retreat like ants from a sabotaged anthill as British redcoats marched into Philadelphia in 1777. The Americans had no time to carry or destroy the armies' supplies stored in mills along the main road. Washington sent Alexander Hamilton and Captain Henry Lee with eight cavalrymen on the extremely dangerous mission of destroying these supplies.

They had almost completed their mission when the British discovered them and they were forced to scatter. It became evident to Captain Lee as he saw Alexander and some men trying to escape in a boat that was suddenly showered by enemy fire that his friend was dead. Lee communicated this to Washington, but just as Washington sadly read Lee's message, his tent flap opened and in stepped Alexander Hamilton dripping wet . . . sadly informing Washington that *Lee* was probably dead! In a few minutes the two "ghosts," thoroughly rattled, were shaking each other's hands.

On other important missions, such as negotiating with the British for an exchange of prisoners, Washington always sent Hamilton. Washington also relied on Hamilton's detailed and accurate descriptions of what was happening on the battlefields so that he could better formulate his strategy. When the British General Burgoyne surrendered his entire army at Saratoga, New York, to General Horatio Bates, France entered the war on the American side. Hamilton then served as Washington's go-between with the important European leaders who came to aid the Americans.

After 1778, most of the major battles of the war were fought to the south, away from Washington's camp and Hamilton began to consider the very real financial problems of the emerging nation. Hamilton convinced the Confederation that it was necessary to take out a foreign loan in order to stay in the war and slow inflation. Finally, money was obtained from France and Spain which kept America in the war.

In 1780 Washington's troops stayed the winter at Morristown New Jersey. Sometimes there were parties and dances. One day, General Philip Schuyler and his wife came with their very pretty daughter, Elizabeth. Alexander fell in love with the intelligent, kind girl and they soon became engaged. On December 14, 1780 Alexander and Elizabeth were married in Albany, New York.

By this time, Alexander was tired of the drudgery of being Washington's secretary. To fill the boredom, Hamilton was continually writing down his ideas. The greatest weakness among the colonies, in his view, was a lack of unity; each colony thought of itself as a separate ruling body. Hamilton outlined, too, what role Congress should and should not have, insisting that Congress could not be both a lawmaker *and* executive. A separate executive branch was needed. This was to be the office of President. Incredibly, Hamilton was only twenty-five when he formulated these ideas.

In February, 1781, Hamilton decided that he would leave his post as Washington's aide-de-camp. Washington who treated Hamilton more like a son than a soldier, granted him his dearest wish a few months later, putting him in charge of an infantry battalion. At last Alexander Hamilton was back on the front line were he longed to be! Washington even gave Hamilton a commanding role in attacking a key fortification which resulted, on October 19, 1781, in General Cornwallis' surrender at Yorktown. The Revolutionary War was practically over.

Hamilton now returned to Albany where the first of his eight children, Philip, was born. Hamilton decided to go into law. Studying hard, he passed the New York State examination.

In November, 1782 Hamilton was chosen as a delegate to Congress and travelled to Philadelphia. He continued to rally for a strong central government. In 1783 he opened his first law office at 57 Wall Street. Nearby practiced Aaron Burr, a retired army major. Hamilton would one day deeply regret ever setting eyes on the unscrupulous Aaron Burr who, in 1807, was even tried for treason.

As a lawyer, Hamilton earned wide recognition, particularly after his brilliant defense of a Loyalist named Benjamin Waddington. Very few lawyers after the war dared defend Loyalists even if they were innocent of the crimes of which they were accused. Hamilton, though, always did what he thought was right, not what happened to be popular. Boldly he defended Waddington and won!

Hamilton was elected a member of the Assembly, New York States' lower house in 1786. He was among those who wanted to see the Articles of Confederation replaced by a Federal Constitution. These people became known as "Federalists." It was Alexander Hamilton in 1786 who called for a convention in Philadelphia with delegates from each of the thirteen states. This would become the famous Constitutional Convention. In May 1787, fifty-five delegates came together. Most understood the need to create a central government, but the problem was getting the individual states who liked having their own power to ratify, or approve, the Constitution. Without a strong central government, Hamilton was sure there would be civil war and the states would break into small, weak countries.

In getting the Constitution adopted by the various state conventions, the Federalist essays proved invaluable. Probably Hamilton's brainchild, these eighty-five essays, most of them written by Hamilton, put forth convincing arguments as to why a Constitution was so necessary. Through his efforts, New York, which for so long had refused to even consider the Constitution, finally moved towards ratification.

On April 30, 1789 George Washington took the oath of office to become the first president of the United States of America, on a Wall Street balcony in New York. As he appointed members of his cabinet, there remained the most important cabinet post of all, the Secretary of the Treasury. This person would have to develop a workable system to solve the nation's financial difficulties. Washington chose Robert Morris who had been the Congressional Financier. It was a logical choice, but Morris — who did not want to take on the enormous task — suggested Alexander Hamilton instead. Without a second thought, Washington approached Hamilton, who accepted. At age thirty-four he became the first U.S. Secretary of the Treasury.

Hamilton's first big problem was paying back war debts. Some people wanted to forget all about these debts, but Hamilton remained firm: all debts had to be repaid. In January 1790 Hamilton told the House of Representatives that he had come up with a solution to the national debt. He offered to deliver his plan in person. Upon hearing this, a debate immediately broke out in the House. Many members who knew Hamilton personally also knew that he was an exceptional speaker. They were afraid that his sheer ability as a speaker would persuade them to accept his proposal. So it was decided that Hamilton should submit his report in writing. To this day no cabinet member has ever come in person to present proposals to Congress. As it turned out, Hamilton's proposal was approved anyway.

Hamilton also wanted to establish a National Bank. There was great protest against his plan. Some claimed it was unconstitutional. But the House, on February 8, 1791, voted 39-20 in favor of Hamilton's idea. Hamilton still needed Washington's signature on the bill before it could become law — and Washington had some doubts of his own. Washington asked Edmund Randolph, his Attorney-General and his Secretary of State, Thomas Jefferson what they thought of Hamilton's plan and they, too, claimed that the National Bank was unconstitutional. Even more uncertain, Washington then turned to Hamilton. With his usual vigor, Hamilton outlined the entire plan . . . and Washington's doubts were laid to rest. He signed the bill into law, and the National Bank was born.

In 1791 Aaron Burr was elected to the Senate. Hamilton knew that Burr was not only ambitious but utterly ruthless. Realizing that Hamilton disliked him, Burr openly declared himself Hamilton's enemy. Hamilton did not see eye to eye politically with Thomas Jefferson either but when Jefferson and Burr had the same number of electoral votes in the race for president, it was Alexander Hamilton's efforts that got Delaware to switch its vote, making Jefferson president over Burr.

Always busy, Hamilton helped found *The New York Post* newspaper. In 1801, when Hamilton's house "The Grange" in upper Manhattan was almost finished, he was looking forward to some peace and quiet and spending more time with his growing family. It was not to be.

Hamilton's son, Philip, then nineteen, was attending the theater one night in November, 1801. Beside him sat George Eacker a lawyer and good friend of Aaron Burr. Eacker began making loud, insulting remarks about Hamilton's father. Finally Philip challenged Eacker to a duel. Hamilton knew nothing about his son's duel. It was fought in New Jersey. Shot in the side, Philip was taken home to die. Hamilton was devastated.

When Burr decided to run for governor of New York, Hamilton vigorously fought against his election. Burr subsequently challenged Hamilton himself to a duel.

On July 11th Hamilton sailed across the Hudson to Weehawken, New Jersey; his second in the duel was his friend, Nathaniel Pendleton. Dr. Hosack, a surgeon, accompanied them in the boat. When they found a clearing in the woods, Hamilton and Burr wordlessly loaded their pistols. As he walked the ten paces, picture-flashes from St. Croix, the bloody battlefields, his life in New York, his family, crowded Hamilton's memory. He wondered, as he turned to face Burr, if the country he had helped create would one day be as great as he imagined.

Burr's bullet, when it came, lodged deep in Hamilton's abdomen. He died, in agony, the following day.

Abandoned and utterly poverty-stricken as a child, Hamilton was fiercely determined to break out of the dark corner where he had been thrust by life. Standing but five feet seven inches tall when he reached full height, Hamilton grew to become a giant in American history. His achievements, ideas, and visions for the future are remembered and cherished by his countrymen still.

Scott Hamilton   (1958 -)
Olympic Skater

People, too many to count, filled the stands at the Bowling Green State University ice skating arena. They were cheering for him — Scott Hamilton. He leapt high into the air and performed a series of dangerous, extremely difficult whirls with apparent ease. Loudly the cymbals smashed as his skates returned to the ice. He was skating, no floating, on top of the world. Then suddenly a door squeaked open, bright sunshine poured in and the fans vanished — but not the dream.

Somewhere, probably in Toledo Ohio on August 28, 1958, a baby boy was born. He weighed five pounds and seven ounces. His mother, perhaps hoping that her child would have a better life than she could possibly give him, put him up for adoption. When Ernie and Dorothy found out that there was a baby boy waiting to be adopted they excitedly drove twenty miles to the Lucas County Child and Family Services Agency in Toledo.

Ernest and Dorothy had married in the summer of 1951. Their daughter Susan had been born a few years afterwards. Receiving his Ph.D. in botany Ernie began teaching at Bowling Green State University in Ohio. Although the Hamiltons had planned on having a large family, over and over again Dorothy miscarried. They were heartbroken.

51

But at the Lucas County Child and Family Services Agency, when they saw the tiny baby they knew their prayers had been answered. He was the most beautiful baby boy they had ever seen. However, they could not bring him home right away as they would have liked. The rule at the Agency was that they had to go home and think about the adoption one last time. Of course the Hamiltons did not have to think twice. The next day, waiting in the deserted parking lot for the Agency to open, the Hamiltons, several hours later, brought their baby home. They named him Scott Scovell Hamilton.

The baby had a room of his own with a large crib out of which he was forever trying to climb. Finally Scott's father had to build a lid making the crib into a cage to keep the active, curious little boy from hurting himself. One summer, when Scott was two years old, his father was working on the roof and left the ladder next to the house when he went to a neighbor's home. When he returned, little Scott was hippety-hoppeting on the roof and waving cheerfully to his bulging-eyed father below. Fortunately Ernie was able to climb up the ladder and net the little boy before any other ideas popped into his head.

In the Hamilton home there were always dogs and a succession of cats named Puffy Buttons. When Scott was about three years old, his parents adopted another baby boy whom they named Steve. The Hamiltons now had three children. They were happy but for one thing — Scott's parents noticed that their three-year-old son had stopped growing. Concerned, they took Scott to many different doctors. The doctors believed that Scott's body was not digesting and absorbing food properly but they were uncertain as to how to help him. For much of his early childhood, Scott was in and out of hospitals and to this day he dislikes them.

At age five, Scott entered kindergarten and was the youngest member of his class. His teacher thought that maybe his youth made his progress a bit slower than that of his older classmates, but Scott worked hard and managed to keep up. But by the end of Scott's first grade year he was a very sick little boy. In the second grade he was so small that he had to use a first grader's desk. His teacher made sure Scott learned his multiplication tables very well. She thought that Scott could become an accountant or a bookkeeper when he grew up — it was evident that he would never be able to hold down a job that required much physical activity. Looking into a crystal ball, how surprised and pleased Scott's teacher would have been to see her once frail, sickly pupil skating up to accept an Olympic gold medal!

When Scott was in the third grade he had a feeding tube that came out of one nostril from his stomach and was taped behind his ear. In the unforgettable fall of 1967, doctors informed Scott's parents that he had cystic fibrosis. They said Scott had about six months to live. The Hamiltons were devastated.

Dr. Klepner, a friend of the family, however, was skeptical. He was not at all convinced that Scott had cystic fibrosis. He advised the Hamiltons to take Scott to the Boston Children's Hospital in Massachusetts. Like Dr. Klepner, Dr. Schwachman, a Harvard Medical School professor, believed that Scott did not have cystic fibrosis. Scott was seen also by a psychologist who told Ernie and Dorothy that Scott was very worried and frightened about his illness and scared that his parents might die. In Dr. Schwachman's opinion, psychological care and better eating habits were all that Scott needed to improve his health.

As if by fate, that same year, in 1967, Bowling Green State University built a huge ice-skating rink. At Dr. Klepner's suggestion, Scott participated in Saturday skating lessons with his big sister Susan. Doctors today believe that the increased physical activity and the coolness of the rink may have contributed to Scott's recovery. But whatever the reason, Scott started growing — and so did his love of skating. Soon people watching from the rinkside were commenting on Scott's natural ability. He seemed to make even difficult moves appear easy.

But skating — especially competitive skating — costs money. It requires proper equipment and expert training. The Hamiltons, however, were convinced that the skating had helped cure Scott and they were willing to do anything to allow him to continue. They would sell their house, Dorothy insisted, if necessary.

At age thirteen, Scott went to live and train with Pierre Brunet who was an Olympic gold medalist and figure skating coach at the Wagon Wheel Figure Skating Club in Rockton, Illinois. Scott worked very hard, practicing at least six hours each day. Coach Brunet who had lost his own son Jean-Pierre in a highway accident some years before took a special interest in Scott.

Travelling constantly as he trained, Scott attended many different schools. His senior year of high school he moved three times, finally graduating in 1976. Also in 1976, in Boston, at the Jimmy Fund benefit exhibition, Scott met Kitty and Peter Carruthers. Scott was the Junior National Champion and Kitty and Peter were getting their own skating careers underway. Scott and Kitty began dating at the 1978 National Championships in Portland where Scott won third place and a spot on the U.S. World Team. Just like Scott, Kitty and her brother Peter, who formed a skating pair, had each been separately adopted. Kitty's ancestors were Lebanese while her brother was from Dutch and English ancestry. Both had been adopted as babies from the New England Home for Little Wanderers. Scott and Kitty had much time to get to know each other. They enjoyed many happy moments together but the strain of competition and skating eventually drew them apart although they remained very good friends.

Having finished high school, Scott decided to quit competitive skating forever and become a student at Bowling Green State University. For the last time, Scott hung up his skates in his room. Whenever he walked in, however, the silver blades would catch the sun, sparkling in the silence. Sadly Scott shoved his skates in a box deep in his closet; he did not want his parents spending any more money on him and his skating. Before classes at Bowling Green started, though, an anonymous rich couple came forth and said they would financially support Scott so he could continue skating. Bursting with happiness, Scott made a dash for his room.

Then — tragedy. Dorothy Hamilton was diagnosed with cancer. Not wanting to upset her children, Dorothy remained optimistic about her illness. At the United States National Figure Skating Contest early in 1977, Scott placed only ninth. He was very disappointed. Shortly after, when Scott was nineteen, his mother succumbed to cancer.

Scott was crushed. For days he sat alone beside the pond in the Hamilton backyard. People had often commented that Scott looked like his adoptive mother. Dorothy had always liked it when they said that, and, smiling, she would reply that children grow up to look like the people who love them. Scott felt terrible that he had placed so low in the competition; he felt he had let his mother down. Suddenly the pond seemed to freeze over and Scott saw himself standing on the ice. People were cheering. In his heart Scott wanted to show the world that his mother's faith and encouragement had given him the inner strength to become a champion.

Over the next few years Scott skated as he never had before, spending hours and hours practicing. One judge, however, bluntly told Scott, who is five feet, three and a half inches tall, that he would never be taken seriously because of his small size. Scott was hurt and even alarmed by the judge's unkind words. He had to win! Determined, Scott continued working. He changed his jumping style on the ice to give people the impression of greater height. Then in 1980, Scott won third place in the national competition to become part of the U.S. Olympic figure skating squad. Because of his strong will in the face of so many obstacles, the American team captains chose Scott to carry the U.S. flag and lead the troupe into the arena on the opening day ceremonies of the 1980 Winter Games at Lake Placid New York. Scott finished fifth at the 1980 Olympics and again at the world championship a few weeks later.

But at the international meet in Connecticut in March 1981 Scott took first place. Later in the same year he won an individual gold medal at the first annual Skate America tournament. Scott was voted Male Athlete of the Year by the U.S. Olympic Committee.

Scott had a lot of time off the ice to think. He was determined to safeguard his national and world championships for the next three years. He would do it for his mother. Scott practiced eight hours a day six days a week under the careful guidance of Don Laws at the Colorado Ice Arena in Denver. Through sheer work, persistence, and talent, Scott did manage to hold onto his national and world titles in 1982 and 1983. At the 1983 world championship, Scott stunned his competitors with his spectacular free skating, doing six triple jumps. His outstanding performance of the difficult routine earned him nothing but 5.8s and 5.9s (with 6.0 being a perfect score) — and even an unheard of 5.9 for artistic impression from a Soviet judge.

Scott had won an impressive fifteen straight championships since 1980 and was the likely candidate for the gold medal in men's figure skating at the 1984 Winter Olympics in Sarajevo, Yugoslavia.

On the big day Scott was very nervous. He wanted to win so badly that he was having trouble concentrating. As Scott Hamilton glided onto the ice, the spectators leaned forward in their seats. Skating flawlessly Scott earned a first-place finish in the school figures part of the competition. But as Scott continued, some spectators noticed, puzzled, that he appeared to be slightly off-balance. What they did not know, was that Scott had picked up an ear infection which was affecting his balance on the free skating. But he had decided that he was not going to use the infection as an excuse if he did not skate his best. However Scott skated his compulsory figures so perfectly that he soon had an impressive lead over other competitors including the Canadian National Champion, Brian Orser. In brilliant style, Scott captured the gold, becoming the first American since David Jenkins in 1960 to win this honor. After skating the traditional victory lap, Scott held up an American flag and led his fellow medalists on one more spin — this one was for his mother, the greatest influence in his life.

Scott won another spectacular victory at the world championships in Ottawa, Canada a month later. Not long after, Scott announced that he was going to retire from amateur skating.

Scott was swamped with million-dollar contracts from all the big ice shows and even a tempting offer to head his own touring company. But Scott finally decided to become part of the Ice Capades, and has been with this famous ice show since August of 1984. Although Scott Hamilton misses the challenge of competitive skating, he loves performing in front of large, enthusiastic crowds, bringing children into a magical, make believe world and watching adults, at least for a couple of hours, forget their worries.

Hamilton has never learned much about his biological parents. Once, when he was a boy he asked his mother who they might have been. Dorothy was so hurt that

Scott vowed never to ask any more questions. He decided that it was the Hamiltons who had loved and cared for him as a little boy — heard his first words, helped him take his first steps, and taught him right from wrong. This is where his life's history really began. Now, even as an adult, Scott has never felt the need to find out more about his past. Perhaps as a child, during a dark moment, he might have wondered if his mother and father could possibly love him as much as biological parents could. But in his heart he would have known the truth; he had been chosen by the Hamiltons as their child to love and he had given them the precious gift of his childhood.

Scott Hamilton is a fan of the Denver Broncos and, whenever he can, he attends their games. He also likes to listen to music in his spare time. Each year Hamilton, who has met with former President Ronald Reagan, returns home to skate in the Bowling Green Skating Club's annual show. At these performances, money is raised for a very important cause: cancer research.

John Lennon   (1940 - 1980)
Singer/Songwriter for the Beatles

It was 1963 and music history was about to be made. Four young men walked onto the stage as the support act for the famous American singer, Chris Montez. But the audience soon made it resoundingly clear just who they had come to see. In amazement, the Beatles suddenly found themselves the main act of the performance. In March of that whirlwindish year the song *From Me To You* written by John Lennon and Paul McCartney entered the charts at number six and in a matter of days climbed effortlessly to number one. A new word entered the English language: beatlemania. Coined by astounded reporters, this word was an attempt to express the fanatical following the Beatles inspired in people of all ages. Just before Christmas of 1963, the song *I Want to Hold Your Hand* heralded the Beatles' arrival on American shores. In fact Beatles expert Neville Stannard estimates that this song in single, EP, and LP form sold an incredible 21.5 million copies worldwide. Early the next year the Beatles flew to the United States and on February 9 and 16 appeared on the Ed Sullivan Show before an audience of 70,000,000 Americans. According to statistics, on that night, the national crime rate, particularly for juvenile offenses, dropped lower than at any other time in a half century.

On August 15, 1965 the Beatles, by now far-famed, performed at New York's Shea Stadium in front of the largest audience in history: nearly 60,000 roaring fans. For safety reasons, the Beatles were taken from the stadium in an armored Wells Fargo van and it seemed to John Lennon at that moment, his ears ringing from the screams of adoring fans, that he was wanted by the entire world. There had been a time, however, when he had felt just the opposite.

John Lennon was born on October 9, 1940 at the Oxford Street Maternity Hospital in Liverpool England during an air raid by bombers of the German Luftwaffe; when such raids occurred John and the other babies were quickly put underneath the beds for protection.

Julia Stanley Lennon, John's mother, was a fluttery, rather absent-minded person. Against her family's better judgement she married Alfred Lennon who worked, whenever he could find work, as a ship's waiter. "Freddie" Lennon was not present at his son's birth. It came as no surprise to Julia's family when, one day, Freddie Lennon simply disappeared. He turned up again, though, when John was famous.

"Who needs you now?" was John's attitude.

Taking advantage of John's feelings, Freddie publicly declared that his son was ignoring him. Anger filled John. His fans, too, believed that Freddie Lennon was being unfair. Angry, John told Freddie that there was more to being a father and a son than sharing the same blood type — there was sharing sad times, hard times, and something as goofy as love.

Although John knew in his heart that Freddie's hand was probably extended more out of greed than affection, he nevertheless decided to help his father financially. Even as a child John was known for his generosity, often sharing his candy and toys with friends.

When John was four years old his mother realized that her marriage to Freddie Lennon was over and she moved in with a man named John Dykins, a hotel waiter with children of his own. Unwanted in this new family, John was sent to live with his mother's older sister, Mimi, and her husband George Smith. Bewilderment, jealousy, and hurt strangled John and forced angry tears from him. He felt abandoned and betrayed. Although John's mother lived not even ten miles away, she did not make a point of visiting him regularly. But whenever John cried, he cried alone, keeping his true feelings hidden from Aunt Mimi and Uncle George. They had no children of their own and were very happy to have him stay with them.

Aunt Mimi and Uncle George lived in Woolton, a suburb of Liverpool. Nearby was a Salvation Army Children's home called Strawberry Field where John often played as a child. Later it became the inspiration for one of John Lennon's best-loved songs, "Strawberry Fields Forever." It was Uncle George who bought John his first musical instrument, a harmonica which the little boy played day and night. Later, when he was older, his Aunt Mimi bought him a steel-stringed Spanish guitar. Remarkably, John Lennon never took lessons and did not even know how to read music.

But although Aunt Mimi loved John very much, she believed in discipline. She wanted John to grow up properly. When he was a bit older and Aunt Mimi got mad at him, John would heatedly reply that one day he would be famous and she would be sorry. Uncle George, though, was a softie. Whenever John got a hands-on-hips-talking-to from Aunt Mimi, Uncle George would give him a secret wink or a nod that meant "look under your pillow upstairs." There Uncle George would leave candy or cookies for John, especially if he thought John might need a smile. When John was four and a half years old, Uncle George took him on his lap and taught him to read and write.

Soon it was time for John to enter Dovedale Primary School. The school was located very near "Penny Lane," a street in Liverpool which later became the title of another popular Beatles song. John was a bright student who especially enjoyed art and creative writing. Some of his crayon artwork from Dovedale Primary, lovingly saved by Aunt Mimi, would later find its way on the cover of his 1974 solo album called *Walls and Bridges.*

When John was twelve years old, in June of 1952, his beloved, gentle Uncle George died suddenly of a brain hemorrhage. In his child's heart, John felt not only grief but anger at being abandoned a second time by a father. John's behavior took a turn for the worse. In the fall of that same year, John entered Quarry Bank High School. Becoming the class clown, his grades soon deteriorated. His best friend, for whom John would later buy a supermarket, was a boy by the name of Pete Shotton, and together they delighted in playing practical jokes on their teachers and classmates. They soon gained the reputation of troublemakers with John always the ringleader. Shaking a finger in the air, parents warned their children to steer clear of John Lennon, whom they considered a bad influence.

In school, where there was little freedom, John Lennon felt trapped and he often threw himself into the limelight for all the wrong reasons; he tossed erasers out the windows, gambled on school grounds, played hooky, and disrupted classes by passing around cartoons. When his teachers ran out of patience they sent him in a dither to the headmaster for caning. Trudging down the halls John told himself that if this was the worst they could do to him it wasn't much. Steadily John's grades sank lower and lower.

In his third year at Quarry Bank, John Lennon failed every subject — including art. Although John was a good artist, he hated doing assigned drawings. When it came right down to it, John detested doing anything if he was *forced* to do it. He only did well those things he wanted to do, like drawing caricatures of his teachers. At the yearly school festival John and Pete Shotton would put up a booth where people threw darts at John Lennon's drawings of the Quarry Bank teachers. Without fail, their booth always raised more money than any other.

John Lennon loved swimming and running but was not very good in sports like football because of his nearsightedness. He enjoyed the company of friends like Pete Shotton but at times John felt very alone. Sometimes he thought there was something wrong with him; he noticed a lot of things other people did not seem to notice at all.

The year 1956 was significant for John Lennon. It was the year he first heard Elvis Presley's *Heartbreak Hotel* and was instantly captivated by Elvis' energy and style. In a flash he knew the type of music he wanted to make and decided to form his own band.

Lonnie Donegan, a British singer was easier to imitate than Elvis Presley. Lonnie's music, influenced by rock n' roll was known as "skiffle" and could be played with inexpensive guitars and makeshift instruments. Forming a skiffle group with Pete Shotton and some other friends, John Lennon decided to name his band the Quarrymen, after his school, Quarry Bank High and a rock quarry where as children, John Lennon and his friends would meet. Because John Lennon wanted to perform at school events and dances, his behavior in school improved.

The beginnings of the Beatles go back to those early days of the Quarrymen. One member whom John invited to join was a fifteen-year old boy named Paul McCartney who was in the audience for the group's first important public perform- ance on July 6, 1957 at the Woolton Parish Church. John Lennon took an instant liking to Paul who could sing, actually tune a guitar, and even, John thought, resembled Elvis Presley. But John did not immediately ask Paul to join the Quarrymen; there was the very real danger that with Paul's talent and musical knowledge, he would naturally take over as leader of the band. Still, despite these misgivings, John Lennon asked him to join and, thus, John and Paul commenced their famous songwriting partnership.

Yet although John Lennon and Paul McCartney grew to become very good friends, their personalities were considerably different. Paul was generally hardworking and good-tempered, whereas John was often lazy and hotheaded — qualities which had never endeared him to adults. Having failed his eight examinations at Quarry Bank High, John left the school and in September of 1957 enrolled in the Liverpool College of Art. His teachers had suggested he enroll, as art seemed to be the only subject that interested him. John's Aunt Mimi said she would help him financially while he went to art school, hoping that he would get better grades than at Quarry Bank. Paul McCartney, in the meantime, attended the Liverpool Institute close by.

Although John enjoyed art, he enjoyed making music more. Living in Liverpool, Europe's busiest port, sailors often brought with them the latest records not yet available in England. John and Paul heard many new songs at parties which enormously influenced the music the Quarrymen played and the type of songs John Lennon and Paul McCartney were writing.

It was in 1958 that John first met George Harrison, a fellow student of Paul's at the Liverpool Institute. George was fourteen years old and an avid rock 'n roll fan who had taught himself to play the guitar by listening to Buddy Holly records over and over. Soon George was playing lead guitar with the Quarrymen. Paul, George, and John were now the band's principle musicians.

On July 15, 1958, tragedy again entered the life of young John Lennon — his mother, Julia Lennon, was struck and killed by a car in front of Aunt Mimi's house. John was seventeen. Once more John Lennon was filled with a sense of loss; he had just begun to establish a relationship with his mother and now she had left him again — this time permanently. In his anger, pain, and frustration John grew increasingly aggressive toward other people.

However, at the art school, John met two special people. One was Cynthia Powell, and the other was Stuart Sutcliffe. Cynthia was a quiet, even-tempered person, almost John's exact opposite in character. Cynthia says that as an art student she tried hard to follow all the rules while John tried equally as hard to break them. Neither did the dedicated Stu Sutcliffe resemble John Lennon, who usually went about his art work with lazy disinterest. Winning an art competition, Stu used the prize money to purchase a bass guitar and then he too joined the Quarrymen. Patiently John Lennon tried to teach his friend how to play the bass guitar but Stu, although a gifted artist was not as talented a musician. Whenever the Quarrymen performed in public, Stu would turn his back to the audience so they could not see what he was doing. But in the year 1959 the Quarrymen were far from being an exceptional band. Frequently they did not even have a drummer.

During the summer, for the audition of *Carroll Levi's TV Discoveries* talent show, John decided to change the band's name to Johnny and the Moondogs. Though they were not selected, John remained determined to keep improving. Stu Sutcliffe, inspired by Buddy Holly's group, the Crickets, suggested the band change its name to the Beetles. Associating the name to beat music, John changed the spelling to the "Beatles." Trying to make their name more high-sounding, they changed it, one more time, to the "Silver Beatles." It was as the Silver Beatles that they met Allan

Williams, their first professional manager, who owned the Jacaranda coffee bar in Liverpool in whose cellar they performed.

Early in 1960, Larry Parnes, a concert promoter and manager from London, approached John Lennon after hearing the band play and told him that he would like to hear them without Stu Sutcliffe, who it was evident, did not know the first thing about playing the bass. But John, remaining loyal to his friend, replied that if Stu did not play, the band did not play. Thus, the Silver Beatles missed the golden opportunity of possibly touring with the popular singer Billy Fury. Still convinced that the group had talent, Parnes offered the Silver Beatles — John, Paul, George, and, of course, Stu — a job as support to the singer Johnny Gentle which they accepted. For several weeks they toured northern England.

In 1960 John Lennon was dismissed from the Liverpool College of Art. He had done so little work that the college officials saw no point in letting him continue. John dreaded telling Aunt Mimi the terrible news.

Life suddenly seemed bleak for John Lennon and the Silver Beatles. They were without a drummer and had very few bookings. But even when life is at its gloomiest, John Lennon was to learn that in turning a corner — or two — one's luck can also turn. Their manager Allan Williams obtained a job for them in Hamburg, Germany. Needless to say Aunt Mimi was appalled to learn that John had been asked to leave the Art College. She was only partly mollified when John informed her that he would be earning - £100 a week (about $300) exaggerating his earnings by £85 ($255). Approaching Pete Best who played drums at the Casbah Coffee Club, Paul McCartney asked him if he would like to play drums for the group. Pete said he would.

When the Silver Beatles arrived in Hamburg and saw the Indra Club, owned by Williams' partner, Bruno Koschmider, they were sorely disappointed. The club was dismal, dark, and damp. They had to perform about six hours each night, while sleeping in less than favorable conditions: the wall in the room in which they slept was located directly behind Bruno's cinema screen.

As the Silver Beatles grew in popularity, however, Bruno decided to have them perform in a bigger club called the Kaiserkeller where they took turns with another band, Rory Storm and the Hurricanes. This group had a drummer named Richard Starkey . . . who went by the name of Ringo Starr.

Astrid Kirchnerr, a student from the local art school, became one of the Silver Beatles' fans, and soon Stu Sutcliffe and Astrid fell in love. One day Astrid decided the Silver Beatles needed haircuts. She cut everyone's hair except Pete Best's — who refused to let Astrid near him with her click-clacking scissors. It was Astrid who gave the group the distinctive hairstyle the world would come to know and many to imitate: the hair brushed down over their foreheads without a part.

By now, too, the Silver Beatles had shortened their name; they were, simply, the Beatles. When a man named Peter Eckhorn opened a new club in Hamburg called the Top Ten and offered the Beatles better pay and rooming conditions, they leapt at the opportunity and left the Kaiserkeller. Enraged, Bruno went straight to the police who suddenly found that George Harrison was only seventeen and as a minor could not work in the clubs. George was swiftly deported and Pete Best and Paul McCartney, after being arrested on an outlandish charge of setting fire to the curtains in their own dwelling, left shortly thereafter for England. Stu took a plane back, and John, with as much of the bands' equipment as he could bring, traveled home by train. The Beatles had been in Germany for five months and were returning with their pockets and stomachs empty.

At first, depressed and exhausted, the Beatles laid their instruments aside. John spent an entire week in bed while Aunt Mimi pried him with hot tea and honey, all the while shaking her head ominously. But neither John nor the other members of the band could stand to remain idle for long. Playing for a dance at the Litherland Town Hall shortly after Christmas, their friends in the audience were amazed at how much the group had improved. The nonstop, teeth-gritting sessions in Hamburg had paid off after all.

Sitting among the spectators, very impressed, was Bob Wooler, a disc jockey who approached Ray McFall, owner of the Cavern Club and asked him to book the Beatles. Soon the Beatles were attracting large crowds to the Cavern Club; there they performed *Hello, Little Girl,* the first song John Lennon ever wrote.

In 1961, the Beatles — Paul, John, George, Stu Sutcliffe, and Pete Rest — were again off to Hamburg to play at the Top Ten. Stu Sutcliffe enrolled in Hamburg's Art School and, after much thought, decided to leave the band. In June 1961 Stu and Astrid were married. But on April 10, 1962 at the age of twenty-one, Stu Sutcliffe died of a brain hemorrhage. John was deeply affected, even embittered, by his friend's sudden, tragic death.

While in Hamburg, the Beatles made their first commercial recording. They cut eight tracks, six playing as back up to the British singer Tony Sheridan, and two of their own: *Ain't She Sweet* with John as lead singer and the instrumental *Cry for a Shadow.* A single from the session entitled *My Bonnie* with Tony Sheridan and the Beatles, became very popular in Germany. Bringing some copies of *My Bonnie* back with them to Liverpool, the Beatles gave one to Bob Wooler who played it often at the Cavern Club where he hosted rock n' roll sessions during the lunch hour.

Brian Epstein, manager of the North East Music Store (NEMS), a record shop located not far from the Cavern Club, became increasingly perplexed by demands for *My Bonnie*. Learning that the Beatles were playing at the Cavern Club, Epstein decided to so some investigating.

Entering the cold, dark club, Epstein expected very little. But he was astonished by the Beatles' talent and was particularly impressed by John Lennon, noticeably the band's leader. Back at his shop Epstein ordered from Germany one hundred additional copies of *My Bonnie* which were quickly snapped up. Instantly recognizing that this band possessed that extra something special, Epstein offered to be their manager. The Beatles agreed — that is, if Epstein agreed not to try and change the kind of music they played. With a wide grin, Epstein laid their fears to rest on that account. Not even with a magic wand, he told them, would he dare touch their style.

Brian Epstein's family owned the NEMS stores and were, therefore, influential customers with the big record companies. Using this connection, Epstein obtained an audition for the Beatles and established the company called NEMS Enterprises.

In January 1962 the Beatles and Brian Epstein excitedly poured into the Decca Records Studios for the audition, only to be turned away. Decca was little impressed with the Beatles and told Epstein that bands with guitars were on their way out; Epstein was flabbergasted at the refusal. But as the studio doors closed with finality behind them, Epstein knew — he just knew — that one day Decca Records would have cause to regret its hasty decision.

By May of 1962, Epstein and the Beatles had been turned down by almost every major record company in the country. It seemed that Decca was right after all, until Epstein approached a producer by the name of George Martin, who ran the EMI-owned Parlophone label, well known for putting out Peter Sellers' comedy records. Martin said he would give the Beatles a chance.

During the audition, Martin took the opportunity to test each member of the band individually. He decided that Pete Best was not a good enough drummer. In their own minds, the other Beatles had come to the conclusion that Pete's style did not fit in with the rest of the group's music. It was Brian Epstein who told Pete what George Martin had determined. John was sad for Pete, who took the news gracefully and left the band, still a very good friend. To replace Pete the Beatles chose Ringo Starr whom they had met in Hamburg.

In August 1962 John Lennon married Cynthia Powell when they learned that she was pregnant. The wedding reception took place quietly at Reece's Cafe' and, because no alcohol was allowed at the cafe, everyone, including Brian Epstein, the best man, toasted to the couple's happiness with tall glasses of water. John Lennon's first son, Julian Lennon (named after John's mother Julia) would be born on April 8, 1963.

During September 4-11, 1962, the Beatles recorded their first songs at the EMI Studios in London. The song *Love Me Do* written by John Lennon and Paul McCartney featured John as lead singer and a harmonica solo. *Love Me Do* reached number seventeen on the British charts. Excitedly George Martin brought the Beatles back to the studio to record *Please Please Me* with John once again as lead singer. This time, their song *Please Please Me* went straight to number one. A week later they released what would become their first number one LP also entitled *Please Please Me*. The album contained fourteen songs, eight of which were written by John Lennon and Paul McCartney. Over 2,000,000 copies were sold. Their second LP *With the Beatles* (which in the United States was called *Meet the Beatles*) also went to the top of the LP charts.

The year 1963 was an exceptionally busy one for the Beatles, or the "Fab Four," as they came to be called. They performed in concerts, appeared on television, and, of course, were making waves on the radio. Their single called *She Loves You* came onto the chart at number two only a week after its release and sold more than 1,000,000 copies in Britain alone, becoming the best-selling record of that year. On October 13, 1963 they made their debut on the then most popular variety show on television, *Sunday Night at the London Palladium* while 15,000,000 people watched, glued to the tube. On November 4 the Beatles appeared at the Royal Variety Performance before Queen Elizabeth, the Queen Mother, Princess Margaret, Lord Snowdon, and many other VIPs.

In late March of 1964, John Lennon published his first book, a best-seller entitled *In His Own Write* which sold, by the end of the year, 300,000 copies. Also in that year the Beatles made their first movie *A Hard Day's Night* which premiered in London's Picadilly Circus and was well received not only by fans but by critics too. On August 5, 1964 the theme song from *A Hard Day's Night* was number one on the singles and LP charts in both Britain and the United States, an astounding achievement.

In 1965 John purchased a beautiful bungalow in the seaside town of Poole, Dorset for his Aunt Mimi who had, all this time, proudly, quietly watched John's phenomenal rise to fame. Harold Wilson, the British Prime Minister, himself from Liverpool, could also be numbered among the Beatles' fans. At Wilson's suggestion, the Queen presented each of the Beatles with the prestigious MBE (Member of the Order of the British Empire) at Buckingham Palace. In 1969, however, John would return the MBE award in protest of British government policies in Nigeria and its support of American involvement in Vietnam.

Yet, the extraordinary pressures of fame were taking their toll on John Lennon and he sought escape them through drugs. Much more is known today than in the mid-1960s of the terrible dangers of drug use. Fortunately for John Lennon and for popular music he realized that drugs were no solution and began to look for other ways to relieve his restlessness. He took part in an anti-war movie called *How I Won the War,* playing the part of "Private Gripweed." But it was a chance meeting in 1966 with artist Yoko Ono at the Indica Gallery in London that completely changed John's life. For the first time he fell deeply in love.

In the year 1967 John Lennon's and Paul McCartney's song *All You Need Is Love* became the summer's smash hit. But also in that summer their manager Brian Epstein died tragically.

In late 1967 the Beatles bought a clothes shop together and decided to launch their own organization, the Apple Company, as a record label and management company. Above the clothes shop they wanted to install offices where different Apple Companies would be located — for movies, publishing, electronics, and the Apple Record Label. After seven months of losing money, though, the Beatles decided to close shop, generously giving clothes away to passersby. The only Apple business that was ever really successful was the record label whose first release was *Hey Jude,* the Beatles' eighteenth British single. The Beatles did establish, however, the Apple Foundation for the Arts, donating large sums of money to writers and artists.

In 1968, John Lennon's marriage to Cynthia ended. Some months later he would marry Yoko Ono. But first, on January 30, 1969 the Beatles made their historic trip up the stairs to the roof of the Apple building with amplifiers and played some songs during the filming of *Let It Be.* It was the last time the Beatles would ever perform together.

John and his new wife Yoko shared much in common. Together they campaigned for world peace and Lennon came up with his well-known song *Give Peace a Chance.* In the summer of 1971 Lennon and Yoko went to live in New York and they soon became actively involved in political rallies against social injustice. Then — the incredible.

In 1972, President Richard M. Nixon was seeking reelection. He feared, however, the political consequences that an outspoken, well-known liberal like John Lennon would have on his campaign. On February 4, 1972, Senator Strom Thurmond sent a secret message to Attorney General John Mitchell urging that John Lennon be deported.

Learning that the extension of his visa, granted five days earlier, had suddenly been revoked, John Lennon demanded to know why. The immigration authorities informed him that they would not extend his visa because of his involvement with drugs in England. In 1983 papers released by the U.S. government revealed that FBI agents had trailed John Lennon everywhere in the hope of arresting him on a new drug charge and thereby deporting him. But John Lennon hired the best lawyers that money could buy. Naturally, however, the realization that a full-scale political machine had been mounted to remove him from the country hurt John Lennon very much. Some of the old feelings of rejection he had experienced as an unwanted child resurfaced.

As legal battles ensued, John Lennon and Yoko continued with their lives. At the Madison Square Garden concert on August 30, 1972, John Lennon and Yoko participated in a special performance for the One to One Organization to collect money for handicapped children. They raised $1,500,000 for the charity.

On October 9, 1975 — John Lennon's thirty-fifth birthday — his wife Yoko gave birth to their son Sean Lennon. A year later, at last, John Lennon received permission to remain in the United States as a permanent resident. John Lennon described this time in his life as extremely happy. He became totally devoted to raising Sean. Remembering how it had felt to be expulsed from his own home as a child and guilty that he had been away in concerts while Julian was growing up, he spent practically all of his time with Sean and encouraged Julian to visit frequently.

But in the midst of John Lennon's new-found happiness came tragedy, the specter that had always hovered on the sidelines of his life. On December 8, 1980, John Lennon, who had so ardently campaigned for peace, was shot to death outside his apartment building in New York. His murderer was a twenty-five year old American from Hawaii. His name was Mark David Chapman.

Idolizing John Lennon from earliest childhood, Chapman had even married a Japanese American because, in his mind, she looked like Yoko Ono. One of the most chilling and bizarre aspects of the murder was that, when Chapman quit his job in Honolulu, he signed out as "John Lennon."

Returning home from a recording session in their limousine neither John Lennon nor Yoko Ono could possibly have known that in the shadows, a gun pressed to his heart, Chapman waited . . . for them. John and Yoko were walking easily towards their building when suddenly a voice in the darkness shouted, "Mr. Lennon!" and then fired five bullets from a .38 caliber revolver. The bullets sliced into John Lennon's shoulder and back.

John stumbled inside the apartment building, followed by a frantic Yoko. A police car rushed John Lennon to the emergency room, but John Lennon was pronounced dead on arrival at Roosevelt Hospital. He was only forty. Chapman was convicted of murder.

Ringo Starr and John's oldest son Julian flew immediately to New York to comfort Yoko and Sean. At Yoko's suggestion, an international silent vigil was held for ten minutes on Sunday December 14th. More than 100,000 people came to New York's Central Park for the 2 p.m. vigil, many with their hands outstretched in the gesture of peace.

As the decade of the 90s unfolds, John Lennon speaks to us still and we can hear him, strong as ever, as he challenges the world to *Give Peace a Chance.*

Hugh Leonard/John Keyes Byrne (1926 -)
Irish Author

Hugh Leonard is the pen name of John Keyes Byrne, who was born on November 9, 1926 in Dublin Ireland, the son of Annie Byrne and a father he never knew.

"I was adopted when ten days old by a working class couple. I knew from the outset that I was not their natural child; living in Ireland and knowing little of the 'facts of life' I knew of no reason why I should feel inferior or underprivileged and could not understand why a neighbor occasionally went out of his or her way to make me feel so. Silly person, I thought!"

He was adopted by Nicholas Keyes, a gardener, and his wife Margaret. One day, without telling her husband where she was going, Margaret left her house in the seaside town of Dalkey and walked all the way to Dublin. She walked hurriedly as if she had an important mission to accomplish. When she returned to her house several hours later, Margaret's usually stern face radiated joy; in her arms was a small bundle, from which peeked a tiny head and stretched a miniature pair of hands. For many years she and her husband had wanted children and now, at last, she had a little boy to love.

Nicholas was very surprised indeed when he came home that evening to find he was a father! Peering into the baby's huge blue eyes Nicholas smiled. And the baby not only smiled but laughed back! Nicholas could not decide if the jolly little chap was laughing with *him* or *at* him.

It was a bit of both a few years later when Jack's "da" (*da* is the shortened version of dad used in Ireland) went to the town hall to pick up a Christmas turkey he had won in a whist drive. Jack stood outside talking with some neighbors who had gathered to watch his father exit with the plucked, sixteen pound turkey. Minutes later jaws were dropping in astonishment as Jack's father scrambled out the door for dear life holding onto a piece of string attached to a big, clucking turkey who was very much alive. Chased down the street by the noisy creature, his father, furious, whirled around to give it a smart kick. But the turkey was too swift and, with its wings outstretched, looking like a girl curtseying in a lively Irish jig, skirted the blow. Holding his fist high in the air with a threatening frown at the subdued turkey his father turned with a "harumph" as if he had shown it a thing or two. Then all at once the turkey flew into the air, digging its claws into his father's legs while its beak clamped onto his bottom. Jack's father made a comical picture indeed as he tried to remove the stubborn bird from its perch.

Another day Jack and his father were returning from the Enderly House where his father had worked as a gardener for many years. The owner had recently passed away. Jack's father was carrying a mass of thirty or more wire eye glass frames that had become fused together during the fires of a San Francisco earthquake. Mr. Jacobs, his late boss, on one of his trips had found the discarded frames in a jewelry shop and had them mounted as art work. Upon his death he left them to Nicholas who was proudly taking them home. Jack stared at what seemed to him a tangled heap of junk. As he walked along he started thinking about the neighbor who had, just the other day, made him feel like a piece of junk nobody wanted. He had thought that meanness and smallness belonged only to the world of children and when a person became an adult he/she was above certain things. It hurt him deeply to find that this was not so.

But not everyone was unkind, he reminded himself, as he looked up at his da. When he revealed his thoughts out loud, his father said to him, "Jack me lad, what we see depends on the glasses we choose to wear. Some people have a twisted view of the world and even what's straight they see as crooked. You know different and so do I. Just be careful you don't find yourself peering back at those people through the same glasses they use."

There was something else, too, that was bothering Jack. He always carried the niggling fear that one day his birth mother might try and take him back. When his father heard this he tensed his muscles and reassured Jack that he belonged with them and no one could ever take him away. He would be like a lion defending its cub, he promised Jack.

Jack went to the Loreto Convent School and Harold Boy's School in Dalkey. At the Harold Boy's School, boys in the sixth class were required to take care of a small flower bed on the grounds. The narrow, individual strips looked like graves to Jack—probably, he concluded, of former students. Feeling like pansies, the gardeners went home asking their parents for flower seeds. Jack told his father that he wanted seeds for the kind of flowers that required absolutely no work and, of course, grew in great abundance (to cover up any weeds or the headmaster, old Tabac, would go into a rage.) One day his father came home with some seeds, informing Jack that he had only to sprinkle them on the ground. (Having a father was a gardener had its advantages.) "And you only need a few seeds to do the trick," his da said.

The next day, as Jack sprinkled the seeds a huge gust of wind blew them all across the school yard. Waiting until the wind died down, Jack dumped all the seeds onto his plot of earth. After all, wouldn't more flowers grow with more seeds? As he turned away, Jack prayed that his flowers would grow. In a few days, sure enough, flowers were beginning to poke their heads up through the soil. They were very pink and very ugly. Each day, more of them grew — and more and more. Soon flowers were spreading into other boys' strips of land, choking all the flowers they had painstakingly coaxed into existence. The other boys were very angry with Jack and his pink flowers — pink no less! Some boys tried uprooting the ugly things from their own beds but it was no use. Jack's flowers seemed to flourish when challenged. Then, suddenly, they started shooting up in every crack and crevice until the entire school yard was in the pink!

Jack felt his knees grow weak as he thought about what Tabac, who was ill, was going to do to him when he returned. When old Tabac did see the schoolyard looking like a pink field that needed some very hungry goats, he was fit to be tied. Someone came and sprayed week-killer over the entire schoolyard and on the flower beds too. It was the end of the boys' gardens for the year. Much to Jack's surprised relief, the headmaster never sent for him. Jack asked his da what the pink flowers were called. Straining to remember, his father finally replied, "Well, they come from Japan and are called . . . Mother o' Millions . . . though I could be wrong."

In 1941 John Keyes Byrne went to Presentation College, a Roman Catholic School on a four-year scholarship. After he left the school in 1945, Byrne worked in a film rental office, then as a clerical assistant with the Irish Land Commission. Whenever he had the time, though, Jack Byrne could be found in the Commission's amateur dramatic society, acting, directing, and then, writing his own plays. One day Byrne decided to send some of his plays to the famous Abbey Theatre Company in Dublin. His first script was rejected.

In the hope of changing his luck, he submitted his second play, *The Big Birthday* under the pen name Hugh Leonard. This play was accepted and staged by the Abbey

Theatre in 1956. From that moment on, Byrne decided to keep writing under his lucky pen name.

In 1960 his play *A Walk on the Water* was staged with the Dublin Theatre Festival. This play earned Byrne a job as a script editor with Granada Television LTD in Manchester, England. But he continued to write stage plays and in 1963 his play *Stephen D* was so widely hailed that he moved to London working as a freelance television writer specializing in adaptations of literary classics.

Yet television did not provide the same kind of excitement as the theatre for Byrne. He loved writing for live audiences. In 1970 the Irish government passed a law exempting writers and artists who lived and worked in Ireland from paying income taxes and Byrne returned to Ireland. He then wrote his most famous and successful play *Da* (about his childhood and his adoptive father.) He has also written a touching autobiography entitled *Home Before Night* published in 1980.

John Keyes Byrne is the most commercially successful playwright in the modern Irish theatre. For him, the chief purpose of drama is to entertain. He calls himself an optimist whose work reveals that life is sometimes bad, but we are able to change it by changing ourselves. Byrne lives with his wife, whom he married on May 28, 1955, in a seaside house in Dalkey, Ireland. They have one daughter named Danielle. Byrne's hobbies include chess, river cruising, and going for long drives in his Porsche.

Gregory Louganis   (1960 -)
Olympic Diver

The grit, determination, and will to succeed so needed for an Olympic athlete sometimes stem from having to overcome obstacles early on in life. Gregory Louganis is one such person who has emerged from many hardships to become an outstanding athlete and sportsman.

Greg's unwed teenage parents who wanted to give him a better start in life put him up for adoption soon after his birth in 1960. When Greg was a few months old, he was adopted by a loving couple, Peter and Frances Louganis who raised him in San Diego, California, along with Despina, Greg's older adopted sister. While still practically toddlers, Greg and his sister were enrolled in dance classes. When the time came for a recital, Greg was usually the star of the show, performing, singing, and dancing in front of large crowds without being scared or nervous. He loved the attention.

If Greg was a star in recitals, though, school was another story. Greg was very shy and had trouble making friends. He was dark-skinned and had dark eyes whereas most of the other children were blond and blue-eyed. At recess, they teased him for being different. When Greg tried to tell them to stop, he stuttered, which just made the kids tease him even more.

In the classroom things were just as bad for Greg. He especially dreaded reading class. Whenever he had to read aloud, the words came out jumbled and he often read words backwards. The snickering of the children around him made Greg feel terrible.

Greg took solace in his dancing. He excelled in it, and it made him forget the misery of school. The dance classes also served another purpose. Looking back, Greg has said that they were invaluable to him in developing the intense concentration crucial to a champion.

Greg also enjoyed gymnastics, which a doctor had recommended to cure his asthma. One day Greg's father saw his son doing flips off the diving board in their backyard pool. Recognizing Greg's talent, Mr. Louganis promptly signed him up for diving classes at the local Parks and Recreation Center. Soon Greg was taking part in diving meets. The competition was fierce and whenever Greg lost, he was deeply disappointed. But his mother, who always came to the meets, would comfort him. "Win or lose," she reassured him, "I'll always love you."

Within two years, Greg was already a winner. He scored a perfect ten in diving at the 1971 AAU Junior Olympics in Colorado Springs. Dr. Lee, two-time Olympic gold medalist in diving, became Greg's coach for the 1976 Summer Olympics in Montreal. Refusing to accept any money, he started Greg on an intensive training program which included no smoking or drinking.

Greg had never felt as though he belonged at school. When the other boys picked on him, Greg's father enrolled him in wrestling classes so he could learn to fight back. But Greg disliked wrestling, partly because his father was so insistent on the classes. Finally Greg quit wrestling altogether. Then he bought himself a pet boa constrictor mainly because he was afraid of the big snake. Wrapping it around his neck he would parade around town. He felt he had to prove to himself, and to others, that he could conquer his fears. After a while Greg actually came to like his snake and enjoyed showing it to other people. But still Greg wanted friends, so he took up smoking and drinking because the "cool kids" at his school encouraged him. To be part of their group, Greg felt he had to do as they did. Greg's parents tried to help him, as did Dr. Lee, and at last Greg realized that these dangerous habits were interfering with his life. He decided to replace the smoking and drinking with goals of fitness and health.

Greg trained for long, hard hours. He moved into the Lee's house so he could train even more. When he had free time he helped Mrs. Lee with her work and cleaned the swimming pool. Greg had already built up important muscles in his previous part-time job, mending nets for the fishing company where his father worked, but now he became even stronger and more fit.

When it came time for the Olympics, the training paid off; Greg qualified for the springboard and platform diving events. However, the day of the springboard final Greg did not feel his best. He found it hard to concentrate, perhaps because he was only sixteen and this was his first international competition. Another reason was probably because he felt that some of the other U.S. divers were angry at having such a young member on the team. Greg had edged out older, more experienced divers in the trials in order to earn a spot on the U.S. diving team, and some of them resented him. Though Greg had earned his spot fairly, they felt he would get his chance in the upcoming 1980 Olympics, so why was he rushing things now? Greg pretended not to notice all these remarks behind his back, but they hurt. Greg felt all alone and kept to himself.

Despite his concentration problems, Greg placed sixth in the springboard competition. Again, some of the U.S. divers started making comments about Greg, saying the older divers should have performed much better. Aware of these comments, Greg felt very pressured about the platform diving competition. Nevertheless, he finished in second place, a mere 23.52 points behind the winner, Klaus Dibiasi, who had previously won two gold medals. The world was now aware of Greg's potential as a diver and reporters were busily writing about the high school boy with the Olympic silver medal.

Yet the return to California after the Olympics was anything but easy. Many of Greg's friends would not talk to him because they thought he had changed. Greg then came down with mononucleosis and, to make matters worse, he started spending time with the wild crowd again, drinking and smoking. Then another special coach came into Greg's life. His name was Ron O'Brien, and he believed in Greg and helped Greg to regain the fulfillment he once felt in diving. He also encouraged Greg to try more difficult dives.

By the spring of 1978 Greg was back in fighting form, capturing many national and international crowns. At five feet, nine inches, with a very low percent of body fat, he seemed destined for greatness. Even his slight bowleggedness became an advantage; Greg could orient himself by peeking through his legs to see the water and thus perfect his timing.

Greg was looking forward to the 1980 Olympics, and was the favorite for two gold medals. The United States, however, decided to boycott the Moscow Olympics when the Soviet Union invaded Afghanistan. Greg's disappointment was immeasurable — now he had to wait another four long years before the next Olympics! Greg had to make a decision. He had planned to retire after the 1980 Olympics and pursue a career as a professional dancer or actor. Now that he could not go to these Olympics, should he put his acting/dancing career on hold and train for the next Olympics?

Greg decided to keep diving. Over the next years, he showed that he was the undisputed champion of the springboard, winning every major national and international title. But Greg still smoked and drank! Then he saw a young diver at the recreation center smoking, though, he went over to stop him. What he found out made him take a hard look at himself. The boy confessed that he had started smoking because he admired Greg and wanted to be exactly like him! Greg decided to take himself in hand. If children going to look up to him, he would have to be a better role model. He stopped smoking and drinking. He learned to be himself and realized he could make friends this way. Concerned that other children might smoke and drink, he gave talks at schools to discourage them from these habits, and told them there was nothing wrong with being shy. He told them not to worry about popularity contests or fitting in. Instead, he told them, be yourselves, proud of your own talents and of who you are.

Greg continued training. One of his new routines on the platform required three and a half reverse somersaults. In, 1983, Greg and a Russian diver were competing in an important meet in Canada. Greg was to dive right after the Russian, so he waited on another platform halfway up the tower. The Russian prepared himself and then dove. Greg felt the tower shake and, looking down, saw a widening, blood-red stain in the aqua-blue water. The diver had hit himself on the platform and was rushed to the hospital. He would die a week later. Greg, however, had yet to perform the same dangerous dive. He was very shaken by what he had just witnessed. Nevertheless, his discipline and courage enabled him to perform the dive. He executed a perfect three and a half reverse somersault. Still, it was sobering to Greg and to everyone to be reminded so tragically of the dangers of diving.

As the 1984 Olympics approached, there was tremendous pressure on Greg Louganis. The judges were expecting nothing less than perfection. Though he certainly felt the pressure, Louganis made a spectacular showing in the springboard competition to capture the gold. Making diving history, Louganis scored the highest number of total points ever.

But if there was pressure on Louganis for the 1984 Olympics, there was even more in '88. Louganis had intended to retire after the 1984 Games, but could not quite bring himself to do so. He resumed training, hoping to become the first man to win two gold medals for diving in two separate Olympic Games.

Louganis' courage and determination were certainly put to the test. While competing for the springboard title, Louganis missed a dive in the qualifying round and hit his head on the board. He had four stitches in his scalp, but would not let that deter him; he dived two more times that same night to qualify and came back the next day to win an Olympic gold medal.

In the platform finals, Louganis faced another challenger, in the form of fourteen-year old Xiong Ni of China. Louganis was losing to Xiong by 85.56 points and had only one dive in which to make up the difference. The pressure was tremendous. Climbing to the top of the platform, his heart pounding, Greg says he suddenly remembered his mother's words when he first entered competitive diving, "Win or lose, I'll always love you."

Clinging to those words, Greg jumped, executing a beautiful reverse three and a half somersault, to just defeat Xiong by 1.14 points. His mother's encouragement had given him the winner's edge.

Gregory Louganis, who was presented with the Olympic Spirit Award, has come a long way from the shy, stammering boy he once was. Not only has Louganis become the greatest diver in history, winning, apart from his Olympic medals, forty-seven U.S. titles and one-hundred and eighteen world class competitions, he has also overcome his self-consciousness and difficulty with reading. His freshman year in college, Louganis realized he had the reading disorder called dyslexia. That was why he read words backwards! Learning to compensate, Louganis began to enjoy reading. He has a 1983 bachelor's degree in theatre from the University of California. The future holds great promise for this Olympic superstar.

Lue Gim Gong   (? - 1925)
The Orange Wizard

Not everyone in China, where Lue Gim Cong was born, was as lucky as he was. He worked hard in a land where there *was* no day of rest every seven, as we have in the Western world. But Gim Gong's father (Lue was his family name) owned a farm. This meant the family could grow vegetables for themselves and had some to sell in the market. And his father was luckier than most, for he also owned a water buffalo and was able to plow his fields with greater ease.

Still, life was far from easy, and Gim Gong was a little child who, like all the other members of his family, had daily chores to do. Day in and day out little Gim Gong could be seen in his family's fields, wearing the loose trousers and jacket that all Chinese boys wore. His hair was plaited in a pigtail which became longer and longer as the boy grew. There was nothing strange in this, for at that time all Chinese men and boys wore their hair in one pigtail that hung down the middle of their backs.

Although life was difficult it was also interesting and busy. The farm animals were Gim Gong's friends, and there was the satisfaction of knowing that he was a contributing member of his family. Gim Gong held his head high.

Part of the Lue farm was dedicated to citrus trees which, years later, would prove of great importance to orange and grapefruit growers in Florida and California.

Gim Gong enjoyed his simple life. He enjoyed especially working with his mother in the orchard. He loved to watch her as she carefully used a small brush to collect the pollen of one plant and brush it onto another. In this way Gim Gong's mother taught her little son how to cross-pollinate plants, and preserve the best characteristics of each plant. No wonder, thought the little boy, that fruits of his mother's orchard were always better and more succulent than those he tasted from the gardens of his friends.

One day which began like all others, Gim Gong's life changed. His father's brother came back to the family! The uncle had been living in the United States for many years, always cherishing the idea of returning to China when he grew old. Finally he was able to join the family as a well-to-do man.

Gim Gong had never heard of many of the things that were commonplace to most Americans. He had never heard of a president . . . imagine! — a president was elected by the people! There were many schools in this country his uncle talked about, and wonder of wonders, girls — almost deprived of rights in China — were allowed to attend school with the boys! Gim Gong knew, after listening wide-eyed to his uncle, that he somehow, someday would attend one of those schools in this far-away land.

Gim Gong found it very difficult to convince his family to accede to his desires. He was needed on the farm. Soon he would be a grown man; he must marry and have sons. That was his duty to his family and to his ancestors. But Gim Gong did not give up, and after much reflection his uncle helped him convince the family.

75

Generously, his uncle also offered to pay Gim Gong's fare, and even gave him some silk to sell in America to get started in the new land. Had his uncle not helped him, Gim Gong would have had to find an agent to pay his way, and once in America he would have had to work for many years just to pay back the cost of his trip.

It was not easy for the young boy to separate himself from his family and friends, from the farm animals he so loved and to start on his journey all by himself. But Gim Gong was also excited. He packed his few possessions: some extra clothes and shoes, his bedding, a bag of oranges and salted vegetables. The oranges and vegetables eaten on the long sea voyage, would prevent him from getting dysentery, an intestinal disease. The trip was not a pleasant one. All the passengers lived for days in tiny cubicles and only occasionally could they come on deck for a breath of fresh air. The food was not the wholesome fare he was used to and the boy was often seasick.

When Gim Gong arrived in San Francisco he was met by other Chinese and taken to Chinatown where he was to live. Chinatown was a neighborhood where only Chinese people lived. They congregated in the same streets where they could help each other, for their customs were similar, and, of course, they ate the same foods and often spoke the same language.

Living in the United States was very hard for Gim Gong. He did not have the comfort of his family, and the first job he was able to obtain, in a shoe factory, paid very little. However, thought the boy, there were other jobs. Chinese men in the United States were not hired everywhere, nor did they all have a command of the English language, which would have opened more doors for them. Mainly they worked on the railroad or in Chinese restaurants, or went around with a small hand cart collecting and delivering the laundry they washed.

San Francisco was an exciting city to the growing boy. He liked it . . . but here he had no opportunity to realize his dream of attending school. Then Gim Gong had another lucky break. A man from New England — whose workers had gone on strike — came to recruit Chinese shoemakers for his factory.

So Gim Gong signed up to go north. This was also a change of climate for him, as the part of China he came from was warm and pleasant. For the first time Gim Gong had to deal with the harsh snow storms, ice, and hail of the New England winters. Mostly the Chinese kept to themselves, until the American community began to worry — if these people were to live among them, they should learn English and be properly instructed in religion. It was agreed that a school should be started. Since the factories were open for long hours, the workers attended school on Sunday afternoon. The teachers were all volunteers — mostly people of good families who did not have to work for a living. The workers were very grateful and were eager and intelligent.

Soon Gim Gong began to wear American-style shoes instead of the clumsy wooden shoes that the Chinese wore when they left their house. And soon, he also adopted Western dress. In school he was among the most advanced pupils, even though he was the youngest worker in the factory. As part of the community effort to integrate the Chinese, the factory workers were invited to church festivals. At one such festival Gim Gong tasted ice cream for the first time. Never did he expect to taste anything better. He let the ice cream melt slowly on his tongue and wished he could share this delicacy with his family so far away.

One day Gim Gong was invited to the home of Mr. Burlingame, a wealthy man who owned a hardware store. One of his daughters — Miss Fannie, an unmarried lady about forty years old — was very interested in the Chinese and liked Gim Gong instantly. Miss Fannie herself was very well educated and had taught school. Her cousin, a lawyer, civil rights and anti-slavery champion, was an authority on China. It was he who had enlightened Miss Fannie with stories of that fascinating country.

Miss Fannie invited Gim Gong to live in her house. In exchange for the schooling, room, and board he would receive, he was to help around the house and in the orchard. Gim Gong could not believe his luck. For the very first time in his life he had his very own room! Back in China no one, no matter how wealthy, enjoyed such a luxury. Usually the entire family lived in one big room, with small partitions. This room became a treasure to him, and Miss Fannie, although never adopting him legally, treated him like a son for the rest of her life.

Gim Gong loved living in the Burlingame house and loved being treated as a member of the family. Best of all, he loved school and working in the orchard. Gim Gong learned English and took courses at a school in town. Not only was he learning about America but — another first in his life — he was learning about China. He wrote his family letters full of all the wonders in America. He could not hope that they would understand, but he knew his uncle would try to explain.

Then something awful happened to Gim Gong. He became very sick with a disease for which there was no cure at that time: he contracted tuberculosis. The doctors were convinced that a warm climate was good for the patients and suggested that Gim Gong return to his family in China. Saddened beyond words, he resigned himself to his fate and dispiritedly sailed back to China. The only bright spot on the horizon was the thought that he would be seeing his family again.

His stay in America had changed Gim Gong. No longer the little farmer boy who had left years before, the way of life in his country of origin now seemed strange to him. He did not experience the warm closeness to his family that he had expected to feel, except towards his mother. For now the grown up Gim Gong realized, as the young boy could not, what an exceptional person she was. The other members of the family had trouble understanding the strange things he described and often times laughed at him. Only his mother and his uncle seemed to take seriously what he said. Perhaps his uncle, like Gim Gong, had made the mistake of returning, and felt homesick for the far-away country. Finally Gim Gong, feeling he could endure living in China no longer, wrote to Miss Fannie asking if he could return to America. Miss Fannie, who missed her foster son, answered by return mail overjoyed and sent him the money for the trip. It was a sad parting, for this time Gim Gong knew he would not come back. He would never see his mother again.

Gim Gong started the trip back with a heavy heart. He did not expect to live long with his disease in the cold climate of Massachusetts. But Miss Fannie, unknown to him, had planned a surprise. As soon as she knew he was returning, she had purchased a grove in DeLand, Florida, and that was to be their new home. Gim Gong was very excited. Good things were again beginning to happen to him, and one of the best was his becoming an American citizen. Proudly he walked that day beside Miss Fannie, whom he always called Mother Fannie, and cast his first vote.

In the orchard, Gim Gong experimented with cross pollination. He was extremely successful in his efforts and stories about him and his fruits appeared in newspapers and magazines. How proud Miss Fannie was of him! At a time when fruit was not, as it is today, readily available out of season, Gim Gong developed a peach that could be picked and eaten in November. He also developed the "Lue Gim Gong" orange, a delicious new variety. One of the advantages of the fruit was that it could be stored for very long periods without loosing flavor or texture and it could travel very well at a time when refrigerated cars had not yet been invented. This orange is still grown in Florida. Nor did Gim Gong limit himself to oranges. He experimented With grapefruits too, and also developed a new variety.

In 1903 Miss Fannie died, and Gim Gong felt alone as he had not felt since his trip to faraway America, or his first days in the new land. He grieved for Mother Fannie and never quite recuperated from her loss. Also, he was very grateful to her. She had given him his start. Now he wished to pass onto others the kindness he had received. He adopted a nephew who came to San Francisco and helped him in every way he could.

After the death of his protector, Lue Gim Gong became more engrossed than ever in his work. Financially, he was very well off, but his best triumph came when in 1911 he was awarded the Wilder Silver Medal for his exquisite new orange. This was the highest honor a horticulturalist could receive — but alas! — Mother Fannie was no longer here to share his happiness.

In this way, always keeping busy, the years went by. Gim Gong continued to work in the orchard and to tend the horses that, it seemed so long ago now, had taken Miss Fannie and him for rides. He corresponded with many people in America and in his native land. Newspapers referred to Gim Gong as the "Chinese Wizard of the Orange;" and his varieties of fruit were grown in California as well.

But there are some dishonest people ready to pounce on the trusting and one day Gim Gong realized that he was in danger of losing his beloved orchard. Only the quick intervention of his friend and admirer, Edgard Wright, saved his orchard. Mr. Wright, the editor of a horticultural magazine launched a campaign to have people buy bonds that would save the orchard. Mr. Wright also made sure that Lue Gim Gong would be cared for during the rest of his life. And so it happened.

After Lue Gim Gong's death on June 11, 1925, he was honored in two world fairs by the State of Florida, for he had truly contributed to its orange and grapefruit growers. But Lue Gim Gong is also remembered — as he undoubtedly wished it — for his honesty, and his love of people and animals, and his devotion to the land he adopted.

Catherine McCauley   (1778 - 1841)
Founder of the Sisters of Mercy

The founder of the Sisters of Mercy, Catherine Elizabeth McCauley — called Kittie by her family — enjoyed a carefree existence for the first few years of her life. She had a younger brother, James, and a sister, Mary. The family was wealthy and the children had many comforts which were denied to most people in Ireland in the 18th century. The house where the family lived was old and beautiful, surrounded by lawns and trees that provided cool, dappled shade where the children could play in the summertime.

Ireland is a beautiful island and Kittie loved to look over its rolling hills dotted by white sheep sewn into the lush emerald green fabric. She especially liked to be the first to spot her father coming home from one of his long strolls.

Mr. McCauley was a very devout Catholic and he dedicated many afternoons to teaching doctrine to his poorer neighbors. Catherine always accompanied her father on these sessions, as she loved to play with the children, and years later those catechism lessons were the guiding light that shaped her life. Mr. McCauley taught his little daughter that along with spiritual nourishment the physical needs of the poor had to be met. This he did, making sure that all who came to him had medicine, food, and clothing.

Little Catherine adored her father, and his early death when she was seven was a devastating blow. Her mother, mourning and bewildered, soon found herself with financial problems that she did not know how to solve. True, she had a country estate, but she could not manage the mansion and lands on her own. Since the death of the master, too, the mansion was thought to be haunted. Transparent white figures were seen on the lawns at night, odd sounds came from the walls, and the servants by the flickering fire in the kitchen told tales of ancient murders until one by one the servants left.

The three children left their home too one beautiful morning, never to return. It seemed to Catherine, who kept looking back, that the figure of her father smiled and waved to her, wishing her well in life. As the carriage climbed a hill and her childhood home was lost from view, Catherine cried bitter tears. She was so distracted that her mother had to reprimand her. "Oh, I wish Daddy were here," sobbed Catherine over and over.

Life in Dublin was new and exciting for James and for Mary. There were well dressed people — quite unlike the peasants they were used to seeing in their country manor — and shops lining the fashionable avenues showing off luxuries and toys that the children had never imagined existed.

Mrs. McCauley, however, decided to send James to school rather than have tutors come to him as they had done in the country. Every night James had homework. When he went to school unprepared — and these occasions were frequent as he preferred playing to studying — the schoolmasters meted out severe physical punishment. Catherine would willingly have gone to school, but in those days girls were taught at home.

Other changes were occurring too. After her arrival in Dublin Mrs. McCauley had converted to Protestantism. She now believed that children should decide for themselves what church they wanted to attend when they grew up. So Mary, Catherine and James did not go to church at all. James and Mary found this lack of obligation very comfortable and soon forgot their religion, but Catherine's was too well ingrained. However, the little girl had to obey her mother and as she was a sensitive child, she suffered deeply for what she considered her mother's abandonment of God and her treason to the memory of her father.

When Kittie was eleven, her mother fell seriously ill. While her brother and sister went out for enjoyable rides, Catherine sat for hours by her mother's bedside, comforting her. It was Catherine, too, who sent for a priest when she saw how grief-stricken her mother was at having neglected her religion. When death claimed her mother a few days later, Catherine had the satisfaction of knowing that she had died a Catholic.

Several of Mrs. McCauley's relatives offered homes to the children, and it was decided that Catherine would go to live with Surgeon Conway. The little girl liked Mr. Conway very much, but in just a few months he was in financial trouble and could not support her any longer. Catherine was sent then to live in the house of Mr. Armstrong, an honorable gentleman and a Protestant who belonged to the Established Church of England. Without hesitation, James and Mary fell right in with the family and attended services at their church. But Catherine could not yield; to her, attending another church was against the faith taught by the father who had loved her so dearly. Nothing could persuade Catherine to change her mind, and indeed both threats and rewards were tried to sway her. In an attempt to be fair — while she could not bring herself to join the family in their worship — Catherine read about their religion in the books and materials Mr. Armstrong gave her.

Catherine's decision elated Mr. Armstrong. He was sure that once Catherine read the books he gave her, she would discard all previous notions. Wishing to please Mr. Armstrong, she continued to read history books and religious treatises and tried with all her might to understand. Perhaps, thought Catherine, if she talked to a priest her doubts would be allayed once and for all. But tolerant in other matters, Mr. Armstrong was adamant on this point; Catherine was not allowed to visit any priests.

And alas! Hard luck once more came Catherine's way. Financial difficulties crushed Mr. Armstrong as his business failed. Gone were the servants, the carriages, the luxuries — the easy life. For the first time Catherine knew what it was like to go hungry. However, not even in his most desperate moments did Mr. Armstrong think of giving up the children; they were a family and they would weather the storm together. But this experience of being poor taught Catherine that happiness comes from within, and does not come from store-bought trinkets. Finally, with his intelligence, skill and hard work, Mr. Armstrong was able to turn the tide of misfortune and as his business gradually improved, life returned more or less to normal.

Another event that proved crucial in her young life took place when Catherine was sixteen. Mr. and Mrs. Callahan, distant relatives of Catherine's mother, came back from India where Mr. Callahan had held a job for many years and where he had made a very large fortune. Of course, they met James, Catherine, and Mary. They were impressed by all three, but Catherine's intelligence, sense of humor, kindness and consideration stole their hearts and they decided to adopt her legally as their very own daughter. It was not that Mr. Armstrong did not love Catherine, for he loved her very much, but he knew that the Callahans could give her opportunities denied to him.

Amid her good fortune one thought constantly troubled Catherine: her adopted mother and father did not understand her religion, nor did they like it. However, they did not forbid her to practice it. But just suppose, Catherine thought, that because of her religion she had been rejected by all? What would she have done then? There should be a place where a young girl could go when she had nobody to turn to, no money of her own. This thought lingered in her mind.

Taking advantage of a shopping expedition, Catherine one morning directed her steps to a nearby Catholic church, knocked at the door and asked for a priest. The gentleman who received her answered all her questions, cleared up all her doubts and asked the girl if she wished to be instructed for her first confession. "Oh yes, Father," Catherine replied joyously. Her First Communion followed shortly and only then did she have the courage to tell her adoptive parents what she had done and how she had struggled all her young life to keep her faith. This news startled her parents but they loved her and did not punish her for such a bold move. However, for what they perceived to be her best interest, her parents did all they could to discourage her from participating in her church, which was nine miles away. But when one Sunday morning Catherine set out to walk those nine miles, her parents — who had counted on the distance to deter her — quickly gave their permission for the use of the carriage and coachman. From then on they also allowed any of their Catholic servants to ride to Mass with their young mistress.

The Catholic religion requires good works of its faithful, and so Catherine, always eager to help others since she was a little child, visited the sick and the poor. On one such visit she was warned not to go into a cabin. But enter she did, and found a once respectable lady — now insane and raggedy — half-starved inside. Catherine took the woman home with her, where she remained until her death.

In the meantime, James and Mary had grown up. James had joined the army and become a surgeon under the Duke of Wellington. After the Battle of Waterloo he left the army and opened his own practice. Mary married very young. Now her physician husband also joined James and his wife in the battle to dissuade Catherine from practicing her religion. Mary loved her sister dearly and tried to convince her to attend parties. Mary's children also adored their Aunt Kittie and were never more delighted than when she came for a visit. Aunt Kittie told them wonderful stories of old Ireland, that spurred their imaginations and kept alive the traditions of the Irish bards. But of late Aunt Kittie's visits had been infrequent for Mrs. Callahan was ill. Surely now that she was so busy, argued Mary, Catherine would put all that religious foolishness aside. "Mary," Catherine replied, "it gives me deep happiness to care for the needy, and instruct those who lack teachers. You know my father has generously given me a fund to use in my charity work."

"But you'll get sick if you visit those dreadful, filthy houses," protested Mary.

"Those visits and the classes I give are my life. You were too young to remember what satisfaction they brought to Father," countered Catherine.

"Promise me at least that you'll come and visit us soon," said Mary. "I'll come as soon as mother is well enough to be left alone," Catherine said quietly.

But Mrs. Callahan did not get well. She remained confined to her bed for two years and Catherine lovingly cared for her. It grieved the girl, though, that her mother did not belong to any church at all. Catherine spent her few free moments in prayer that God would show her parents the way to her faith. And so she was not surprised when one afternoon Mrs. Callahan asked Catherine how it was possible that such a sensible and intelligent girl would practice that strange religion against the wishes of all her family?

Catherine explained to Mrs. Callahan how her father had taught her as a little girl . . . how he had enlightened many children of peasants and seen to their physical needs. Mrs. Callahan was very curious now and wanted to know exactly what Catholics believed. Catherine said she should hear it from a priest and secretly arranged a visit to the house. Mrs. Callahan did not wish her husband to know for fear he might become enraged. As Mr. Callahan did not know his wife's secret he was sorely perplexed to find her so happy when she was so ill.

Soon after her baptism, Mrs. Callahan died, leaving a great void in Catherine's and her husband's lives. Mr. Callahan had no desire to live without his wife and his health began to fail. With the specter of death ever present now, Mr. Callahan called the minister of the nearest church. But Catherine begged that she be allowed to call a priest to talk with him. Mr. Callahan hesitated, but he loved his daughter very much, and consented, just to please her. To his own great surprise, a few months later Mr. Callahan, happy and at peace, was baptized.

How grateful Catherine was to learn that her adoptive father had left all his wealth and possessions to her. Catherine's brother and sister were also happy for her. After taking care of her sick parents for so long, surely she must wish to have some fun . . . especially now as money was no object. Instead, Catherine spent her time on her knees in church or seeking out poor and sick people to help. What kind of behavior was that for a young lady with excellent marriage proposals? But

Catherine was happy. She went to Mass daily and thought of how she could help more and more people. Little by little her plans took shape; she was going to build a large house where poor Catholic children could be educated, where unemployed, homeless women could find refuge. The priests with whom she spoke were enthusiastic and advised her to build in a wealthy part of the city, hoping that seeing the needs of the poor, the rich would help. It was an overwhelmingly complex project for one person alone but Catherine did not hesitate. Wishing her school to be an excellent one, she visited others and observed the latest teaching methods.

One day her brother James had had enough of her strange conduct. What did she think she was doing anyway? She should marry that army officer who had proposed to her so many times and who would soon grow tired of waiting he said. People were laughing at her. A woman's place was in the home, caring for her family.

Catherine patiently explained to James that she was concerned with her eternal life; life in this world did not matter to her except as an opportunity to do all the good she could do.

In the midst of these family arguments, Mary became very ill. With all the skill her husband possessed, he was unable to save her. Catherine dropped all other activities and rushed to her side. She nursed her sister and comforted her spiritually. Her prayers were answered, for before she died Mary confessed to her oldest daughter that she was dying a Catholic and that she wished her children to be instructed in religion by their Aunt Kittie. Her husband, broken up by her death and by his inability to save her, became moody and difficult, taking out his bad tempers oftentimes on his children. When he further discovered that his wife had adopted the Catholic religion before she died, he became furious and attempted to kill his sister-in-law.

He must have admired Catherine secretly, however, for when he died shortly after his wife, he — who had been so outspoken against Catherine — named her and her brother James guardians of the children. Even more astonishing, he left the children free to decide with whom they wished to live. Without hesitation all five children chose Aunt Kittie. The boys were sent to St. Patrick's school where they did very well in their studies. But Catherine's pride in their accomplishments was short lived. The boys, like their mother before them, succumbed to that dreaded disease for which there was then no cure — tuberculosis. Only the youngest boy, Willie, who had gone to sea, survived.

When Catherine finally finished her institution, poor young girls were welcomed and taught cooking, serving, sewing, and keeping house. Then jobs were found for them so that they could lead productive, happy lives. But should anything go wrong, the doors of Catherine's institution were always open. One of the customs of the institution — that of feeding the poor at Christmas time — was begun by Catherine and is still observed by the Order of Mercy.

Catherine had not planned her life the way it turned out. She had not planned to become a nun or to found an order. But she had always wanted to instruct and help those less fortunate than herself . . . the rest followed naturally. The wealthy ladies who came to help many times stayed overnight because they worked until late and wished to begin early in the morning. They had to stop wearing elaborate, cumbersome stylish clothes and choose those that were more comfortable, simple, and utilitarian. Of course they ate together and prayed together. Soon all the ladies were conforming to a daily schedule with set times, and a congregation was born. Catherine called it the Order of Mercy in remembrance of that other ancient Order that rescued Christians captured by the Turks.

Nothing had been easy for Catherine and establishing the Order was not easy either. Her brother James constantly argued with her that she should marry. But Catherine's mind was quite made up and the family at last accepted that she was not going to change. And so one day they said goodbye to her as she went to the Presentation Convent to begin her novitiate. This is a period of training that all nuns must go through. Here Catherine learned the rules of the Order, confirmed herself in humility and obedience, continued to learn about her faith and spent many hours in prayer in the cold chapel. Without true vocation it is impossible to endure this trial. Catherine did endure it and was rewarded with the habit of the Order in a ceremony presided over by the Archbishop and attended by many of her friends. Then she took the vows of poverty, chastity, and obedience and promised to dedicate her life to serve the poor, the sick and the ignorant.

The day that Catherine returned to her home — now properly a convent — December 12, 1831, is officially the founding date of the Order of the Sisters of Mercy. Catherine had been transformed into Mother McCauley, and devoted herself to her many duties, which apart from the feeding, education, and housing of the poor, also included writing a constitution for the Order, and designing a habit that would be comfortable, utilitarian and modest.

One of Mother McCauley's greatest assets had always been a warm, happy, caring disposition that attracted friends. This helped her with her many projects, for though she devoted her entire life and fortune to others, she knew that she could not do everything herself. Many young ladies came to help her in her work and stayed in the convent as nuns. These ladies in turn had contacts who could offer jobs to the girls they trained. One of these young ladies was Catherine's own niece. Mary's daughter was only sixteen, and James pleaded with his sister to let her live in his house for a year. The boys, the parties, the luxuries, the attention, he thought, soon would clear her head of any ideas of becoming a nun. Mother McCauley readily agreed and the young girl had a wonderful time. She was, like her Aunt Kittie, a happy, merry person with a sunny personality. But at the end of the year, the girl was as earnest as ever about entering the convent and, thanking her uncle very much, she went to take care of the orphans. Tragically, she died very young, despite the efforts of all the renowned doctors her uncle summoned to her bedside and the unceasing care of all the Sisters.

Mother McCauley worked hard to obtain some unheard of privileges for her Order, such as being granted visiting rights to hospitals where the very ill and the dying were in need of comfort. Then, in 1833, an epidemic of cholera decimated the city of Dublin. The Sisters of Mercy rushed to help the doctors as they cared for the hundreds that were sick. When the epidemic subsided many were left without homes or family. Heavy-hearted, the Sisters knew that they could not help everyone, nor did Mother McCauley's wealth suffice to cover even the barest necessities of the needy.

But if more money was needed, more money would she obtain.

After thinking for some time, she decided to hold a bazaar. Her brother James was horrified. Hold a bazaar now when almost every one in Dublin had lost a family member to the dreaded disease and the whole city was in mourning? "Suffering," replied his sister, "makes people more willing to help other unfortunates." And forth she went with her idea. First, she needed a patron that all others could follow. Why not aspire to the highest in the country? Catherine wrote to the queen, explaining their needs and asking that she interest herself in this worthy cause. She waited, amazed at her own audacity, sometimes not daring to hope. But not long afterwards, the Queen's messenger arrived with a package. Inside were beautiful embroideries signed by the queen and the princess, who later became Queen Victoria. No more was needed. The bazaar was a great success!

But Mother McCauley had worn herself out through the years in the care of others; she fell ill. But she did not fear death, for she was sure she would join her friends and loved ones in heaven. On November 11, 1841, Catherine McCauley died, leaving behind her the great Order of Mercy which continues to work in every place where the sick, ignorant, and the aged need help. The Sisters of Mercy stood side by side with Florence Nightingale in the Crimea, and have since alleviated the suffering of many, following the vision that Catherine McCauley had so many years ago.

James Albert Michener
(1907 -)
Bestselling Novelist

In the year 1957 James Michener and twelve other passengers were aboard a C-47 transport bound for Iwo Jima when suddenly the plane crashed into a raging ocean. Knowing they had but three minutes to evacuate before they sank with the aircraft to a watery grave, the crew desperately boarded a life raft. James Michener was forced to leave behind his possessions including a notebook full of notes for a new book. The small raft was tossed up and down on the white crested waves, turning on every side, as the passengers gulped more water than air. In the distance was a Japanese rescue launch. Summoning every last ounce of strength, the frantic passengers paddled toward the launch but the sea was too rough and they could not get close enough. Then they saw a Japanese sailor, with a rope tied around him, plunge into the swirling depths. Bravely swimming through shark-infested waters, the sailor reached the raft where he was speedily hoisted in. Grabbing hold of the rope the crew was pulled toward the launch. Not a single life was lost.

James Michener had been at sea before this frightening experience. He volunteered for the Navy during World War II and spent time in the Pacific, and was later awarded the Navy Gold Cross. On one occasion, Michener was assigned to locate a village on a Pacific isle that had been helping Americans shot down by the Japanese. Michener found the village in the person of a girl who paddled out in her canoe to rescue the fliers. From these experiences he wrote *Tales of the South Pacific*, immortalized in the musical "South Pacific" by Richard Rodgers and Oscar Hammerstein II. First produced as a play, South Pacific was then made into a movie that attracted thousands upon thousands of moviegoers.

An aura of mystery surrounds James Michener, but it is known that he was born in New York City about February 3, 1907. For many years he believed that the mother he loved and with whom he lived was his biological mother and that her dead husband, Edwin Michener, had been his father. When the young boy discovered that he did not legally belong to the family, Mabel Michener informed him that he had been abandoned as a baby. She neither knew his name nor had she a birth certificate for him, Mabel told the boy, but she had taken him in and named him James Albert after one of her favorite uncles. James, of course, had a thousand questions — all beginning with who, when, where, and ending with . . . why? After a long time and a lot of thinking, young James must have concluded that he was actually luckier than most people. If Mabel Michener was not his real mother then he had two mothers, one who loved him enough to give him life and another who loved him throughout her life.

But times were often difficult for the Michener family. Mabel received almost all her income from embroidering buttonholes in women's shirtwaists. For dinner, the family would sometimes have mustard sandwiches — without the meat — and dandelion greens soaked in vinegar. They could not afford anything else. Growing up James' diet was so poor that some of his bones never developed properly. When someone was sick in the family James had to live for a while in the poorhouse. Here he saw terrible poverty and partook of the hopelessness of old, tired people who had nowhere to go and nothing to look forward to. The little boy feared that he, too, when he was old would have to live in the poorhouse. Terrified he resolved right then and there that he would make a different future for himself.

Although destitute herself, Mabel Michener never stopped helping others even less fortunate than herself. She opened a boarding house for children who needed some temporary care and a place to stay. Some came from working single mothers, others were the children of travelling parents. Not always was she paid but that never made any difference in the love Mabel gave all the children. In the evenings, Mabel read to them, and while it is true that they lacked material possessions, James, Robert, and any other children who stayed in the Michener home were rich indeed in those things which money cannot buy — love, understanding, encouragement, and a good example.

One Christmas eve, the family had absolutely nothing and Mabel could not afford to buy any presents for the large number of children at her house. Seeing so many sad little faces, Mabel made a decision. She marched to a place where trees were sold, grabbed one and told the seller that he could have her arrested for theft, but her children were going to have a tree on Christmas. Mabel was not arrested. In fact, the tree seller and some friends of his got together and bought presents for all the children.

James possessed an adventurous spirit. At the age of fourteen he hitchhiked around the United States, visiting almost every state in the Union. At fifteen he was writing a sports column, delivering newspapers and working as a hotel watchman, all the while keeping up with his studies. Not only did he receive high grades in his academic courses, but he was also very good in sports. Upon graduation from high school, James Michener won a scholarship to Swarthmore College, from where he graduated with highest honors. Later he obtained a master's degree and a doctorate.

He was also endowed with great curiosity. As a very young boy he used to attend courtroom sessions until he was discovered and chased out. When he wanted to travel, lack of money did not stop him; he merely rode the boxcars. An avid reader, James visited a school teacher sister of his mother's, and spent hours reading the many fascinating books she possessed.

James loved his mother very much but he did secretly miss not having a father. He could not, as other boys did, talk about all the things that fathers can do. Two men were to become father figures to James Michener. One was George Murray — called Uncle George by the boys in Doylestown, Pennsylvania. Murray, an unmarried tinsmith, always had time to chat and answer a boy's questions.

The other was Allen Gardy, a printer, publisher and part-time coach. James loved basketball and there was nothing Gardy loved more than coaching a team to victory. As Gardy taught his team the intricacies of basketball he also taught them trust, loyalty, responsibility and the importance of proper conduct.

When James was not talking to Gardy or shooting baskets, he was in the library. The teachers were amazed at the facts he knew; his classmates thought he was stupid for learning so much and made fun of him. He became the butt of everyone's jokes. As an adult, James Michener said that school is anything but easy for a bright child in America.

James Michener has had a varied and brilliant career. He served as reporter for *Life, Holiday,* and *Reader's Digest.* Once a penniless boy, he became a millionaire, and has received many honors and awards, including the Pulitzer Prize for fiction and the President's Medal for Freedom. Yet it was not until he was forty years old that James Michener actually published a book. Among his best sellers are *The Bridges at Toko-Ri, Sayonara, Hawaii, Caravans, The Source, Centennial,* and *Space.* His fans are innumerable, and his books have been translated into many languages.

Not everything has been easy for James Michener, but if he had written it himself he could not have given his life story a happier ending.

Carlos Montezuma (1866? - 1922)
Indian Doctor

Fire! Smoke! Screaming! Young Wassaja, a six-year old Apache boy was awakened one night by the cries of his people and the smell of their burning campsite. The Apache's arch rivals, the Pima Indians, had crept into the Apache campsite and stealthily set fire to all the wickiups — dome-shaped huts in which Apaches lived. Now the Pima rode up and down the camp, slaughtering Apaches as they tried to run from their burning homes. Wassaja, blinded by terror and confusion, was running, calling out for his family and trying in vain to find them. He was not even aware of the Pima who rode up next to him until suddenly Wassaja felt himself lifted onto the back of a Pima's horse.

At first Wassaja thought the Pima meant to kill him, for Apaches usually tortured and killed the boys and men they captured from enemy tribes. Strangely, though, the Pima took Wassaja to the Pima camp, gave him food, and set him to sleep with his own children. The children, who had flatter faces, looked different from the Apaches. Their houses were square instead of being dome-shaped like the Apaches' wickiups. The Pima also ate different food. For the first time, Wassaja tasted bread and gruel.

After Wassaja had spent a week with the Pima, he realized he would probably not be killed. The worst that had happened so far was that some of the Pima children had taunted him by throwing dirt and rocks. Still, Wassaja did not want to live as a captive of the Pima! He thought longingly of his family and the Apache way of life. He remembered his sisters, one older and one younger, who would follow him as he went into the brush to trap animals. Sadly, Wassaja recalled how he had promised to protect them and hunt for them. He also thought of the meetings at night he and his father had attended. They would gather round the central campfire, with the elders, and boast of the strength and fearsomeness of the Apaches. A few times, Wassaja had been allowed to perform ritual dances and sing. Best of all, Wassaja loved the pride with which the elders spoke of the tremendous feats Apaches had performed in past wars. Wassaja, too, had proclaimed that the Apaches were *N'de* (The People), unconquerable! Now, all of a sudden, Wassaja felt puny and afraid. Would he ever see his family again?

Wassaja had not spent many days in the Pima camp when his captors decided to take him to another strange place. They took him to the white people's town! Wassaja was amazed by the sights he saw there. The people wore coverings on their bodies, whereas Wassaja was used to the freedom of going without clothes. The people also smelled differently and their wooden houses seemed strange compared to the Apaches' wickiups.

Many white people crowded around to see Wassaja. They pointed at him and spoke in a strange language which he could not understand. Wassaja stared solemnly at them. A part of him was frightened, but another part of him felt as though he were inside a terrible dream. The strange, jabbering noises those people made to each other, the hair on the men's faces (Apache men were smooth-skinned), the brown weeds the men chewed seemed unreal and were almost too much for Wassaja to absorb at once. Wassaja was very aware of his hunger and thirst, however, for he had not eaten in a long while. Still he told himself as he stood up straight and puffed out his chest, that he would be brave and not complain, for he was an Apache, and Apaches never show weakness.

Despite Wassaja's resolve, he became increasingly anxious about what was going to happen to him. More and more whites had gathered round him, and now some of the boys were laughing at him. The adults started talking louder and crowding closer. Wassaja wanted to break through the ever-growing circle of people around him and disappear. Suddenly, when Wassaja thought he must surely make a run for it, a man stepped forward. He was different from the rest. His name was Carlos Gentilé, an Italian photographer. Wassaja looked at him and saw kindness and understanding shining from his dark eyes. Mr. Gentilé put a hand on Wassaja's shoulder. Wassaja started at first, but then relaxed. Mr. Gentilé's touch was gentle and comforting, reminding Wassaja of the doe in the forest who nudged her young. For the first time, Wassaja felt that this was someone he could trust. Wassaja then saw Mr. Gentilé give the Pima Indian some round, shiny rocks, which were actually coins. Though Wassaja did not know it yet, he had just been adopted by a generous and caring man who would be his father.

Mr. Gentilé took Wassaja to his home and gave him a new name. He already cared for this tiny Indian boy. His heart had gone out to him when he had seen how Wassaja had tried not to show his fright in the face of what must have been new and terrifying surroundings. Mr. Gentilé decided to call his son — for that is how he now thought of Wassaja — Carlos Montezuma. He called him Carlos so that his new son would have a part of his own name and realize how important he was to him. The last name, Montezuma, was from a powerful leader of the Aztec Indians in Mexico and Wassaja seemed to possess the same qualities of this brave chieftain — he held himself nobly and refused to show any signs of fear.

In the happy days that followed, Mr. Gentilé cared and taught his young son everything he knew. It was sometimes difficult for Carlos in this new world, for there were many things to confuse him. At first he thought that a match made fire magically and that the people he saw in photographs actually lived inside the photographs. Carlos was exceptionally bright, though, and under the careful and patient eye of his father, learned more about this new world. He amazed his father by learning to speak English very quickly. Carlos enjoyed learning and he wanted to please his father, who had shown him nothing but kindness. Carlos still thought sometimes of his Apache family and hoped that wherever they were they might somehow know that he had found a secure and loving home with Mr. Gentilé.

Mr. Gentilé, who recognized Carlos' intelligence, wanted to provide him with a good education so together they moved from their home in Arizona to Chicago, where Carlos could attend school.

At first Carlos was unhappy in Chicago, for the city was dirty, with narrow streets instead of open meadows where Carlos could play with his animal friends. Nevertheless, Carlos set out to learn the ways of the white people, for he knew that this was his home now. He attended Sunday school and public school. In school, he proved once again to be a brilliant student, learning how to read in three weeks! After four weeks of school, his teacher promoted him to a higher grade, for he was ahead of the whole class. This made Carlos very proud, for he was determined to study hard. Maybe he would become a doctor as his father hoped. Mr. Gentilé took great pride in his son's achievements and continued to encourage him in his studies. None of the boys who laughed at the little Apache Indian back in Arizona would laugh at him now!

When Carlos was in his early teens, Mr. Gentilé decided that Carlos could learn more in New York, a more culturally advanced city. They moved, but neither was happy there — the people of New York treated Carlos as an outsider, which hurt both Carlos and Mr. Gentilé. One night there was a fire at Mr. Gentilé's photographic studio and he lost everything. Carlos and his father, disappointed and disillusioned, decided to return to Chicago.

Mr. Gentilé set up a new studio and Carlos helped his father take photographs. Carlos was a very skillful assistant. Nevertheless, Mr. Gentilé remained steadfast in his determination that Carlos, with his sharp mind, should study medicine.

One day, however, Carlos overhead his father telling a friend, the Rev. W. H. Steadman, that the fire in New York had greatly impoverished him and he did not have enough money to continue Carlos' schooling. The Reverend offered to have Carlos live with him and his wife, and he could go to school while Mr. Gentilé saved up more money. Carlos felt a tightening in his stomach when he heard this news — he had not known that his father was experiencing such financial difficulties! Still, Carlos decided that he would accept the Reverend's offer and pretend to be glad, because this would please his father and allow him to pay back all his debts. In his heart, though, Carlos was very sad to leave his father.

Carlos excelled in school once again. Soon, his teachers wanted him to enter college at the University of Illinois, even though Carlos was only fifteen years old! The Young Men's Christian Association (YMCA) offered him a loan.

Carlos Montezuma entered college and studied very hard. He graduated at age nineteen with honors, obtaining a bachelor of science degree in chemistry. Still, Montezuma thirsted for more knowledge, and he immediately entered medical school with another loan from the YMCA. There he became fascinated by the human body and studied long hours into the night. He became especially interested in the stomach and made this his specialty.

When *Doctor* Carlos Montezuma left medical school he wanted to fulfill a deep wish to help other Indians. Most Indians were very poor and were treated unfairly.

Dr. Montezuma determined to start his work at an Indian reservation in North Dakota. There he found many Indians dying because of inadequate medical care. Diligently, he tried to attend to all who needed his help. It was demoralizing work, though, because many Indians *wouldn't* come to him — they distrusted what they called white man's medicine and instead relied on superstition.

Montezuma decided he would have to change his approach: he would first learn more about the practice of medicine by working with white people, and then he could return to the Indians. Montezuma entered a partnership with Dr. Fenton Turck, who planned to retire soon and would pass his practice on to Montezuma. Dr. Montezuma soon became extremely popular among both the wealthy and the poor of Chicago — if people could not afford to pay him, he did not charge them.

One of his patients came in with stomach pains and Montezuma cured her, but somehow he was unable to forget Maria Keller. He started dating her, and showed her such kindness and gentleness that it was not long before they were married. Maria proved to be a wonderful wife, helping with patients and doing much charity work.

After Carlos and Maria had been married for a few years, he told her his dream of helping other Indians regain faith in themselves. He told how they lived, as poor and uneducated dependents of the government.

Dr. Montezuma had set himself a very difficult task. He sometimes met with opposition from both whites and Indians, but nevertheless continued to campaign courageously. Slowly, he made progress, developing improved health standards for Indians and teaching them how to farm and mine more efficiently. He also set up reforms to prevent dishonest people from stealing from the Indians. Word of Dr. Montezuma's tireless efforts soon spread to the White House. President Theodore Roosevelt offered him a position as Director of the U.S. Indian Bureau. Dr. Montezuma declined, however — he felt he could do more for Indians working independently. Instead, he unselfishly tried to improve the lives of other Indians.

Carlos Montezuma, who had been taken from his Apache family when he was very young, forgot many details of his former life. But he could never forget the love and kindness of the white man who became his father. He worked his whole life to give others the same gifts.

Moses
(1250 B.C. - 1130 B.C.)

Receiver of the Ten Commandments

Moses started life in a most unusual way. Many years before the birth of Christ, Moses' mother and father, who were Hebrews, were living in Egypt under the rule of a king, called a pharaoh. As Pharaoh watched the Hebrews increase in number he feared that they might rise up one day and overthrow him. To keep the Hebrews powerless, he enslaved them. He also issued a decree which broke the hearts of all Hebrew parents — he ordered them to drown their baby boys in the Nile River!

Moses' parents already had two children, Miriam and Aaron. Miriam was a girl, so she did not have to be killed, and Aaron was too old for the decree to apply to him. Moses, though, had just been born and would have to be killed. Moses' parents loved him very much, however, and — sensing that there was something special about him — they devised a plan to evade the decree. Moses' mother put her baby in a basket made of reeds and pitch and lowered him into the Nile. Miriam watched the basket and followed it as it floated down the river.

Suddenly, Miriam gasped. The basket had just floated to where the daughter of the Pharaoh, the princess of Egypt, was bathing with her maids! The Princess peered into the basket, and a smile brightened her face. Here was the most adorable baby boy she had ever seen! She gazed at the soft brown hair, and the round face from which shone two big brown eyes filled with tears. Suddenly the baby chortled and a smile crossed his face. The Princess fell in love instantly. She placed her finger in the baby's palm and he grasped it. The Princess felt in that moment a bond as if she herself had seen the baby's natural mother. Her maids gathered round her, each one exclaiming over the precious bundle. They begged the Princess to be allowed to hold him, for never had they laid eyes on a baby as beautiful as this one.

"Here, indeed, is a wonderfully unusual baby," said the Princess, "I shall adopt him as my son. Even if I have to defy my parents and the elders, I shall do so, for already he is worth that and more to me."

Moses grew to manhood in the palace. But seeing the Hebrews enslaved by the Egyptians made Moses very sad. One day, he happened upon an Egyptian task-master beating an old Hebrew slave. The slave's cries for mercy went unheeded by the Egyptian, who seemed to take pleasure in beating the old man. The sight of the old slave's bloodied back and shrieks of pain outraged Moses. Unable to contain his fury, Moses struck the Egyptian who fell to the ground, dead. Moses stared, aghast, but the Hebrew kneeled before Moses. The slave's tears of pain had turned to tears of gratitude.

Word of Moses' deed spread through the community. Realizing that he would be arrested and killed, Moses, with a heavy heart, traveled into the desert. Moses entered a land called Midian. Resting by a well, he saw seven young women come to get water for their father's flock. As they worked, several shepherds spoke to them using rude and spiteful language. They started to bully the women and shove them aside. Terrified, the women fled. But how could they get the water they needed? The desert was very hot and the animals would surely die.

Moses once again came to the defense of those weaker than he. Though the shepherds outnumbered him, he was not afraid, for the knowledge that he was acting out of justice lent him additional strength. Singlehandedly, he defeated the shepherds and drove them away. He found that, like most bullies, they were cowards at heart.

When the young women returned to their father, Jethro, with news of their protector, he immediately suggested that they find Moses and invite him to dinner. As Moses sat at Jethro's table that night, he found his eye drawn again and again to Zipporah, Jethro's oldest daughter. Earlier, he had noticed her solemn eyes and kind and gentle manner. Now, as her face glowed in the candlelight, Moses thought he had never seen a more beautiful woman. Before the meal was over, Moses had fallen deeply in love with her. Zipporah, too, had fallen in love with Moses. Soon Moses and Zipporah were married. Jethro welcomed Moses into the family with all his heart. Moses became a shepherd and he and Zipporah lived peacefully in Midian, tending sheep and starting a family.

Then, according to the Bible, near Mt. Horeb Moses saw God as a fire in a burning bush. Moses was told to lead the Hebrews out of slavery in Egypt and guide them to Canaan, the Promised Land. Although unsure of his ability to carry out such an awesome task, and sad to leave his peaceful life in Midian, Moses could not ignore the call to help his people. Pharaoh, however, would not allow the Hebrews to leave Egypt. To convince him, Moses used the power given to him by God, and visited a series of calamities upon the Egyptians until Pharaoh relented.

Moses gathered his people together and set out across the desert. But they were followed by the Pharaoh's soldiers when Pharaoh changed his mind. Faced with death or returning to Egypt as slaves again, Moses appealed to God, who parted the waters of the Red Sea, allowing the Hebrews to cross safely. When the Paraoh's soldiers attempted to follow, the waters closed again, drowning them all.

As the Hebrews travelled, God provided food for them and directed them to stop at Mt. Sinai, where he presented Moses with the Ten Commandments. When — almost to Canaan — they repeatedly rebelled against Moses and showed they did not fully believe in God, he commanded that the Hebrews roam the desert for forty years. Only then were they allowed to enter the Promised Land. But Moses himself never entered Canaan. At age one-hundred and twenty, Moses passed away. Deeply the Hebrews mourned their loss.

Born a slave, Moses had been raised the son of an Egyptian princess to become the chosen leader of God's people.

This article is based upon stories as they appear in the Bible. Members of different religious denominations may adhere to dissimilar beliefs. No endorsement of one or any individual religion is intended.

Jim Palmer   (1945 -)
Baseball Player

One day in October of 1945 Moe and Polly Wiesen adopted a two-day old baby. Though they could not have known it at the time they had just adopted one of the future greats in baseball history — pitching ace Jim Palmer. Moe was a dress manufacturer and Polly owned a boutique. Jim grew up with his older adopted sister, Bonnie, in their wealthy household, where a butler often served as catcher when Jim practiced his pitching!

The Wiesens lived in a Manhattan apartment and later moved to Westchester County, New York. There was plenty of love in the Wiesen home, and Jim frankly says that he has no desire to discover who his natural parents might be as he was raised by loving people who never gave him any cause to think about another set of parents.

From an early age Jim displayed a great enthusiasm for baseball. Holding his father's hand, young Jim would barely be able to contain his excitement as he skipped along to see the Yankees play. But into Jim's happy life, tragedy struck. His father died of a heart attack when Jim was only nine years old. For a long time nothing mattered to Jim, not even baseball.

Deciding a change was needed, Mrs. Wiesen took her two children to California, where they finally settled in a Beverly Hills house previously owned by the famous actor James Cagney. Mrs. Wiesen eventually married actor Max Palmer, from whom Jim got his last name. At first Jim thought he wanted to be an actor, like his stepfather, but baseball was still his first love. Fondly he remembered the hot summer days when his father had taken him to watch the Yankees. Together they had shared the excitement of chasing foul balls in the stands, eating hot dogs, and sipping cold sodas. Joining a Little League team in Beverly Hills, Jim pitched and played third base.

Then the Palmer family moved again, this time to Scottsdale, Arizona, in order to help relieve Mrs. Palmer's arthritis. At Scottsdale High, Jim was an All-State athlete, not only for baseball, but for football and basketball as well. Until his senior year, Jim's batting average was excellent. But then he developed an astigmatism in his left eye which lowered his batting average. This also led him to focus on pitching because perfect vision is not as critical in pitching as it is in batting.

If Jim stood out because of his exceptional athletic ability, he was like many young people his age in another sense — he had a sweetheart and her name was Susan Ryan. Jim and Susan were married on February 25, 1964. From this marriage Jim has two daughters, Jamie and Kelly.

Right after graduating from high school, Jim was sought after by the Houston Astros, the L.A. Dodgers and the Baltimore Orioles. Turning down a basketball scholarship from UCLA, he signed up with the Orioles. Jim's first professional game was for a Baltimore farm club, the Aberdeen (South Dakota) Pheasants on May 1, 1964.

Jim Palmer, later known as king of the high fastball, rapidly made history. As a starting pitcher for Baltimore, he became the youngest player to ever pitch a complete-game shutout in a World Series. He was also the youngest player in fifty years to pitch the entire series game himself.

But despite Palmer's stellar performance, arm and back injuries forced him to leave the major leagues and play in the minors. Then, baffling everyone, Palmer played thirty-seven innings without a single win. Physicians finally discovered the problem — Palmer had been born with one leg shorter than the other — and, by padding one shoe he was again ready to do battle on the pitching mound.

Soon he was setting records again. His high fast ball — clocked at eighty-eight to eighty-nine miles per hour, with its last-second dip or rise — could strike out even the best of batters. Wearing number 22 for the Baltimore Orioles, Jim Palmer became the winningest pitcher in the American League during the 1970s. Three times he was awarded the Cy Young Award. Palmer also set other records by winning at least twenty games each season for eight years. Palmer finished his brilliant career with a club record of 2,212 strikeouts over 3,949 innings pitched, and recording fifty-three shutouts.

Palmer has claimed that baseball to him is not a job but a joy. Throughout his career he was meticulous about maintaining his good health and taking care of his pitching arm. He would put his arm in ice water after every game. As he pitched with his right hand, Palmer tried to use his left hand for all other activities. He ate and played tennis with his left hand. He even slept on his left side. During the off season, to keep his body in peak physical condition, Palmer would take up running.

Even though baseball is one of Jim Palmer's great passions and occupies much of his time, he has also found time to open his heart to help others. He supports the Cystic Fibrosis Research Foundation and has served many years as its national sports chairperson. He has also donated his poster earnings to aid the Foundation.

Palmer remains very active today. He models for Jockey International, has done some broadcasting, and has appeared on various talk shows. His favorite pastimes are golf and gardening. For Jim Palmer, the saying "diamonds are forever" has particular significance — on January 10, 1990 this superstar was named to the Baseball Hall of Fame.

Edgar Allan Poe (1809 - 1849)
American Author

Edgar Allan Poe, possibly the most famous American author, was wretchedly poor throughout most of his adult life. Bottling up the feverish desire to write poetry, he was forced to work long, tedious hours as an editor, critic, or writer in order to put food on the table. Shivering in winter winds and drenched by summer rains in threadbare clothes, hunger would burn in his stomach. No one but a genius could have produced the writings Poe did under such miserable conditions. Edgar Allan Poe was a genius — brilliant and driven, but also tormented and troubled.

Historians have worked out much of Poe's life story, but many details still elude us. The mystery and darkness which enshrouds his life also permeates nearly all of his tales and poetry.

Poe was born in Boston in 1809 to two actors, Elizabeth and David Poe. Poe's mother was talented and popular, sought after for leading roles in Shakespearean plays. David Poe, by contrast, was a former law student whose performances on stage were lackluster at best. In 1810 David Poe abandoned his family, possibly because he was embarrassed at failing where his wife had succeeded, though no one knows for sure.

Elizabeth, impoverished and expecting a child, tried to care for Edgar and her other son, Henry. After her daughter Rosalie's birth, Elizabeth was forced to join a travelling acting company based in Richmond, Virginia but the strain of traveling and acting without any rest soon took its toll. Elizabeth contracted tuberculosis and little Edgar, now age three, watched perplexed and helpless as the disease slowly reduced his once lively mother into a weak, bedridden invalid. He would remember the sight of her, coughing and moaning, all his life.

Upon Elizabeth's death in 1811, the children were split up. Edgar went to live with John Allan, a rich tobacco merchant of Richmond, and his wife Frances. The couple had no children so Frances transferred her love onto the handsome, precocious child who soon started calling her "Mama." Mr. Allan, a hardheaded man who made no hasty decisions, did not formally adopt Edgar, who was now known as Edgar Allan Poe, but did take him in as a foster child and provided him with excellent schooling. In a matter of days Poe's lifestyle changed dramatically from one of poverty and stress to one of leisure and comfort.

When Edgar was six years old, Mr. Allan and his business partner decided to open a branch of their firm in London. So the family set sail for England aboard the *Lothair*. Edgar was enchanted by the ocean voyage. He spent his days reading books and following the sailors, asking them all sorts of questions about their lives on the high seas.

When they arrived in Liverpool, the adventure continued for Edgar. Always eager for knowledge and new experiences he explored all the sights of Liverpool. Visiting John Allan's family in Scotland, Edgar delighted in playing with his cousins on the misty, heather-covered hillsides under fire-breathing dragon clouds. Too soon the Allans were back on the road. They stopped at Glasgow, Edinburgh and finally London.

Mr. Allan then decided it was time to send Edgar back to Scotland for schooling. The unwilling Edgar balked at "Pa" for sending him away from "Mama" and declared that he would escape to the U.S. Mr. Allan finally relented to Edgar's and his wife's pleading, and Edgar returned to London to eventually attend the Manor House School, an exclusive boarding school. Edgar particularly excelled in French, history, and literature, for which he would do much extra reading. Looming in front of Edgar's school was an ancient castle-like building which the young boy found fascinating in a dark, forbidding way. Creating his own world out of the shifting shadows, many an afternoon Edgar's fertile imagination would wonder at the strange and terrifying secrets hidden deep within the stone walls.

Edgar spent much of his free time by himself, for his schoolmates made fun of the way he spoke and were far ahead of him in the British sports which they had been playing all their lives, but which were new to Edgar. Though athletic and willing to try any new games, Edgar often found himself excluded. So Edgar's free hours were spent reading and dreaming. Then one day he discovered the joy and release to be found in writing. Like any other eleven-year-old, he enjoyed sports and getting into mischief; but unlike most other boys his age, Edgar thought frequently about life and death and started recording his feelings on paper.

Meanwhile, Mr. Allan's business venture had failed dismally. In 1820, he decided to move his family back to Virginia. To the other twelve-year-olds in Richmond, Edgar seemed like an exotic celebrity. His friends would listen, wide-eyed as he told them tales of fantastic sea adventures and other stories. He was also anyone's equal in sports, and amazed the townspeople by swimming six miles upstream on the James River. Popular and outgoing, he excelled in school. Poe was growing into a polished and eligible Southern gentleman. However, he was not allowed to forget his origins — he was the son of two actors at a time when acting was considered not quite respectable. Poe was very quick to use his fists if anyone dared insult the memory of his mother, Elizabeth Poe.

Soon he found a willing ear for his poetry in his friend Rob Stanard's mother. Mrs. Stanard became a sort of surrogate mother to Poe. He was mesmerized by her intelligence and genuine, warm concern. It was to her that the fifteen-year old Poe wrote his great poem "To Helen" which he would continue to revise throughout his life.

But in sharp contrast to the encouragement Poe received from Mrs. Stanard, neither Mr. nor Mrs. Allan could appreciate his poetry. Frances Allan, though loving, was by no means an intellectual, and Mr. Allan, the consummate businessman, was too practical. Poe, however, did not mind this state of affairs so long as he had Mrs. Stanard's understanding. But then, with horrible swiftness, death robbed him of Mrs. Stanard. She died in 1824 of a brain tumor. Grief-stricken, Poe would go day and night to visit her grave.

Meanwhile, life at home was becoming increasingly strained for Poe as he and Mr. Allan started to clash. One day the fifteen-year old, out of loyalty toward his foster mother, confronted his foster father with having romances outside of his marriage. Mr. Allan responded by writing to Poe's brother Henry, with whom Poe had started corresponding, to tell him of Poe's ingratitude and moodiness. These incidents spurred the growing animosity between Poe and Mr. Allan. Then suddenly, the tension eased when Mr. Allen's uncle died, leaving him a small fortune. The vain Mr. Allan moved his family into a mansion and, for a brief period, there was peace.

Poe was a very eligible bachelor, but he remained largely aloof until he met Sarah Elmira Royster. Her hair was midnight black and her eyes tinged with sadness —

Poe was entranced. After spending many an afternoon in their secret shaded garden, the two became secretly engaged in 1826. To the seventeen-year-old Poe, it seemed the future held nothing but happiness. He dreamed of literary fame and starting a family in genteel Virginia.

To prepare for his career, Poe enrolled in the University of Virginia in 1826. Unlike many of the students, who were young Virginia aristocrats intent only on drinking and gambling, Poe studied hard. He took first place in French and second place in Latin. Yet Mr. Allan barely gave Poe enough money to cover his expenses and refused to give him any more. Too proud to satisfy his guardian by begging, Poe tried to earn the money by borrowing and gambling. Bad luck resulted in his owing over two thousand dollars in debts. To console himself, Poe started drinking. His tolerance for alcohol was extremely low, however, and even one drink was enough to make him ill. Often, he could not remember anything he had said or done while drinking. Turning to Mr. Allan, he asked for financial help. Mr. Allan refused to help him. No one knows for sure why this wealthy man suddenly grew so tight-fisted with his foster son.

When Poe left the University of Virginia after the fall term, he was pretty sure he would not be allowed to come back. Poe could not know, of course, that his room, #13, West Range, would later be preserved as a memorial to him.

As he headed home, Poe also had a terrible premonition that his romance with Elmira was over. Sure enough, Poe learned that Elmira had married the man of her family's choice and Poe could not get in touch with her. Meanwhile, his debts were still outstanding and his relationship with his foster father was growing steadily worse. Mr. Allan suggested law to Poe but he remained adamant that he wanted a literary career. Affairs reached a climax when, on March 18, 1827, Mr. Allan raged at Poe for his drinking and gambling, while Poe countered with accusations of Mr. Allan's infidelity to his wife. As the argument escalated, Mr. Allan finally yelled at Poe to disappear from his sight. Shocked, Poe left the Allan house, never to live there again.

From a tavern, he drafted a formal letter telling Mr. Allan that he would rather try his luck in the world than remain at his home. He then asked for a trunk with his clothing and books, but received only a note telling him how ungrateful he was. By now, Poe was hungry and sent a note beseeching Mr. Allan to give him money to leave Richmond. He never got a reply.

Poe probably received the needed money from Mrs. Allan, and made his way up to Boston, where he published *Tamerlane and Other Poems* in 1827. Though delighted to have his name in print, Poe received no recognition. He found shelter and three meals a day by enlisting in the army as Private Edgar A. Perry, to keep his creditors from knowing his real name.

Poe made an excellent soldier. Educated and intelligent, he soon moved up the ranks. He took delight in exploring Charleston, South Carolina, where he was stationed, but he worried that he did not have enough time for writing, and his most creative years were being squandered with nothing to show for them.

Then a series of events developed which changed Poe's life. Mrs. Allan became very sick, and pleaded with her husband to help their foster son and bring him home. To gain Mr. Allan's favor, Poe offered to enter West Point and become an officer. Also, Poe thought, since the life of a commissioned officer was one of leisure, he would at last be able to dedicate himself to his writing.

News then reached him that Mrs. Allan was gravely ill and her dearest wish was that she gaze upon her foster son one last time before she died. Poe raced home, but death once again deprived him of a mother — Mrs. Allan had been buried even before he reached home. Grieving, Poe visited her graveside and wept bitter tears.

In December, 1829, Poe published a rather melancholy collection of poems called *Al Aaraaf, Tamerlane, and Minor Poems,* with no help from Mr. Allan.

Poe then went to live in Baltimore with his grandmother, his brother Henry, his aunt Maria Clemm, and her seven-year-old daughter Virginia. There was hardly any money coming into the house, but Poe was made to feel welcomed and loved. Finally, one day, he received his acceptance into West Point. He went to visit Mr. Allan one more time but once again sparks flew between them. Both were glad when he set sail for the north.

At West Point, Poe's superior education and previous experience in the army set him ahead of his classmates. But once again, his life was fraught with tension and frustration — the tension of not having enough money to cover even his necessities, and the frustration of the rigid schedule which completely disrupted his writing. While other students relied on their families for financial support, Poe had no one. He took to drinking again. As always, even a small drink had devastating effects on him.

Unhappy and restless, Poe decided that if Mr. Allan would not help him, he would get himself discharged from West Point, which now seemed like a prison, by breaking all the rules he could. Then, at last, he could turn to his writing.

Poe succeeded in getting himself discharged, and February 19, 1831 found him a wretchedly ill, shivering, penniless wreck, waiting for the steamboat to take him to New York. The details of the next three years are hazy, though we know he lived for a time with his aunt, Mrs. Clemm, and his cousin Virginia in Baltimore. He searched for work but found none and was often reduced to borrowing from friends. He grew increasingly attached to Mrs. Clemm and Virginia, both of whom adored him. There was plenty of love in their household, but no money. Poe wrote a humble letter to Mr. Allan for some help, but received no reply. It was only when Mrs. Clemm wrote, detailing their misery, that Mr. Allan sent some money without even a note attached.

Finally in 1833 Poe received first prize in a short story contest sponsored by *Saturday Visitor* magazine for his tale *MS Found in a Bottle*. He would also have captured first prize in the magazine's poetry contest for his poem *The Coliseum,* but the judges decided against giving both prizes to the same author. One of the judges, John P. Kennedy, especially took a liking to Poe and would later help him with his career. Though still oppressed under severe poverty, Poe had finally received some recognition.

In spring of 1834 Poe received news that Mr. Allan was near death. Hoping that, for the sake of the affection they had shared in Poe's younger years, they might be reconciled, Poe went to see Mr. Allan. Hurrying past servants who tried to prevent his entry, he was told by the dying Mr. Allan to leave immediately. When Mr. Allan's will was later read, there was no mention of his foster son.

Poe obtained a position as editor of T. W. White's *Southern Literary Messenger,* a Richmond-based magazine. But alcohol started to play an increasingly important role in Poe's life. Even though it always brought him trouble, drinking helped him forget his problems. Finally White fired Poe for drunkenness and he was again penniless. Ashamed, he returned to Baltimore, where he and thirteen-year-old Virginia could no longer hide their affection for one another. (It must be noted that in the age in which Poe lived, it was not unusual for men to marry much younger women.) After Poe married Virginia Clemm, he wrote to Mr. White, asking his forgiveness. Mr. White agreed to give Poe his old job back only if he promised not to drink.

Back in Richmond Poe toiled unceasingly as an editor and critic, and soon made Mr. White a very wealthy man. Unfortunately, Poe did not share much in the profits; at best all that could be said was that he had a steady income. Poe became more and more frustrated by the drudgery of his extremely long days with hardly a second to devote to his own writing.

He had words, thoughts and ideas stopped up inside him, just waiting to be released on paper, but as usual, he was forced to work for someone else in order to survive. His writing — especially his beloved poetry — always had to take second place.

·

Depressed and terribly frustrated, Poe twice broke his promise not to drink, and Mr. White fired him for good.

After a short time in New York City, Poe moved his family to Philadelphia. He worked for a while as editor of *Burton's Gentleman's Magazine,* meanwhile publishing *Tales of the Grotesque and Arabesque,* which yielded neither fame nor profits. In December 1840, George Graham bought the magazine. Poe now wished to start his own magazine, *Penn Magazine* and felt sure he could get the backing. Graham, however, persuaded Poe to stay on with the promise to increase his salary in six months, make him a partner, or help him start his own journal.

Poe's great skill as an editor and the excellent short stories he wrote for the magazine — among them the immortal *Ligeia* and *The Fall of the House of Usher* — created huge profits for Graham. The number of subscriptions rose from 3,500 to 37,000 the largest in the world for any monthly magazine. Poe, however, wished to pursue his own writing full-time. Graham only paid Poe, his best writer and editor, a meager eight hundred a year, while the going salary for most editors was $1,500 to $2,000 a year. Graham's earlier promises to help Poe never materialized.

Poe became more and more concerned with money as his wife's health started to falter. Always sickly, in January of 1842 Virginia burst a blood vessel in her neck while singing and never quite recovered. In powerless agony, Poe was forced to watch as Virginia — like his mother years before — grew weaker with each passing day.

In the meantime, to keep the wolf from the door, Poe tried to get a job with the federal government. He failed, but managed to survive by publishing *The Murders in the Rue Morgue, The Mystery of Marie Roget, The Gold Bug,* and other stories. But he wished to escape the misery of witnessing his wife's declining health. Instead of being practical and trying to hold down a job, Poe turned to drinking. He missed many work days, until finally Graham replaced Poe, hiring the Rev. Rufus Wilmot Griswold, a poet anthologist whose works Poe had criticized. With this turn of events, Poe's drinking increased.

After the summer of 1842, Poe decided to sober up and start writing again. He received financial backing for his magazine *The Stylus* from Thomas C. Clarke, a Philadelphia publisher. He went to Washington to get government officials to subscribe to his magazine, and even managed to arrange a visit with President Tyler through Tyler's son, a poet. Unfortunately for American literature, Poe decided to calm his nerves before these important events by having a drink of wine. It was his downfall. He never met with the president, and the government officials whom he had hoped to impress instead viewed him with great disfavor.

Disgraced, Poe returned to Philadelphia and was reduced to begging Griswold for a five dollar loan. Griswold gloated to see his erstwhile critic brought so low. Poe's life now seemed a great, yawning abyss of despair and he sank deeper into his melancholy. Then, in 1843, he won a one hundred dollar prize for *The Gold Bug;* the crucial money seemed like a godsend, the first ray of hope to break the perennial shadow dogging Poe.

He decided to move back to New York City to try his luck there again. At this time, he also wrote *The Raven,* published in 1845. With this poem, Poe became an "overnight" sensation — fame was suddenly his! People stopped him in the street to ask for his autograph and he was well-received both in the United States and Great Britain. The year 1845 also saw the publication of *Tales by Edgar Allan Poe.* He became partner and editor of *The Broadway Journal* and in October of that same year bought the magazine. Unfortunately, despite having led other magazines to success, he failed with his own. The details as to why are uncertain, but it is known that Poe had started drinking yet again.

In the beginning of 1847 Virginia's health worsened considerably. Aching with pain, cold, and hunger, she had only her husband's old West Point overcoat to use for a blanket. Virginia died in 1847 at the age of twenty-four.

After his wife's death, the grieving Poe launched into a spree of writing, drinking, and romances. He returned to Richmond in 1849 to lecture, and there, still poor as ever, proposed to his childhood sweetheart, Elmira Royster, who was now a widow. Elmira accepted after some deliberation, and the wedding was arranged for October 17, 1849. Poe was delighted. A few days before the ceremony, Poe set out to New York, for reasons still largely unknown, and then made a stopover in Baltimore. On October 3, he was found, half unconscious, in the streets of Baltimore. He was taken to a hospital where he was delirious for four days. On October 7, 1849 Poe died at the age of forty. Only Mrs. Clemm and a few other people attended his funeral.

Edgar Allan Poe had led a tragic life. But there was one more disturbing chapter to follow. Poe had made the mistake of making Griswold his literary executor. The jealous Griswold wrote biting and vicious attacks on Poe's life, defamed his character, destroyed important letters, and changed parts of Poe's writings. In response to Griswold's pettiness, many of Poe's fans leapt to his defense. The subsequent accusations, attacks, and counterattacks between Poe's friends and foes created such confusion that even today we have not been able to decipher the complete truth about the life of Edgar Allan Poe.

Yet what would have happened if Poe had continued the life of ease in which he was raised as a foster child? What sublime stories and poems could he have penned

.

105

if he had only the leisure time and money to write as he so desperately wished? Or would he have lost that dark and forbidding style that so identifies his work? Could he have been as popular otherwise? Why not read some of the works above and decide for yourself?

Eleanor Roosevelt (1884 - 1962)
First Lady of the World

Eleanor Roosevelt, who would be much later called "First Lady of the World," was born into a wealthy family in New York; a family admired, respected, and famous for its contributions to the American nation.

Who could wish for more? But her mother was beautiful and her father handsome and charming. Perhaps because of this, Eleanor's looks as a child were a disappointment to her parents — who had, in any case, wanted a boy as their first child. Eleanor always remembered the sadness she felt at an aunt's unkindness in calling her an "ugly duckling."

In spite of all the wealth and servants that surrounded her, little Eleanor was a very lonely child. The happy moments in her life were few. Eleanor had to stand aside, unwanted, while her mother played with her two younger brothers, Elliott Jr. and Hall — not understanding why the mother she loved so much was always distant to her. She wished so much to be wanted! Her father, who did play with her, and called her "Little Nell," was the only family member who showed her any affection. As a result, Eleanor loved him very, very much. Because she was a very intelligent child, Eleanor early in her life realized that she would always be plain and that she could do nothing to change her looks. So she tried hard to please everyone around her in other ways: she was always polite, courteous, and unselfish.

The little girl had nobody to care about her, and nobody — if her father was away — to calm her fears . . . and she had many fears. When she was two and a half years old she had to be rescued from the ship she was on, and, although she was taken safely ashore in a lifeboat, Eleanor remained afraid of water. Most children outgrow fears quickly, but because she felt unloved Eleanor was very afraid of being left alone in a dark room. Snakes terrified her and she was also afraid of dogs, horses and strangers. All too early in her life the only person who showed her affection, her father, had to leave home — Eleanor learned when she was older — to enter a treatment program for alcoholics.

At that time, too, her mother began to suffer from severe headaches, feeling better only when someone stroked her head. Although only seven — in her desperate search for affection, the little girl stroked her mother's head for hours. She was happier; at last her mother needed her. But the very next year first her mother and then her brother Elliott died from diphtheria. Then Eleanor, sadder and more lonely than ever, was sent with her younger brother to live with Grandmother Hall. The house, large and elegant, with plenty of servants, was a dark and gloomy place for Eleanor.

The only bright spot in her life were her father's rare visits, which also ceased very soon . . . for when Eleanor was ten her beloved father died. This blow added to many the little girl had suffered, making her even more determined to live her life as her father would have wished.

Without friends, little Eleanor spent much time in her room, reading. Often she cried herself to sleep at night. To make things even worse for little Eleanor, her governess delighted in shouting at her and in pulling her hair to make her cry. Eleanor was so terrified of her that she did not dare tell her grandmother of the cruel treatment. And yet another fear haunted Eleanor: when her Uncle Vallie, who had shown her kindness and taught her horseback riding, began to drink heavily, he too was subject to violent outbursts.

Grandma Hall believed that girls did not need an education. They had to be accomplished in music, dancing, sewing and good manners. Fortunately, before her death, her mother had outfitted a schoolroom in the house, hired two teachers, and asked other wealthy families to send their daughters to classes with Eleanor. It was lucky for Eleanor that her grandmother decided to let the little school continue. Eleanor proved to be an excellent student. She was curious and well behaved and had great will power. Also, having no friends, she did not have outside distractions.

Eleanor did enjoy, however, the family visits to Long Island, to the house of her Uncle Theodore Roosevelt, later president of the United States. With her Uncle Ted she could relax and be herself and he became very fond of her.

Grandma Hall was not a warm, loving person, nor did she understand children. A very wealthy lady, she only allowed Eleanor to have two school dresses. Eleanor, wealthy in her own right, on one occasion had to go to school with a big ink stain on her dress until the other dress came out of the wash. Eleanor was mortified but too proud to let anyone know. Only later, alone in her room, she cried and cried and wished her father were with her.

.

And then a most wonderful event took place in Eleanor's life when she was almost fifteen. Her grandmother decided to send her to boarding school in England. Apprehensive at first, Eleanor soon began to enjoy Allenswood immensely. The discipline was strict, but then Eleanor had never been pampered. She kept her room clean, as demanded by regulations; her bed was always made and her clothes were in good order. Of her own free will and to strengthen her determination, Eleanor took a cold shower every day. The headmistress, Mademoiselle Marie Souvestre, a very intelligent and cultured person who really did understand young people, was the greatest influence in Eleanor's young life. Mlle. Souvestre instilled in young Eleanor the desire for justice and the need to fight for the rights of the underprivileged. She also taught the girls to think for themselves, to search for the truth. Eleanor decided that it was her duty to make the world a better place.

Young Eleanor flourished. At Allenswood teachers and students liked her, and she could look up to Mlle. Souvestre. She stopped biting her fingernails and she began to take care of her appearance. She was taught good eating habits and the importance of exercise. Her self-confidence increased and with it came a sense of inner peace and accomplishment. All too soon her grandmother recalled her.

Eleanor was almost eighteen, and in her grandmother's opinion she had had enough schooling. As the daughter of one of the most prominent families, Eleanor had to take her rightful place in society. Eleanor, if consulted, would have stayed on at Allenswood, but she had to obey her grandmother.

Back home once more, all her self-doubt and unhappiness returned. To make matters worse, Eleanor was presented in society together with four other cousins — one of whom, called "Princess Alice" by the family — was very beautiful. It was painful for Eleanor to compare her plain looks with those of the other girls, so Eleanor attended only those parties that she could not refuse and looked for other horizons. She became active in the Junior League, an organization composed of wealthy young women who did good works for poor people. Eleanor elected to work with the children in the Lower East Side of New York, where she taught dancing and gymnastics to girls. At last she was beginning to put into practice the ideals acquired at Allenswood.

And then came the happiest moment in Eleanor's young life — she found love. The man she fell in love with she had known since she was a baby: her fifth cousin Franklin Delano Roosevelt. Eleanor was ecstatic and could not believe that the popular, athletic young man had chosen her — plain Eleanor. But the family did not think it was a good match and tried to dissuade Eleanor from the marriage. They thought that Franklin was dominated by his mother and that his character lacked depth. Both Franklin and Eleanor politely but stubbornly refused to change their minds and in the end the family had to consent to the wedding.

The ceremony was beautiful. President Theodore Roosevelt, — "Uncle Ted" — gave Eleanor away. The couple had to wait for the summer before going on their honeymoon voyage to Europe as Franklin was still attending Columbia University.

When the couple returned from their honeymoon, they lived in a house rented and furnished by Sara Roosevelt, Franklin's mother. Eleanor had three servants and found that as a newlywed, she could not compete with the efficiency with which her mother-in-law ran the house. Always domineering, Mrs. Roosevelt ran their lives too. Still, Eleanor loved Franklin and wanted to win the approval of Sara, so Eleanor went along with any decision her mother-in-law made. Over the next ten years Eleanor was busy with her children. Franklin and Eleanor had six children, although one died in infancy. Now Sara Roosevelt was making decision for the children as well. Still, Eleanor kept quiet.

But when Franklin got bored with the practice of law, he ran and was elected to the New York State Senate and the family moved to Albany in 1910. Shortly afterwards Franklin was appointed Assistant Secretary of the Navy and once more the family uprooted itself, this time to live in the nation's capital. Eleanor, loyal as ever, was an excellent hostess and was always supportive of her husband, but she herself was not happy in an environment of constant parties and entertaining.

When World War I broke out in 1914, Eleanor wanted to help and she did, both with the knitting at the Navy Department workroom and at the Red Cross. She learned accounting so that she could keep books for worthy organizations and she learned to drive a car at a time when ladies were driven by chauffeurs.

Those years of the First World War were busy years for Eleanor. She was in many ways very different from her husband, who was a fun-loving, popular man. Eleanor, who was always serious and punctual, wanted her household run in a businesslike way with the bills paid promptly. Franklin frequently was late for appointments and forgot to pay the bills.

In 1920 Franklin was chosen by the Democratic party to run for vice-president with James Cox for president. Eleanor, as was expected of a candidate's wife, accompanied her husband on his innumerable public appearances, sitting through the same speech time and again, never showing that she was tired. Although Cox and Roosevelt lost that election, Eleanor had learned much. Franklin's adviser, Louis Howe, made Eleanor aware of her value, not just as a support for her husband — the candidate — but of her own value as a person with her own opinions.

In 1921 Eleanor faced yet a new crisis. Franklin fell ill suddenly. He had a high fever and his legs were paralyzed. Several doctors were consulted before the terrible news was discovered: Franklin had polio.

Slowly Franklin's health improved but his legs were paralyzed for life. This was a terrible blow to a man who had loved sports. However, he did not give in to the disease; rather he continued to exercise with his arms and so conditioned his muscles that he was able to propel himself a few steps with the aid of crutches. While he was convalescing he had time to think about things that he had never considered in his entire life. Born to a life of ease he was not always understanding of the poor and unfortunate. But the tragedy that befell him opened his eyes.

Franklin's mother wanted her son to retire to their estate of Hyde Park and live as a country gentleman. But Franklin, backed by his wife and by his adviser, Louis Howe, decided to continue his career in politics. This decision was right for Franklin, and it was right for Eleanor. For the first time she had won a struggle with her mother-in-law, and this victory strengthened her determination to be herself, to live her own life, although never forgetting her husband and her family. She made speeches to women's groups — at first short, nervous remarks, but slowly gaining confidence and poise. Eleanor made many friends and for the first time since Allenswood met people intent on social reform. Eleanor joined in their dreams and she talked to Franklin about them. One of Eleanor's priorities was to stop children from working in factories and send them to school instead; another was to make working conditions better and shorten the working hours for women. In this way, while Franklin was recovering he was also learning about aspects of life which he had never encountered, and which helped him eventually to be a better leader.

Eleanor enjoyed the next several years. With her two friends, Nancy Cook and Marion Dickerman, they established a small factory in which local farmers would create copies of early American furniture. In this way the three friends hoped to create an industry that would help keep farmers in the country and not crowd the cities. Eleanor also bought the then Todhunter School in New York City. Her friend Marion was the principal and Eleanor the vice-principal. Eleanor taught social studies and literature. As she herself had done at Allenswood, she insisted that the girls learn to think for themselves. The time she spent with her pupils was happy and rewarding for Eleanor.

Then in 1928 Franklin was elected governor of New York and the family moved to Albany. In order to fulfill her role as wife of the governor, Eleanor had to abandon her school. This was not an easy thing to do. Also, Franklin was unable to visit schools, hospitals, factories; it was therefore Eleanor who had to do this for him, and inform him of what she saw.

It was a hard time for all of the United States. The country was in a deep depression. Many people — wealthy and poor alike — found themselves with no jobs, no houses and no money. There was nothing to eat. People would stand in long lines to get a cup of soup from a soup kitchen. There was no money for clothes or shoes, so people were cold. Families, evicted from their houses when they could not pay the rent, set up tents in the parks.

Franklin's campaign slogan was the song "Happy Days are Here Again" . . . and he genuinely wanted to restore the country to its former prosperity. He took over the presidency from Herbert Hoover in 1933. Meanwhile Eleanor, working in soup kitchens herself and mingling with the needy, really knew the sufferings they endured. She also tried to make a warm home in the White House in spite of constant visitors and the thousands of pieces of mail addressed to her. She sincerely believed, however, that out of the depression a better world would emerge in which people would care more for one another.

Eleanor had weekly press conferences in which she answered questions; she also wrote a newspaper column she called "My Day," and she established her own radio program too. Since she wanted to reach the American women, she discussed subjects that would interest them. She had succeeded at being both the wife of the president and very much her own person.

In 1936 Franklin Delano Roosevelt won the presidency again by a great majority. But the depression was still not over, although the president had indeed worked hard to create jobs and put the country on its way along the road to recovery. And now there was something else for the president to worry about: Germany, Italy and Japan had invaded and conquered other countries in Europe, Asia, and Africa. Franklin thought that America should prepare itself for war, but many Americans opposed him. Eleanor, too, saw the danger and thought that every person in the United States should be ready to contribute his or her share, small or large, to the welfare of the nation.

In the midst of all this Franklin decided to run for a third presidential term. Again, he won the 1940 election. But the country continued divided as to whether it should help Britain in the war or whether it should remain neutral. The decision was made for the United States when the Japanese attacked Pearl Harbor, a naval base in Hawaii, in December 1941. Congress declared war the next day.

Now Eleanor had to contribute her own personal sacrifice to the war: her four boys were in the armed services. Once again, in spite of her worry and pain, Eleanor helped the war effort by selling war bonds, giving blood, visiting hospitals in England, flying to the theater of war in the Pacific in 1943 and reporting back to the president. The demands of his office were affecting Franklin's health; in 1945 he decided to take a rest. The war in Europe was about to end, but he never saw it . . . for on April 12 Eleanor was informed by telephone that her husband was dead.

Once more she was alone . . . but over the years she had developed a fortitude, an inner strength that allowed her to go on with her work. With characteristic selflessness she called vice-president Truman — now president — and asked what she could do for him.

After her husband's death, and in respect of his wishes, their home at Hyde Park was made into a museum. Eleanor kept the cottage on the property as her dwelling, but much of the time she spent in an apartment in New York. And though sadder, she continued her public life. President Truman asked her to be one of the delegates from the United States to help establish the United Nations. She proved to be an excellent choice. When the Soviet Union demanded that people who had left the countries they now controlled during the war be forced to return, it was Eleanor who — as head of the social, cultural and humanitarian affairs committee — spoke up to say that people should be free to choose where they wished to live. And, by vote, she won! Eleanor served as chairman of the United Nation's Commission for Human Rights. The Commission wrote a Declaration of Human Rights in which, through Eleanor's efforts, the needs of people were given priority over the needs of governments. She travelled all over the world on her mission of peace. She wrote books, contributed to magazines, and gave many lectures.

When Eleanor Roosevelt died on November 7, 1962, the entire world mourned. Eleanor, who devoted her life to the cause of human rights, is buried in Hyde Park next to her husband Franklin Roosevelt.

Sir Henry Morton Stanley   (1841 - 1904)
Explorer

Dick Price told the small boy — who continually wanted to stop and pick up pretty rocks as Dick impatiently jerked him along — that he was going to visit his aunt. This was not true. The boy was being taken to the St. Asaph Workhouse.

On January 28, 1841, Elizabeth Perry of Denbigh, Wales gave birth to a son. She named him John Rowlands after the boy's father who probably died shortly after the boy's birth — although nobody knows for sure. Elizabeth, a selfish, unfeeling woman, did not want her child, and ran off to London. She left the infant with her father, Moses Perry, who worked in a local slaughterhouse. When Moses died, John, then four, was sent to live with some uncles who boarded him out to an old couple named Price. After two years, when John's uncles stopped paying his board, the Prices' son Dick left him at St. Asaph's. There John came under the charge of a brutal schoolmaster named James Francis, a one-handed ex-miner given to insane rages, who would eventually be carted off to a madhouse. For the slightest offense Francis would furiously whip the children like sacks with switches and canes and knock and kick them down on the stone floor. John received his first of many terrible beatings when, as a small boy, he could not pronounce the name "Joseph" correctly in Bible class.

One day Francis came to John in the dining hall and pointed to a tall woman standing by the door. Francis asked John if he recognized her. John did not. Scoffing, Francis informed him that she was his mother. John again looked over the heads of the other children towards the woman who was surveying him with a cold expression. He waited to feel a surge of love. He had always been told that a mother was someone you naturally loved. But he felt nothing. He thought the woman would come in but, without speaking to him, she turned on her heel and disappeared.

John was very sensitive about the way he looked. He was short and, even though the workhouse food was meager, he was rather chubby. Usually John took his beatings from Francis and sat back down at his desk, his throat raw and his chest tight, but too proud to cry. One day when John was fifteen, however, Francis went too far in one of his beatings and drove John to strike back. As they fought, Francis struck the back of his head on the stone wall and lost consciousness. John knew he must escape, for he was terrified that he might have killed Francis. But before John and another boy ran away, John sent someone to check on the schoolmaster to make sure he was all right. John was informed that at that very moment Francis was washing his bloodied face with a murderous expression. John knew he must go. Learning by chance that his paternal grandfather lived nearby at a large farm, John arrived there full of hope and told the old man who he was. The man's face turned red and he shouted at John to go back where he came from, that he never wanted to lay eyes on him again. Then he slammed the door shut.

John had no better luck with any of his other relatives. In fact, one uncle even took the little money John had managed to scrape together. Feeling utterly worthless and unwanted, John drifted to Liverpool. On the streets, strangers hurriedly passed him by. At last he found a job as an errand boy for a butcher. Then one day John made a delivery that was to change his life. He brought a package to David Hardinge, captain of the ship Windermere bound for New Orleans. Seeing the strong boy, Captain Hardinge offered him a job as cabin boy. Eagerly, John accepted — he would not miss the short-tempered butcher.

On December 20, 1858 John Rowlands was off to America. But then he found that he had been tricked. A fellow shipmate secretly told John that all new sailors were part of Captain Hardinge's plot to get cheap deckhands. They were to be treated

·

so badly during the long voyage to America that the moment they hit port, the new sailors would jump ship, not wanting to endure the return trip to England and therefore not collecting their wages.

The six-week voyage seemed endless. With alarming speed, Nelson, the second mate, barked orders and cracked his whip. On one occasion, shuddering, John saw a large group of sharks trailing the Windermere as they did the African slave ships, hoping that people would be tossed overboard into the churning waters. At last the ship wound its way up the Mississippi to New Orleans. Just as Harry had predicted, all of the new sailors disappeared, never to return. Except one. In amazement, Nelson watched as, a few days before sailing time, young John Rowlands strode up the plank ready for duty. Nelson's face grew dark. How was it possible that anyone could endure the beatings he had meted out and still come back as if it had been nothing? Nelson inwardly promised to leave John a quivering wreck by the time he was through with him. After five days of constant battering for no reason, John gathered his few clothes, and as Nelson watched with grudging admiration, walked away straight and proud.

Without money or friends John knew he had to find work or starve. Approaching a man sitting in front of a customs house, John self-consciously asked him for a job. The kindly-looking man was actually a wealthy traveling merchant by the name of Henry Morton Stanley. Happily married for many years, Stanley's one heartfelt disappointment was that he and his wife had no children. Although he had no need of an employee, Stanley did not send the boy away. Instead, he questioned John about where he had come from and why he was seeking work in New Orleans. John told him about his unhappy experiences aboard the Windermere.

Henry Stanley took John, who seemed very hungry, to breakfast and then to get his shaggy mop of hair cut. John was then brought back to the store where he had first met Stanley and introduced to the owner, Mr. James Speake. On Stanley's recommendation, Speake agreed to take John on for a week's trial period.

John thrived in his new life in a new country. He impressed Mr. Speake so much that he was made a permanent employee and his salary raised. John rented a room in a nearby boarding house and still, for the first time in his life, had extra money to spend. He decided to use the money for books.

Henry Stanley often invited John to breakfast at his large house. Mrs. Stanley, a very small and delicate lady, had taken an immediate liking to the serious boy. But during the summer of 1859 New Orleans was stricken with one of its regular bouts of yellow fever. Mr. Speake caught the disease and died. Ellison, the cold and selfish man who bought the business was very different from Mr. Speake. While Henry Stanley was away, his wife became ill. When John asked for a few days off to help take care of Mrs. Stanley, Ellison flatly refused. Angry, John quit, and himself watched anxiously over Mrs. Stanley, day and night. But in a few days, she died. The day after her death Henry Stanley's brother, a ship captain from Havana, came and took over. John, feeling utterly heartsick and unwanted, miserably left.

After various odd jobs, John found work on a flatboat. He had much time to study river navigation, not knowing how very necessary the knowledge would be to him one day. As soon as he returned to New Orleans, John headed straight to the Stanley house. When Henry Stanley saw him, he was extremely happy and embraced him warmly. Stanley's brother had told him of John's concern and helpfulness during his wife's illness, and Stanley promised to take full charge of John's future. Unable to help himself, John broke down sobbing. No one had ever shown him such kindness before. Stanley, who had once been a preacher, dipped his fingers in water and made the sign of the cross on John's forehead. He recalled that the name "John" comes from the Hebrew and means "gracious gift of God." Throughout his life John felt that he was guided by God and perhaps it was no coincidence that "Henry" and "Morton" are both names that mean "home." When his new father asked him to take his name, John realized that his own name, John Rowlands, meant nothing to him. But the name Henry Morton Stanley represented a man who cared about him. This name he could say not only from his head but also from his heart.

Stanley became the father John had never had. For the next two years Stanley and his son traveled up and down the Mississippi River together. This was the happiest time in Henry Stanley's life — for that was John's proper name now. His father's kindness and devotion gave him new direction. No matter where he went or what he did later on, Henry always carried the knowledge that at least one person had truly loved him and believed in him.

Sometime in mid 1860 after collecting a large sum of money, father and son were traveling on the steamer Little Rock. The evening sun was sinking its pink and orange splendor into the river when young Henry glimpsed a thin, hatchet-faced man pressing his ear up against his father's cabin door. Puzzled, Henry watched as the stranger quietly depressed the door handle and crept inside the darkened room. Reacting quickly, Henry found the evil-looking stranger fighting with his father. When the thief saw young Henry ready to pounce on him, he pulled out a knife but only managed to slash the boy's coat as he fled. Both his father's life and money were saved because of his son's swift actions.

A few months later, Henry's father learned that his sea captain brother in Havana was not well. He decided to go to Havana, making arrangements for his son to first visit Major Ingham, a friend of his who owned a large plantation in Saline County, Arkansas, and then work as a clerk in a store at Cypress Bend, until he returned.

Quietly Henry cried into his pillow the night before his father, the only person who had ever loved him, was to leave. The next morning Henry was still terrified that his father might not come back. Trying to appear more cheerful than he felt at their departure, Stanley tried to allay his son's fears.

As promised, Major Ingham took Henry to his plantation. One day on the Ingham plantation, Henry was helping the major's slaves cut down pine trees. The overseer, a brutish man, was in a very bad mood. While a slave named Jim, along with Henry and some other men, was carrying a heavy log, huffing and puffing, the overseer asked Jim a question.

Unable to answer — under the tremendous weight of the log — as politely as the overseer thought he should, the overseer cracked his lash across Jim's naked shoulders. The lash flew so unexpectedly close to Henry that both he and Jim dropped the log, causing the others to drop it as well and it fell, crushing one man's foot. The unjustified, ruthless actions of the overseer infuriated Henry. Shouting loudly, he told the overseer what he thought of him and they came close to fighting. Indignant, Henry went straight to Major Ingham. Henry listened, shocked, as well-educated Major Ingham informed him that the overseer was merely doing his job. Without another word, Henry Stanley packed his bags and left.

Henry went then to Mr. Altschul's store in Cypress Bend which turned out to be a swampy, unhealthy area. Henry soon came down with a disease called "Arkansas ague." While in bed, sick, he read over and over again the letters that came from his father in Havana. The last one reassured him that his father's brother was recovering and that father would soon come up to Arkansas to stay with his son. Henry Stanley never returned; he died in Havana in 1861. His son waited and waited for a visit that never came. In fact, he did not even hear about his father's death for years because he himself became embroiled in a war he did not even understand.

A foreigner by birth, Stanley took little interest in American politics. Young men of his age were enthusiastically rushing to enlist in the "Dixie Grays" while Stanley merely continued to clerk in the store. One day Stanley received a note saying he was a coward. When a recruiter came that same night, Stanley, humiliated, and perhaps wanting to make his father proud, replied that he was no coward and joined the Confederate Army.

The fighting was intense. In the Battle of Shiloh, men were dying all around Stanley. Suddenly a bullet struck Stanley squarely on his belt buckle and threw him violently backwards onto the ground. The buckle probably saved Stanley's life. The next day there were only about fifty Dixies left to do battle with the Union Army. Stanley's commanding officer singled him out and ordered him to stand up smartly and march forward. Stanley did. As the Union troops rushed in on him, Stanley suddenly found himself abandoned in an open meadow. He was forced to drop his gun. On the long walk to the prisoner's camp Stanley thought not only of possible death but also that in a field somewhere lay his knapsack containing his father's letters, lost forever.

As a foreigner Stanley had no deep loyalty to the South. After about six weeks in Camp Douglas, Stanley agreed to join the Federal Artillery. But his stint as a Union soldier lasted only three days. He was stricken with dysentery and some unknown fever. He was sent to a hospital and from there, on June 22nd, he was discharged.

After working various temporary jobs, Stanley managed to save up enough money to leave war-torn America and return to Denbigh, northern Wales, to see his mother. Stanley was still suffering from severe attacks of fever, he was penniless, and he was dressed in ragged clothes, yet he wanted to show his mother that he had grown up. Maybe now she would want him. His mother took one horrified look at the run-down, sickly figure at her door and told him that he was an embarrassment and that he should leave immediately, before the neighbors saw him. This time his mother's cold-blooded rejection left an even deeper scar on Henry Stanley than when he had been originally abandoned as a child. Terribly ill, Stanley turned away. Searching for his adoptive father, he traveled to Cuba, only to find that his father had died there nearly two years earlier.

Completely disheartened, Stanley returned to the sea, its chaotic rages matching his own state of mind. In August 1864 he enlisted in the U.S. Navy and first got the idea of becoming a journalist as ship's writer. But late in February 1865, inactivity caused Stanley to walk away from the Minnesota, the ship on which he was serving. Two months later the war ended and by then Stanley was working as a journalist. Once again, this time dressed up in his Navy uniform, Stanley knocked on his mother's door. For the last time in his life he called himself John Rowlands in an attempt to please his mother. She was not happy to see him, but this time he was clean and did not ask for anything, so she let him stay a couple of days. Stanley, still young, questioned his mother's indifference and kept searching for defects in himself. Why did his mother not want him? What was wrong with him? It would take a much older Stanley to realize that there was nothing wrong with *him*. Yet even though Stanley was admittedly hurt by his mother's uncaring attitude, he was warmed by the memory of the man whose name he now bore. Becoming even more determined to be like his adoptive father than ever before, Stanley realized that he was his own person, separate from his mother and in complete control of who and what he would become.

In 1867 Stanley was writing for the well-known newspaper, *The New York Herald*. On October 28, 1869, the owner and editor of the *Herald*, James Gordon Bennett summoned Stanley and sent him on the most remarkable assignment in newspaper history. Bennett was sure that with Stanley's toughness and determination, he could carry out the task he had in mind. Bennett told Stanley that he wanted him to find Dr. David Livingstone and interview him. Stanley's jaw dropped in astonishment. Livingstone was a British explorer who, in 1866 had ventured into deepest Africa to map central African lakes and to find the source of the Nile River. No one had heard from Livingstone in quite some time and there was concern over his safety. It took Stanley only a few moments to consider the terrible dangers of Bennett's request. Lifting his chin, he told Bennett that he would find Livingstone. But as he walked out of Bennett's office into the heart of the African jungle, Stanley was not so sure.

Livingstone himself knew nothing of this rescue mission when, on October 23, 1871, after gruesome months of traveling he reached the settlement of Ujiji. He soon realized that all of his supplies had been sold or stolen. But two days after arriving at Ujiji, Livingstone learned to his amazement that a white man had recently passed through Unyanyembe, two hundred miles east of Ujiji. Who this white man was, where he was going, or what he was doing, nobody knew. Livingstone could not help hoping that this stranger, whoever he was, would come to Ujiji. He was well aware that without help very soon, he might not live much longer.

In early or mid-November, shots rang outside the village, announcing the arrival of a caravan. Soon Livingstone could see a long line of men dressed in white robes and turbans. Separating themselves from the crowd, a huge native carrying the American flag, was followed by a white man who was impeccably dressed in a freshly pressed flannel suit and a helmet flashing its white brilliance in the strong sun. The crowd parted and Livingstone moved towards the white man who lifted his hat and said, as politely as he could, in a voice that nevertheless shook with excitement, "Dr. Livingstone, I presume?"

Livingstone shed tears of gratitude. This stranger, braving death and danger in unexplored Africa, had saved his life.

Stanley and Livingstone spent five months together in the wilds of Africa. But when Stanley suggested that Livingstone return to England with him, Livingstone refused to even consider the thought. He would not rest until he found the source of the Nile he told Stanley. Back in England in 1872, Stanley published a book entitled *How I Found Livingstone* which became a worldwide best-seller.

When Livingstone died in 1873, Stanley decided to take up the exploration of Africa and the perilous search for the source of the Nile himself. In 1874 Stanley led an expedition of about three-hundred and fifty men into Africa. The group explored Lake Victoria and many other lakes. Then Stanley followed the Congo River all the way west to its mouth at the Atlantic Ocean. By 1877 more than two-thirds of Stanley's men had died or deserted. Henry Stanley's toughness as an explorer earned him the name "Bula Matari" which means "Breaker of Rocks" in Congolese. Stanley helped establish the Congo Free State, eventually the Belgian Congo, an area ruled by King Leopold who had become fascinated by Stanley's reports and wanted to establish colonies for Belgium in Africa.

On his last African expedition, Stanley courageously helped rescue a government official, Emin Pasha, a colonial ruler whom African rebels had cut off from civilization during a revolt to drive Europeans and Egyptians out of the country. On this expedition, in which there was starvation, disease, horrible attacks by wild animals and hidden Pygmies, Stanley succeeded in locating the Ruwenzori range — the Mountains of the Moon — which is the source of the Nile River.

On July 12, 1890, forty-nine year old Henry Stanley married Dorothy Tennant, a beautiful, talented woman of thirty-six. A few years later, the Stanleys adopted a baby boy. They named him Denzil and Stanley loved him very much. He wanted to return some of the love he had received from his own adoptive father. In 1899 at the age of fifty-eight, Henry Morton Stanley was knighted.

But Stanley's health was deteriorating. On April 17, 1903, Stanley suffered a stroke that left him paralyzed. It was not until the fall that he was able to speak and walk a bit. Almost exactly a year later Stanley came down with a serious attack of pleurisy. Not long after, Sir Henry Morton Stanley, who many consider the greatest and most fearless explorer the world has ever known, was dead.

His wife Dorothy insisted on a twelve-foot-high, six-ton headstone to mark the final resting place of this extraordinary man. Carved into its surface are the words:

Henry Morton Stanley Bula Matari
1841-1904
Africa

The little boy holding Dick Price's hand would have stopped in amazement before the huge monument. He would have wondered who Henry Morton Stanley was and what the strange African name meant. He could scarcely have imagined the travels and adventures life held in store for him. Finally he would learn that what his mother or others thought of him was less important than what he thought of himself. If she would not give the love and support he deserved, there certainly were others willing to do so.

R. David Thomas

(1932-)

Founder of Wendy's International

"The dictionary is the only place where success comes before work" said David Thomas, the extremely successful businessman who founded the Wendy's hamburger chain, and whose friendly open face smiles at millions of viewers from the television screen.

Mr. Thomas was not always a "grown-up" — rich and successful. At one time he was a vulnerable, trusting five-year-old who wanted more than anything to be loved and who could not understand why his mother was taken from him, even if the place she was going to was heaven.

But the little boy had, by the time he was eight, a dream bigger than himself. One day he was going to own the nicest, friendliest restaurant in the world, where all the employees and the customers would be happy. All would walk about with a smile, simply because the employees would want to please the customers, the customers would smile in appreciation, and everyone would be especially, especially pleased when he, David, walked into the restaurant. At that time the mechanics of running a business did not boggle his young mind; he only knew that he would make his dream come true.

Already life had taught the boy some harsh lessons: that nothing is easy, that hard work is the necessary ingredient to achieve any goal. Later on he also realized that honesty and fairness, and the rare ability to bring out the best in people, are essentials for the businessman.

At the time the story begins, little David spent the summers with his adoptive grandmother, Minnie Sinclair. These weeks were the happiest in his life, and during these stays in the farm in Michigan Minnie told the young boy stories and listened to him. Here, too, he learned not to "cut corners" and the value of hard work and, very important, to have fun while working toward a goal. Much later in life, Mr. Thomas made Wendy's hamburgers square, literally not "cutting corners."

Minnie was a strict person, but very loving, and very religious. She was hard-working and from her David absorbed valuable moral lessons that he continued to apply as an adult.

As a child David's life was not easy. He never knew his biological parents. His adoptive father moved from place to place always looking for a better job, and it was impossible for the boy to make friends or to have a stable life. Also, David always came last in the family's list of priorities, either because his father's wives preferred their own children or, never having had children, they did not understand the boy, or even because his father was too preoccupied with his own affairs. Young David felt lonely and sad but he was determined to prove to his father and to himself that he was capable of holding a job, of succeeding. Nobody, other than Minnie when he was young, encouraged him; there was no one to pat David on the back and to tell him how proud they were of him. David had to find the inner strength to go on by himself.

As a little boy David had loved the Saturday outings with his grandmother, who had to work the rest of the week. Together they went to the five-and-ten store where David gazed in wonder at so many beautiful things! Colorful threads, sweet-smelling soaps, ribbons, pencils, toys! And the treat for the week: lunch at the counter! David's favorite drink was root beer, his favorite foods a barbecue sandwich, a hot dog or a sloppy joe. The counter of the five-and-ten store was the boy's first introduction to the exciting and challenging world of the restaurant. But the marvels of Saturday were not over for before leaving the store, Minnie bought bridge mix and she and David shared it on the way home riding in the old model-T Ford that Minnie drove.

There were times in the young boy's life when he and his father were alone. On such occasions they ate in restaurants and if his father was not completely focused on David . . . well, David enjoyed the bustle of the restaurant, intrigued by how they food was prepared and served and by the million things that make a restaurant "tick."

David was a shy boy who worked to overcome his shyness. By the age of ten, when most children are still immersed in their toys, David decided that the time had come for him to get a job. He watched a gasoline station during lunch so that the owner could eat. The job was short-lived and David tried his hand at several others: he took on a paper route, which failed because of lack of guidance; became a caddy in a golf course; and set up pins in a bowling alley before automation took over that task. But Dave's real ambition never wavered: he still wanted to work in a restaurant, but no one would hire him. He was too young!

One day when David was twelve his father told him to get a job. The family had just moved and David knew nobody in the new community. David resorted to lying about his age: he told a store owner that he was fifteen and was glad to be hired at twenty cents an hour! The work was difficult for a child; heavy grocery packages had to be delivered to homes without elevators, many times situated on the tops of steep hills. But David did find until the owner decided to close the store for some weeks. He returned unexpectedly and wanted David to come back to work. The boy, who had thought that he would have some free time, excused himself explaining that he had already made plans for his time off. David lost his job but learned a very valuable lesson: when you are the employee you work when the boss needs you — if you wish to keep your job.

The next job that David obtained he quickly lost when the manager discovered his true age. This made his father furious. Sad, nor understanding his father's reaction, David was nonetheless determined to move onward. And soon he got his chance, the first real break. The family was living in Knoxville at the time and David, passing himself for a sixteen-year-old, though only twelve, was hired at the Regas Restaurant. Here David had to learn to balance plates and cups, never spilling a drop, and take orders by memory, making sure that each customer received what he or she had ordered. In between orders he had to keep the counter clean. Nor were the checks added by a machine, as they are now — even telling the cashier what change is due the customer. Rather, the sums were added mentally by the boy. The salary that David was so proud to be earning was twenty-five cents an hour!

There was little free time in young David's busy life. But when he had an afternoon free he spent it at the movies, watching a cowboy show or a comedy. Although the work was hard, David was happy and doing what he had always wanted to do. He was working on his dream. However, one more time his father moved the family to be closer to his own job, and David found himself having to travel sixty miles a day. This may not seem a lot in today's world where teenagers own cars, but in the 1940s it was a tremendous distance. Also, there was a little baby in the family, born to David's father and his wife Viola. To make matters worse, the family was living in a trailer with Viola's two daughters from a previous marriage; the quarters were cramped indeed!

No difficulty every daunted David for long nor did he spend time feeling sorry for himself. Rather he focused on the future and on his dream. Before long David had a job in the Hobby House Restaurant in Fort Wayne, Indiana. Shortly thereafter, David separated from his family when his father decided to move again. There were no hard feelings; both understood their positions. David assured his father that some day he would be proud of him, and his father sincerely wished him luck. It was at this point in his life that David did something that, he admits, he would not recommend that anyone do: he quit school after finishing the tenth grade. If more choices had been offered to him in school, he would have probably remained in school. But there was little vocational education in those days and David had marked a clear path for himself. For a while he lived at the YMCA, then with a family. This was a good experience for David, for the family was warm and caring and gave him a sense of belonging. Finally, he joined the Army. Always resourceful, alert and willing to learn, David made the best of what the service offered. He was then eighteen.

In his 1991 book, *Dave's Way,* Mr. Thomas says that contrary to the commonly held view of never volunteering in the army, young people should indeed volunteer. During his first weeks in the army, David had trouble with his teeth and when an infection developed, he was released from duty by the doctor. Since it was not his way to stay idle for long, he volunteered for mess hall duty. He performed his job so sell that he was sent to Cook and Baker School and promoted to staff sergeant. David was constantly looking around asking himself what could be improved, what he could do to smooth things out, to make the surroundings better. The path to his goal was not always easy. While with the Army in Germany, his assistants were older than he was and it took initiative, courage, and tact on his part to run an operation giving orders to people who perceived him as a youngster. But David, at times pretending to a self-confidence that he did not feel, came through the experience with flying colors.

Time was passing and in 1954 a wonderful event took place in David's life. He married Lorraine Buskirk. Theirs was what could be termed an old-fashioned marriage. She stayed at home, keeping house, supporting him morally, and raising their five children. He went to work, oftentimes having only a few hours for the family. But he never wavered in his values: family, religion, and vocation.

For the next few years David was very busy with his enterprises, moving ever onward and upward. In the course of his career David has met many interesting people. One such person was Colonel Sanders and his "Kentucky Fried Chicken" which was featured in the Hobby House Menu where David worked. Soon David was regional head of operations for Kentucky Fried Chicken stores east of the Mississippi, from Florida to Michigan. But the little boy that still lived inside the grown man had not given up on his dream. He still wanted to have his very own restaurant.

Every successful businessman attests that success is most often a matter of timing. One day during the rush lunch hour in downtown Columbus, David saw that it was almost impossible to get a meal that was both well cooked and quickly and cheerfully served. This was his opportunity. This the location. Certainly the timing was right.

Once he was able to obtain a site, David's next decision was what to call the restaurant. To be remembered a name must be catchy, short, and easy to pronounce, but it must also have "something," some attraction that will make a customer walk in for the first time. After that, the food, the cleanliness, the courteous service, should bring the customers back. David also wanted his restaurant to be a reflection of his family. The idea was excellent, the restaurant would be called Wendy's, in honor of his daughter Melinda Lou. It might appear that there is no connection between the two names, but when she was born, her older brothers and sisters, very young themselves, were unable to pronounce her name and called her Wenda, which naturally became Wendy. Her attractive freckled face was a godsend as an advertisement and a friendly, homey, welcome sign to hungry and thirsty customers. At the beginning the menu at Wendy's was very simple — service and quality were first priorities.

Wendy's was a great success, and the little boy David who swiveled around him looking with longing eyes at the merchandise on display at the five-and-ten store had achieved and surpassed his dream — for now he owned not one but many restaurants. A millionaire, Mr. Thomas looks back on his life and thanks those people who instilled in him the values and the moral courage never to give up. It is true that his adoptive father did not have the time for him that the boy yearned for, but he had excellent care from his adoptive mother before she died, and later he had Minnie, his adoptive grandmother who taught him that if a person works hard he or she can make good things happen. To this day Mr. Thomas proclaims his love for his grandmother and his debt of gratitude to her.

Currently Mr. Thomas devotes much time and energy to his role of national spokesman for "Adoption Works . . . for Everyone," an adoption awareness campaign — for who could serve as a better example?

Maria von Trapp (1905 - 1987)
Singer and Refugee from Nazi Germany

From the very beginning, little Maria Augusta — later Maria Augusta von Trapp — seemed destined to a life of adventure and travel. She was born in a train on the way to Vienna when her mother was returning to join her husband after visiting her family.

Maria's father had been married before. He had lost his first wife in a very tragic accident; while taking a drive in the countryside, the horses had shied and thrown Mrs. von Trapp into a waterfall. Maria's father then took his ten-week old son and left him with an elderly cousin in Vienna. Maria's mother also died very young, and as Maria's father was an engineer who had to travel extensively, he could not care for his young daughter himself; so he took little Maria to the same elderly relative who had raised his son Karl.

Maria's first years were spent in a little village which had recently been incorporated into the city of Vienna, but which was, nevertheless, very rural. The stone house where Maria lived did not have running water and every afternoon Maria went to the public spring to bring home water for the family.

Maria's foster father also died when she was very young. But her foster mother was very loving and kind. A very devout woman, she would sit the little girl on her lap and teach her to pray. But her four children were all grown up, so there were no playmates for Maria. But no matter — if there was no family, then Maria would make one up! And she did — she invented a big, happy family with eleven children.

In a few years, Maria's natural father came back, but the little girl continued to live with her foster mother. Visits to her father's house were always intriguing — one of the rooms had been turned into an aviary, with all kinds of birds flying around. Another room was full of instruments and another contained many different books. But her father, not used to children, was rather impatient when Maria did not demonstrate sufficient interest or was not quick enough to learn the French or Latin grammar that he taught her. He also took her on trips, but these were invariably learning trips and the little girl was always happy to return to the loving and patient warmth of her foster mother.

One day when she was nine years old, Maria was told some very sad news: her father had died. And now the little girl's troubles began — Maria's guardian was "Uncle Franz," a judge married to the oldest daughter of Maria's foster mother. The judge, now living in the same house as Maria, spanked the little girl daily, for he imagined, wrongly, that she lied to him. Later "Uncle Franz" was declared insane and committed to an asylum. In the meantime Maria decided she might as well do the things she was spanked for so she began to skip classes and endure, too, punishments from her teachers. Maria was, however, a bright girl. After graduating from high school, she had planned to attend the State Teacher's College of Progressive Education.

Her uncle Franz had other ideas — and besides, he said, where did she think the money would come from? This did not deter Maria. She already had a scholarship that covered her tuition, room, and board. She simply would *earn* the rest of the money she needed. A friend from school took her into her house and spoke of the money to be earned working in a big hotel.

Maria found no work in the hotels, but she was asked if she could teach tennis. She knew nothing about the sport, but she accepted the job, asked a few pertinent questions and discharged her duties beautifully. Now, with the money they earned, the two friends went to college. Maria needed still more money, but she earned it by doing embroidery, for which she was paid by the inch. Her grades in college were excellent.

125

Now she also had the freedom to enjoy her passion for music. Although she had no money for concert tickets, Maria went to churches where she listened to the Mass of Mozart and Haydn.

She was also a superb hiker. One morning, during one of her hikes, as she was contemplating the magnificent view and wondering at the beauty of nature she realized that the great outdoors was what she liked best in life. So, she decided, this freedom and beauty, this enjoyment of nature . . . she would give up and offer as her sacrifice to God; she would enter a convent. But which convent? Never one to do things by halves, Maria asked a passing Capuchin monk to direct her to the strictest convent. He pointed her steps to the Benedictine Abbey in Nonnberg and there Maria went, carrying her knapsack, her climbing ropes, and her ice pick. That same evening she was admitted to the convent as a candidate.

Maria was so different from the other girls, who were docile and subdued, that for a while she had to be assigned her own mistress of novices. Maria was willing enough to do the will of God and make sacrifices, but many times forgot the proper demeanor; her natural exuberance led her to slide down the banister, to whistle (after all, thought Maria how can it be wrong or bad to whistle religious tunes?), or climb to the roof where she could jump over the chimney. Filled with all the new theories from the State Teacher's College of Progressive Education, Maria argued with the mistress of novices about her antiquated methods. To show repentance and humility for the insubordination of questioning a nun, the novices were made to kiss the floor. Maria would obediently kiss the floor . . . but then continue express her opinions! Many a time she went without a meal, the punishment for breaking a dish or utensil — for wasting the common good. Yet, for the first time in her life, she was made to realize the value of self-discipline. In the convent, Maria began to feel at home, as she had with her foster mother when she was little — loved, and secure. Maria performed a valuable service for the Abbey as well: she taught fifth grade in the little elementary school run by the nuns. Her methods were progressive and innovative, and she was highly praised by the school's superintendent when he visited her classes.

And then Maria's life changed drastically. One day Mother Superior summoned her. Maria's heart did somersaults as she went over and over in her mind all her latest transgressions. Very rarely was a novice sent for by the Mother Superior. Maria hoped she was not to be sent away from the convent. She was trying hard. Besides, she loved the 1400-year-old Abbey in its beautiful setting in the Austrian mountains.

The news was both good and bad: Maria had demonstrated her love and competence with children and the Mother Superior wished her to tutor the little daughter of Captain Georg von Trapp, who was recovering from scarlet fever. Maria was horrified. She, in the home of this . . . hero? This widowed aristocrat? Leave the convent for ten months? Besides, what could she wear? All the worldly possessions of new candidates were given to the poor; the convent only kept the set of clothes from the last candidate, to be given away when another presented herself. However, humbly, Maria said that if it was the will of God — as expressed by Mother Superior — that she leave her beloved Abbey, she would do it and look forward to the day of her return. Sad, but determined, with her guitar, and her few books in a satchel, she ventured forth.

But although Maria had not expected to enjoy her assignment, she immediately fell in love with the children, who ranged between four and fourteen years of age — two boys and five girls. Baron von Trapp was often away, but when he was home he loved to partake in family games and outings. On one of these occasions while the Baron was at home, Father Wasner — who had come to say Mass in the family chapel — was so impressed by their singing that he suggested the von Trapps form a family choir. Soon after, opera singer Lotte Lehman heard the family sing and obtained the Baron's consent for the von Trapps to appear in the Salzburg Festival. As a result, the family was offered contracts everywhere, which the Baron laughingly collected and pasted in a scrapbook. In the meantime Georg von Trapp had surprised Maria by proposing to her. She accepted and love entered her life.

But their happiness was tragically shattered when on March 13, 1938 Austria was incorporated into the German "Third Reich." The Baron and his family were forced to confront a vital issue: they had to choose between preserving their material possessions or their honor. And if they chose not to cooperate with the Nazis, then they would have to leave Austria. Knowing that their butler was a member of the Nazi Party, the family pretended to leave on one of their usual hikes in the mountains. That meant that they could only take a knapsack with them. The Baron, however, brought with him what proved to be their most valuable possession: the singing contracts.

It was hard for the family who had led a life of luxury to adjust to poverty overnight. They were now refugees instead of honored guests, and by now the family had nine children and Maria was expecting yet another baby. As a family, they sang wherever they could, even at a birthday party or wedding.

But soon another shadow pursued them. People asked themselves why — if the family was not Jewish — did they leave Austria? Inevitably, many reached the wrong conclusion: the von Trapps must be spies for Hitler! And so the Italian government ordered them to leave the country, and other countries treated them in the same way. Yet they had to sing, for every penny counted if they were to pay for their fare to the United States where they had a contract. Finally, after many struggles, they arrived in America . . . with only four dollars in their pockets.

Fortunately, their concerts in the United States were very successful. However, their visa expired in three months and they had to leave. They travelled to Denmark, Sweden, and Norway.

Then, on September 30, 1939 the Second World War broke out. The von Trapp Family Singers' manager in the United States sent them tickets so that they could come to America to sing again. For the first time since leaving their country, the family felt safe, for the United States did not expel anybody during the war.

The success of Maria's family was tremendous. After the second concert, the family showed a profit of one thousand dollars! Clothes, shoes, and other necessities were high on the family priority list but, after much consideration, they decided to ignore the necessities and invest their money on land — they would buy a farm! Their home in Stowe, Vermont was among lush green hills that reminded Maria of her beloved Austria.

Soon the family experienced other changes: the two sons of military age were drafted. But Father Wasner adapted the music to suit the women's voices and the one male voice and the von Trapp family continued its career on stage. After the return of the boys and the end of the war, happy years followed for Captain von Trapp, who saw the triumphs of his family and his own contribution toward its success. When he died, the family buried him on the farm.

Maria was very saddened but she knew that she had to be strong. In 1950 she went to Europe and back — for a little while — to her Austria, reliving so many memories. Then, to the South Pacific, Australia, and New Zealand. Maria and some of her children, answering the call of Archbishop Carboni in Sydney, became lay missionaries in Budoga. Her foster mother would indeed have been proud of her, as it was she who very early in Maria's life instilled in her the love of God.

All over Maria made friends. Once while happening to swim in shark infested waters, Maria found herself surrounded by village women who had come out to protect her. These natives had learned to make an explosion-like sound with their hands underwater that frightened the sharks away.

Back in the United States once more Maria continued her work in the von Trapp Family Lodge: reaching out with her friendliness and warmth to all guests, who partook as much as possible in the family's life. Christmas was a beautiful celebration in the Lodge. At dusk on Christmas eve, the guests and family would enter the living room to get a first look at the tree, its home-made decorations and its real candles. All together they would sing *Silent Night,* read *The Christmas Story* and present gifts to the help. All during the week-long celebration, the children were allowed to take candy from the tree.

Although no longer young, Maria learned to ski and to ride on horseback . . . and soon the Lodge bought horses that the guests could ride. Maria also opened a gift shop at the Lodge, where the guests could buy gifts and where souvenirs could be obtained by people interested in seeing the von Trapp Family house.

In 1949 Maria wrote the story of the von Trapp Family Singers. Most bookstores, seeing the word singers placed the book in their music sections and sales were not as high as expected. Then Rodgers, Hammerstein and Lindsey and Kraus made a musical based on the book! It was a resounding success. Later a movie, *The Sound of Music,* was made and it too was highly successful. These productions could have made the von Trapps rich indeed but, unfortunately, years before when the family had needed money, Maria had signed away all rights for nine thousand dollars, itself a large amount at the time.

After many years, Maria passed the running of the Lodge to her son Johannes. She died in 1987, but her memory and music live on.

Edgar Wallace   (1872 - 1932)
Novelist

In the year 1872 a baby boy was born in a poor London neighborhood. His mother was a young actress who named her child Richard Horatio Edgar Wallace. The identity of his father is unknown as there was no father's name on the child's birth certificate. The child's mother knew that she had to support herself and that the theater was no place for a tiny new-born, so wanting the best for little Edgar his mother was forced to give her baby away.

Edgar was a happy child. Adopted by a couple with ten children of their own, he grew up in a loving family where there was always a playmate available and where an older brother or sister would always lend him a helping hand. Edgar's father sold fish in the market and the family was not rich, but the children did not go hungry and, whenever they could, they too worked.

Edgar was an alert, enterprising child who very early showed a liking for reading and a lively imagination. An observant little boy, he filed away in his head what he saw on the London streets and this knowledge of human nature appeared later in his novels and plays.

As a young boy, Edgar sold newspapers in London; later he worked in a printing office, all the while helping the fishermen and meeting people of all social classes. Not many of them seeing the boy in his tattered clothing would have guessed that they were looking at a future best selling author and the inventor of the "thriller" as we know it today. Yet that time lay in the future and many years of toil awaited the boy.

When Edgar was of sufficient age, he enlisted in the Royal West Kent regiment and was sent to South Africa. This exotic environment with its new animals, plants and people, and its glittering sun so unlike that of England, added an important dimension to Wallace's development as a writer. He began contributing to a Capetown newspaper, and soon became the correspondent of the *London Daily Mail,* a newspaper with a large circulation. In Capetown, too, Edgar Wallace married the daughter of a missionary. It was this African sojourn that inspired Edgar Wallace to write one of his many best-sellers, *Sanders of the River,* the stories of an adventurer in Africa, plotted while Wallace himself was in the heart of the Congo. His tales and novels, although complex and suspenseful, are very clearly written with exciting conclusions and an underlying humor that keeps the reader smiling throughout each book.

Back in London, Edgar Wallace wrote many successful books, among them *The Four Just Men, The Crimson Circle, The Flying Squad,* and *The Terror* — altogether one hundred seventy-five books. Edgar Wallace also wrote comedies and plays. Two of the most successful were *On the Spot,* based on the life of Al Capone, famous Chicago gangster, and *The Case of the Frightened Lady* which appeared on Broadway under the title of *Criminal at Large.*

Edgar Wallace was invited to Hollywood and offered a fabulous contract. He co-authored the script for the very successful horror film *King Kong* featuring a gargantuan-sized ape who climbs to the top of the Empire State Building and beats his mighty chest as he plucks a plane from the sky.

Edgar Wallace died suddenly in Hollywood in 1932. He left behind a wife and four children who formed the company Edgar Wallace Ltd. Wallace will be remembered not only for his superb mystery novels but for creating one of the memorable animal giants of film.

Phillis Wheatley   (1753? - 1784)
Black Poet of the American Revolution

The history of the slave trade is one that ranges from casual disregard for the basic rights of fellow humans to incredible emotional cruelty and physical violence. And although slavery has been common in many cultures, from China to the South Pacific to the natives of North and South America, to ancient Egypt, Greece, Rome, and Britain.

Native chiefs in Africa themselves often held slaves, and sometimes became involved in the lucrative trans-Atlantic slave trade. Setting fire to the huts of other villages at night, they could entrap the men, women, and children as they ran screaming in terror from their blazing homes and then turn this "black ivory" over to white slavers for a handsome profit. Despite the widespread occurrence of slaves in primitive cultures, thee can be no justification for it, and we hope that, as cultures mature — particularly our own — humans develop more concern for others than themselves, and leave these barbaric practices behind.

Mrs. Susannah Wheatley walked arm and arm with her husband, a prosperous tailor merchant, down Beach Street in Boston, a bustling town in the New World. On this beautiful June morning in 1761 a breeze stirred the branches of some poplars whose silver-backed leaves seemed suddenly like a school of sparkling fish that had been startled and were flitting away against the deep blue sky. Docked in the harbor, not far away, a large ship named the *Phillis* nodded sleepily on the gentle waves, its timbers creaking tired snores. But inside the ship, below the water line, without portholes or other means of ventilation, were masses of black humans, too sick, too feeble to moan their agony.

Some were packed so closely together that despite the swaying of the ship on the high seas they had not moved an inch from where they had been wedged at the start of their journey from Africa. Chained, like animals, water was passed and food thrown down a hole into the ship's lower regions where no sailor ever ventured.

After the horrific voyage, if they survived, the people were hastily washed down and then, still in chains, dragged across the cobblestones to the wooden platform where they would be sold into slavery. Most slaves were sold down south to work on the plantations, but many white families in New England owned slaves too. In the south, however, there were laws called slave codes which made it unlawful for blacks to own property, to testify against whites in a court of law, and even to defend themselves against an unjust, brutal owner. It was not a crime for a white master, though, to beat a slave unconscious or even to death while teaching him or her a "lesson."

Just then Mrs. Wheatley spotted Prince, the black man given to the Wheatleys to pay off a debt owed them. At this moment Prince was anxiously peering into the faces of the newly arrived slaves to see if he recognized any of them. There was always the chance that a friend or family member had been captured and brought to America on a slave ship.

Mrs. Wheatley ordinarily avoided the ghastly sights of a slave auction but her eyes were drawn to a little black girl who stood trembling on the wooden auction block. She had no clothing except a bit of dirty carpet she held round herself.

"Take a look at this monkey," the auctioneer's voice boomed to the people crowding around the platform, "Plucked straight from the African jungle. Buy 'em young and you can train 'em right. Wanta watch the monkey dance? Ha-ha! Dance, monkey, dance!" Cackling, he flicked his whip with lightening speed repeatedly across the small child's feet. In painful protest the child cried out and jumped, pulling against the rope encircling her middle. The auctioneer, tightly holding the other end of the rope suddenly jerked the little girl forward so that she stumbled and fell. Some people in the crowd laughed.

"I'll give you a pound for her," one man yelled, cupping his mouth with both hands.

"And I'll give you a pound and a half," a mean-looking woman returned. Mrs. Wheatley's heart constricted. The child looked so frail and frightened.

"Two pounds!" Mrs. Wheatley suddenly called out. Startled, Mr. Wheatley turned to his wife. "Oh, John," she pleaded, "I'm past fifty. You know I've been saying that I need a younger servant to help me with the household chores. Why not her?"

"But Susannah," her husband said, "She's only a child and a mighty small one at that. Besides, she looks sickly."

"But I want her, John. I want her. She belongs with us. I don't know why but she does."

"Two and a half pounds!" the same woman issued forth, fixing Mrs. Wheatley with a menacing glare.

"Three pounds!" Mrs. Wheatley pressed, staring back. She would not allow the child to go to that nasty-looking woman. Moments later, Mr. Wheatley, still amazed, found himself handing over three pounds as his wife was handed the other end of the rope to which was attached the little girl. Mr. Wheatley, unknowingly, had just purchased a future poet whose writing abilities would become a century later one of the prime examples used by the anti-slavery movement to prove that blacks were sensitive, intelligent human beings who could profit from education.

Clip-clopping down the Boston streets in the horse-drawn carriage, Mrs. Wheatley could see that the child was terribly frightened by the strange sights, sounds, and smells which were so alien from her little village in Africa. Taking the girl's hand in her own, Mrs. Wheatley tried to comfort her.

The Wheatleys had two children — twins named Mary and Nathaniel — who were then eighteen years old. When they saw the little black girl with the beautiful, velvet eyes their mother had bought, they were entranced. The Wheatleys guessed that she was about seven or eight years old because she was losing her first teeth. They gave her some warm, soft clothes and named her Phillis Wheatley — her first name coming from the slave ship that had brought her to Boston. At night Mary tried to soothe the trembling girl who could think only of the horrible kidnapping, the horrible voyage in utter darkness, and, of course, her home and family back in Africa.

One morning very early, Mary and Nathaniel watched as Phillis crept out of the house. Alarmed, they thought she was running away. But Phillis filled a small pot with water and then poured the water on the ground. Puzzled, they saw her kneel and touch her forehead to the ground and then stand, smiling, her arms outstretched towards the rising sun.

"She's greeting the new day!" Nathaniel exclaimed in a burst of insight, "It's probably a ritual from Africa!" Later, the image of the rising sun would appear frequently in Phillis' poetry.

The Wheatleys lived on King Street (today State Street) in a large house that would be Phillis' home for the next fourteen years. Soon Phillis proved to the Wheatleys just how bright she was. With astounding rapidity she learned the English language — and, using a piece of charcoal — began copying on the walls letters that Mary had taught her. Most people would have severely rebuked their slave for attempting to write. Some even would have been frightened to have such an intelligent slave living under the same roof, but not the Wheatleys. Beaming with pride Mrs. Wheatley encouraged Phillis to learn. It was decided that Mary would become Phillis' tutor. While most black girls were learning how to cook and clean, Phillis was learning how to read and write. She even began studying Latin.

Nor was this the only way in which Phillis received special treatment. The other Wheatley slaves lived in the carriage house behind the Wheatley home but not

Phillis. She ate with the family and was even given her own room. One day, in fact, when Phillis was visiting at another Boston home, the temperature suddenly dropped. Worried, Mrs. Wheatley sent Prince to bring Phillis back home. When Prince returned, Mrs. Wheatley was furious at him: Phillis was sitting up in the driver's seat with him instead of inside the carriage . . . never mind that was where people of higher quality sat!

Never very strong, probably due to asthma or tuberculosis coupled with the horrendous voyage on the slave ship, Phillis was sent to the country from time to time to relax. *Very* few slaves received such treatment in the 1700s. When Phillis was twelve years old and started to write poetry, Mrs. Wheatley let her keep a candle, paper, a quill pen, and an ink bottle on her night table in case Phillis had a sudden idea for a poem. Because of her special position in the Wheatley house, Phillis would belong to neither the black nor the white world.

The only housework Mrs. Wheatley allowed Phillis to do was, occasionally, some dusting or polishing. Sometimes Phillis also helped out with dinner parties. At these parties, Mrs. Wheatley would invite prominent politicians, merchants, clergymen and proudly show them how much Phillis had learned through her studies. Before long, many important Bostonians began to regard Phillis as a brilliant young woman and gave her expensive books to help her with her education. As these wealthy whites listened to Phillis and her enthusiasm for learning, they marveled at how much like themselves Phillis seemed . . . but very few ever bothered to ask themselves why. If they had they would have realized that Phillis, like themselves, was a human being!

Raised a congregationalist, Phillis attended the Old South Meeting House, where blacks were confined to segregated sections. It was here that Phillis first came into contact with the ideas of the "Great Awakening," a religious revival movement that spread through the American Colonies during the 1700s. Today, the Old South Meeting House — where Phillis was baptized in 1771 — still stands.

Clergymen of the "Great Awakening" traveled widely hoping to "awaken" people's interest in religion, teaching that all people could attain salvation. Phillis wholeheartedly accepted the ideas of the Great Awakening. When she was just fourteen she wrote a poem, fifty-six lines long, entitled *An Adress* (sic) *to the Atheist* which came from her new faith. Phillis used Alexander Pope, an English poet, as a model for her writing.

Phillis did not generally write poems about the injustices of slavery, partly because she did not want to hurt the Wheatleys who had treated her so kindly. In one poem, however — which she sent to William Legge the Earl of Dartmouth when he became secretary of state for North America — Phillis described her kidnapping

134

and revealed her longing for freedom, the same freedom the colonies desired from England. But Dartmouth, although astounded by Phillis' talent, like most people of his time, did not share her views on slavery.

In August 1765, a group of men proclaiming themselves the "Sons of Liberty" marched through the Boston streets, passing right in front of the Wheatley home, protesting the Stamp Act. Three years later, in the autumn of 1768, two regiments of the British army came ashore and, they too, marched in their bright red coats up King Street. Watching the men with their shiny muskets striding in perfect unison, fifteen-year old Phillis excitedly wrote a poem entitled *On the Arrival of the Ships of War, and Landing of the Troops.* Unfortunately, this poem has become lost to time.

Not far from the Wheatley mansion, on March 5, 1770 some boisterous colonists were standing in front of the customs house on King Street. Jeering, they began throwing snowballs at the severe-looking British guard posted at the door. Soon twenty other British sentries appeared, for by now the crowd of stone-throwing colonists had swelled to the hundreds. Humiliated beyond endurance, one of the British soldiers, without waiting for orders, took aim at a throng of colonists and fired. Swiftly more shouts exploded into the crisp air and moments later, five Americans lay dead. Under the dark blue sky, the white snow soaked with blood. This tragedy, known as the Boston Massacre of 1770, seemed a vivid portrayal of the colors of the future American flag — but only seemed. Face down in the snow, half-forgotten in the hysteria was the first man to die in the struggle for American freedom — Crispus Attucks, a black man.

Despite the unrest, Phillis continued studying diligently. Learning astronomy, she would trace the constellations with a finger in the night sky, whispering their names, marveling that people centuries before her had observed the same stars. She studied, too, history, geography, mythology, Latin, and literature.

Eagerly she read the Bible and continued attending the Old South Meeting House where an English clergyman George Whitefield — whose stay in the colonies was sponsored by the British Selina Hastings, countess of Huntingdon — preached powerful, spellbinding sermons on the true meaning of Christianity: the love and acceptance of all people. Whitefield died unexpectedly at the age of fifty-six.

Saddened, Phyllis wrote an elegy (a poem mourning someone's death.) Her elegy was published in Boston, Philadelphia, New York, and Newport, Rhode Island, and was hugely successful. Soon Phillis' writing abilities were talked about not only in Boston but in other colonies too.

Although Phillis Wheatley was undoubtedly a talented young woman, it is unlikely — because of the time in which she lived — that she could have become as well-known as she did without Mrs. Wheatley's constant encouragement and devotion. Had Mrs. Wheatley been any less determined than she was to collect Phillis' poems and publish them in a book, Phillis' book would probably never have been published. In the 18th Century, printers required that authors get a list of three hundred people who guaranteed to buy their book once it was published. Mrs. Wheatley advertised for subscribers in the *Boston Censor*. But many people, as they read the advertisement in the newspaper suddenly felt uncomfortable and some even experienced indignation at Phillis' high-nosed endeavor. After all, that a slave should print a few isolated poems was one thing, but now a book? Phillis Wheatley, they felt, was getting above herself and Susannah Wheatley was taking her slave's talents beyond reasonable limits. Because Mrs. Wheatley was unable to obtain the required number of signatures, no publisher would accept Phillis' book.

Undaunted, Mrs. Wheatley decided to publish the book if not in America, then in England. Speaking to Robert Calef, the captain of the Wheatley ship *London,* she asked him if, when he got to England he could search around for a printer.

Arriving in London, Calef was given directions to the shop of a little-known printer named Archibald Bell. Very impressed with the poetry Calef gave him to read, Bell nevertheless looked up at Calef and the corners of his eyes crinkled with mirth. This was a joke, of course. Poetry of this quality could not possibly have been written by a black. Calef assured Bell that it was true but Bell remained unconvinced. At last Bell said he would publish the book on the condition that Calef present him with undeniable proof that Phillis Wheatley was who Calef said she was — a black woman poet.

Returning to Boston, Calef told Mrs. Wheatley what Bell had said. Immediately, Susannah Wheatley got to work. Attached to a statement which affirmed that the poems were the work of Phillis, a young black girl, were eighteen signatures of some of the most important people in Boston including the governor of the Massachusetts Colony, Thomas Hutchinson, and a person who would soon sign another important declaration, John Hancock.

With Phillis' book all ready to be published she needed now only a person to whom to dedicate the book. At this time dedications were important because the name of a prominent or leading person increased the book's prestige and sales. Probably in her heart Phillis wanted to dedicate the book to Mrs. Wheatley who, had done so much for her, but Mrs. Wheatley would hear nothing of it. Remembering that the Countess of Huntingdon had been very impressed with Phillis' elegy to George

Whitefield, Mrs. Wheatley urged Phillis to dedicate the book to her. When the countess learned of this, she was very pleased and told all her important friends.

Mrs. Wheatley again placed advertisements in many Boston newspapers, this time announcing Phillis' upcoming book and encouraging people to witness for themselves the talent of this young black girl.

In the spring of 1773, Nathaniel, the Wheatley's son, was preparing to sail to England on business. Phillis, at the time, was feeling unwell. The Wheatley's doctor recommended that the air of an ocean voyage would be good for Phillis' health. Concerned about Phillis and realizing that a trip to London would probably help her career, Mrs. Wheatley sent Phillis with her son Nathaniel to England.

When the Countess of Huntingdon found out that Phillis was coming, she set the literary circles abuzz. Phillis, meanwhile, wrote a poem entitled *A Farewell to America* which was addressed to Mrs. S. W. and reveals Phillis' strong affection for Mrs. Wheatley.

On May 8, 1773, Phillis, twenty years old, was on a ship for the second time. But this time, she was not chained by the neck and fed like an animal; she was travelling to London, a poet, awaiting the publication of her first book. Among the many important people she met was Benjamin Franklin who was in London as the colonial agent for Pennsylvania. One of the most treasured moments of Phillis' stay occurred when the city's Lord mayor, Brook Watson, presented her with an elegant edition of John Milton's *Paradise Lost.* This copy which Phillis cherished is now in the Harvard University library.

The Countess of Huntingdon invited Phillis and Nathaniel to visit her at her mansion in South Wales. But just as Phillis was excitedly making plans to go, an emergency message arrived from Boston — Mrs. Wheatley was seriously ill and she wanted Phillis to come home.

Phillis was terribly disappointed. Not only did she miss witnessing in person the publication of her book but she never met the Countess of Huntingdon whom she so admired. The publication of Phillis' book, after all, was a historical event. To be entitled *Poems on Various Subjects, Religious and Moral,* her book was only the second published by an American woman (the first was a book of poems published in London in 1650 by the colonist Anne Bradstreet) and the first by a black person — and incredibly, by someone so young! Phillis was even to have visited the King of England, George III which would have greatly helped her career. But for Phillis duty came first. On July 26, 1773, Phillis was on her way back to Boston — she had been in England not even a month. Nathaniel, however, was unable to accompany her. He was engaged to the daughter of a well-to-do merchant and remained in London to get ready for his wedding.

When Phillis' book appeared in September of 1773, it received high praise in many English and Scottish newspapers. Some, however, pointed to the hypocrisy of the Wheatleys and other Bostonians for recognizing Phillis' talents and intelligence yet keeping her a slave. Perhaps hurt by such comments, the Wheatleys freed Phillis shortly after her return from England. Although Phillis' life was more or less the same, as a freed woman she now had to provide for herself. Her book sales became even more important. But Bell, who was frantically trying to meet demands for the book in London, did not send Phillis the promised three-hundred copies until 1774. In the meantime, Phillis devotedly cared for Mrs. Wheatley who was now very ill indeed. At night, when she had at last a spare moment, Phillis would write her poems by the light of a sputtering candle.

Sampson Occom, a forty-one-year-old Mohegan Indian, was a Christian missionary and one of Phillis' friends. Late one evening Phillis wrote Occom a powerful letter. In this letter she cried out against the hypocrisy of a society that called itself Christian but believed in slavery. Probably at Occom's suggestion, Phillis Wheatley's statement was published on March 11, 1774 in the *Connecticut Gazette*. In the weeks that followed, the eye-opening statement was reprinted in several New England newspapers.

But a week before Phillis' letter to Occom was published, she suffered a painful loss. Mrs. Susannah Wheatley, the woman who had treated Phillis more like a child than a servant, died on March 3, 1774.

Only a year after Susannah Wheatley's death, the battling of the Revolutionary War had begun. British troops, under the Quartering Act, were housed in the homes of Bostonians. It appears that two British naval officers who had been stationed in Africa were quartered at the Wheatley home. These officers probably spoke to Phillis about their experiences in Africa. Phillis wrote a poem entitled *Reply* which may have come from her conversations with the two officers. This poem is the first written by a black American looking back on her African heritage with pride and affection.

Boston was in an uproar in that year 1775. Weapons were gathered, and minutemen — men who could go and fight at a minute's notice — were trained. After the battles of Lexington and Concord, over 10,000 Bostonians, mostly Tories (people whose sympathy lay with England), left the city either for England or the countryside. John Wheatley moved to the neighboring town of Chelsea and Phillis came too. Although Phillis was a devout Patriot, she probably left Boston because her former owner wanted her out of harm's way.

During a stay with Mary Wheatley and her husband John Lathrop, a minister, in Providence Rhode Island, Phillis wrote a poem about General George Washington and sent it to him.

On a blustery day in March of 1776, General George Washington was receiving important visitors at his headquarters in Cambridge Massachusetts as he busily prepared for war. The general was extremely pressured for time . . . yet he set aside thirty minutes to speak with one visitor he had personally invited. She was twenty-three-year-old Phillis Wheatley, a black woman poet. A month after their meeting, Wheatley's poem about Gen. Washington was published at the insistence of the patriot and editor of *Pennsylvania Magazine*, Thomas Paine. Phillis, in December of 1776, returned to Boston alone. Most of her friends and admirers had either left the city or colonies or were dead. As the war raged, her financial situation grew steadily worse.

John Wheatley died in 1778 and not long after, his daughter Mary also died. Phillis had grown up with the Wheatleys and now they were gone, except for Nathaniel — but he was married and living in England. That same year, Phillis Wheatley married an ambitious man named John Peters who was to try several different occupations, from grocer to lawyer, barber, baker, and doctor. While expecting her first child, Wheatley wrote a prayer entitled *Sabbath, June 13, 1778* asking God to grant her strength to bring a child into the world. Tragically, the baby died shortly after birth.

Then, four months later, Phillis Wheatley tried to publish a second book of poems which she wanted to dedicate to Benjamin Franklin. Wheatley put notices in the newspapers asking for subscribers to her book. Unfortunately, with the war, not many people had money to spend on such luxuries as books of poetry and of course, many of Phillis' supporters were no longer in Boston. Although her second book was never published, five of the poems and some of the letters were later printed.

After Massachusetts abolished slavery in 1780, Wheatley and her husband were living in a fashionable house on Queen Street (today Court Street). Phillis Wheatley continued to enjoy some notoriety. Jupiter Hammon, a slave who lived with his owner in Hartford Connecticut, on August 4, 1778 published a twenty-one verse poem addressed to *Miss Phillis Wheatley, Ethiopean Poetess, in Boston, who came from Africa at eight years of age, and soon became acquainted* (sic) *with the Gospel of Jesus Christ.* Clearly Phillis had become an inspiration to other blacks.

In the early 1780s, Phillis, her husband, and now a child (who, sadly, would also die), moved to the town of Wilmington, north of Boston. Most likely, the family had been forced to move due to financial hardship. The increased amount of physical work Phillis had to do soon became a strain and her health deteriorated.

In 1781 when the British general Charles Cornwallis surrendered to General George Washington in Yorktown, Virginia. The war for Independence was, for all intents and purposes, over. Finding it extremely difficult to support his family in Wilmington, John Peters decided it was time to go back to Boston. In 1784, according to records of the Massachusetts Historical Society, Peters was sent to the county jail due to an outstanding debt.

In the autumn of 1784, Phillis had her third child. She had recently written a poem entitled *Liberty and Peace* which welcomed the end of the Revolutionary War. The poem was published in December 1784 but by the time it appeared, Phillis Wheatley was dead.

Tragically, the end of Phillis Wheatley's life was spent alone in utter poverty. Her husband John Peters was probably in debtor's prison again and Wheatley, who had achieved international literary fame and had met such illustrious people as Gen. George Washington and Benjamin Franklin, was now working as a scrub woman in a poorhouse.

We can only imagine the poems left unwritten when, on December 5, 1784, in a narrow bed, shivering in the bitter cold, Phillis Wheatley died. A few hours later her child would die too. Phillis Wheatley's death was announced in the *Massachusetts Independent Chronicle and Universal Advertiser,* but no mourners came to her funeral and there was no stone to mark her final resting place.

But today in Boston there is a monument dedicated to Phillis Wheatley. On February 1, 1985, the arts and sciences building at the University of Massachusetts officially became Wheatley Hall. Former Massachusetts governor Michael Dukakis declared February 1 "Phillis Wheatley Day" in honor of the mother of black literature. But Phillis herself would have been the first to acknowledge that Susannah Wheatley deserved a place too in history as her mother.

(For more information about this individual, see *Black Americans in Defense of Their Nation,* National Book, 1992.)

Daniel Hale Williams (1856 - 1931)
History-Making Surgeon

One day many years ago, a little boy called Daniel Hale Williams was crying. He was all alone in the world. His father had just died and his mother had apprenticed him to a shoemaker in Baltimore, Maryland, and then gone to live with family in Illinois.

Daniel missed the warm and loving family he had so recently known. He especially missed his father. He could still remember clearly the way his father's face would light up as he spoke of rights and equality for blacks. Mr. Williams had served in the National Equal Rights League, working and lecturing tirelessly. He had crusaded in particular for the right to education, proclaiming that the black race must become educated in order to progress.

Though his health had suffered and his family pleaded with him to rest, Mr. Williams refused, for he insisted that there was too much work to be done. Upon returning from one of his trips, Mr. Williams collapsed. Gradually he grew weaker until all the strength left him and he died. Mrs. Williams split up the family; all of the children went to live with relatives, except for Dan. He was to remain behind in Baltimore and learn the shoemaking trade.

The smell of hides, the art of sewing leather — none of this appealed to Dan. He had always thought he would be a barber, just like his father, so now his apprenticeship seemed like a prison term. His famous cousin Frederick Douglass had escaped from slavery and now young Dan intended to make his own escape. He persuaded a railway agent to give him a ticket so he could return to his mother in Illinois.

His reunion with his mother and sisters was a happy one. Dan once again felt part of a secure and loving household. Unfortunately, this was not to last. Dan's mother grew restless and decided to return to Annapolis, Maryland. Her mother and younger children lived there and she missed them. She told Dan he could come with her.

Dan decided to remain in the Midwest rather than be uprooted again. For the next few years he boarded with several of his cousins and worked part-time jobs in order to pay for his keep. By the time Dan was sixteen, he decided to move to Edgerton, Wisconsin, where he opened his own barbershop. But Edgerton did not have a school for him, and — remembering his father's words about the importance of an education — Dan intended to find a school. He moved to Janesville, Wisconsin, and asked for employment at a barbershop owned by a black man, Harry Anderson.

Learning that Dan had no place to live, Mr. Anderson immediately opened his home to him, inviting him to stay with his wife and their children. Mr. Anderson and his daughter Traviata taught Dan how to read music. Many a night they all sat up and filled the house with their singing and laughter. Soon Dan was also playing with Mr. Anderson's twenty piece string band. Dan was completely happy. He studied at the local school, helped Mr. Anderson in the barbershop, and spent his nights as part of a loving family. He realized just how much he meant to the Andersons when Mrs. Anderson named her newborn son after Dan and asked him to be the godfather.

Soon Dan began thinking about college. He knew he would have to enroll in the Janesville Classical Academy in order to get proper training. Mr. Anderson encouraged Dan and the headmaster, Professor Haine, welcomed the serious, intelligent young student. Soon thereafter, an angry father came bursting into Professor Haine's office, outraged that Dan, a black, had been admitted to the school. Furious, he stated that he would withdraw his daughter if Professor Haine did not dismiss Dan at once. Professor Haine stood his ground; he would not send away an excellent student because of another man's prejudice.

Dan enjoyed his years at Janesville Classical Academy and graduated in 1877. One day, while reading the local newspaper, he saw an article about the heroic life-saving efforts of Dr. Henry Palmer, the surgeon general of Wisconsin. As he continued reading, Dan's heart leapt in excitement and his mind raced with ideas. He had found his goal! He too would become a doctor.

Dan went out to Dr. Palmer's home. With confidence and not a little boldness, he asked Dr. Palmer if he would accept him as an apprentice. Dr. Palmer agreed and there began a marvelous two years of discovery for Dan. He accompanied Dr. Palmer on all his house calls and helped him tend to the patients. With each passing day Dan became more and more convinced that he had chosen the right profession.

Then one day Dr. Palmer told Dan that it was time for him to enroll in medical school. Dan realized that he did not have the money, but his determination to become a doctor would not allow him to consider even this a stumbling block. He had accumulated a small store of cash from his barbering job and from playing in Mr. Andersons's band. He also got a job putting up telephone wires and installing lighting along the streets of Janesville — anything to gain extra money. But even then he did not have enough money to pursue his dream.

Dan sent a letter to his mother asking for financial aid, but she wrote that she did not have the money. Who could help Dan now? The man who had taken him in as a son! Mr. Anderson did not have the money on hand, but he took out a loan in his own name so that Dan could go to the Chicago Medical School.

Once he got to Chicago, Dan went to stay at the home of Mrs. John Jones, a wealthy widow whose husband had worked on the Equal Rights League with Dan's father. With great enthusiasm, Dan studied physiology, anatomy, biochemistry, and histology texts. Mr. Anderson, though he had little enough as it was, sent Dan money every month. In his weekly letters to the Andersons, Dan expressed his gratitude again and again. Without the Andersons, Dan's dream of becoming a doctor would have floundered and the world would have suffered a great loss.

When it came time for the final exam, Dan took the written and oral portions with confidence. He was able to continue his studies and graduated with high marks in 1883. He then decided to open his own practice in Chicago's South Side.

"Dr. Dan" as his patients affectionately called him, became a popular and well-known figure. He set up office hours at the most convenient times for his patients, and made house calls for all those too sick to come to his office.

Dr. Dan's name became even more well-known when he was asked to be a demonstrating physician for a clinic operated by the Chicago Medical College — an opportunity offered to few black doctors. Dr. Dan's prestige also increased when he took up a volunteer position as assistant physician at the Protestant Orphan Asylum. When all the children — two hundred fifty in number — contracted measles at the same time, Dr. Dan certainly caught the attention of the media! The governor of Illinois was so impressed by Dr. Dan's dedication that he appointed him to the Illinois State Board of Health. Dr. Dan was the first black doctor to serve on the Board.

Despite these successes, Dr. Dan would not allow himself to rest. Like his father before him, he wanted progress for all blacks, not just for himself. What he witnessed in his years of doctoring in Chicago's south side only deepened his resolve. He was shocked at the appalling lack of adequate medical care available to blacks. Often operations were carried out on kitchen tables and in unsanitary conditions because Chicago hospitals would not permit black doctors to use their equipment or rooms.

It was then that Dr. Dan decided to establish his own hospital. His heart swelled with happiness and anticipation as he planned; the hospital would be open to doctors and patients of all races. No longer would blacks be denied entrance into a hospital just because of their color! No longer would black doctors be prevented from practicing in one of the city's hospitals! In 1891, Dr. Dan fulfilled his wonderful plans: Provident Hospital — the first interracial hospital in the United States — opened its doors.

Provident Hospital was also the site of another historic event. Dr. Dan became one of the first surgeons to repair a rip in the pericardium, the sac which surrounds the heart. Dr. Dan received the patient, James Cornish in July of 1893.

James had been stabbed less than an inch from his heart. Dr. Dan made an incision, detached the fifth rib and examined James' heart. He saw that the pericardium had been punctured and the left mammary artery damaged. The wound did not seem deep, but the patient claimed he had pain around his heart. Dr. Dan debated what he should do. On the one hand, medical experts advised against opening the chest and heart surgery was unheard of. On the other hand, Dr. Dan thought, if he did nothing, the patient, who was coughing and hardly had a pulse, would die.

Dr. Dan — who had no journals or books to consult about heart surgery — decided to do what hardly any other doctor would have dared: he decided to operate and try to save James. Though he noticed the heart muscle had been nicked, he decided it did not need surgery. He tied off the left mammary artery to stop its bleeding and then concentrated on suturing the pericardial sac. He was operating in an opening which was two inches by one and a half inches! The delicacy and precision required for such an operation are astounding.

The operation took a long time, after which Dr. Dan sutured the chest opening closed. For the next four days, James was between life and death; he had a very high fever and his pulse was erratic. He successfully came out of the crisis period, however, and three weeks later Dr. Dan performed a minor operation to clear out some fluid from James' pleural cavity, the sac around the lungs. After another month of resting, James was fully cured and lived at least another twenty years.

Dr. Dan had saved James' life in a history-making operation. The publicity which followed was tremendous. Some prejudiced people refused to believe that a black doctor could have performed such surgery, but Dr. Dan remained unfazed.

Dr. Dan's influence spread. In 1893 President Grover Cleveland asked Dr. Dan to be surgeon-in-chief of Freedmen's Hospital in Washington, D.C. Dr. Dan was loathe to leave his beloved Provident Hospital, but he realized his services were needed more at Freedmen's. The largest black hospital in the country, Freedmen's had been set up after the Civil War as a place where blacks could go for medical care. Since its establishment, though, it had largely been ignored by the government. It was incredibly understaffed. There were no nurses; patients administered medicine themselves, and those well enough would get up, do the work for the hospital, and then go back to bed! When Dr. Dan saw the death rate, he shook his head in dismay.

In his five years at Freedmen's, Dr. Dan established a nursing school and enlarged outpatient clinics. Dr. Dan persuaded doctors of all races to volunteer as consultants to Freedmen's.

When the black doctors and interns of Meharry Medical College were refused positions in white hospitals, Meharry made its own hospital, following Dr. Dan's guidelines. Soon other hospitals and training schools appeared in Dallas, Atlanta, Knoxville, Memphis, and in many other cities.

Much of Dr. Dan's last years were spent in the tranquility of the country. Years before, while he was at Freedmen's he had treated a lady with cancer. Her daughter, Alice Darling Johnson, was a beautiful woman who had captured his heart. Gentle and serious, she made a wonderful wife for Dr. Dan. During these peaceful days Dr. Dan and Alice reflected on the wonderful people who had touched their lives. One man in particular, Mr. Anderson, held a special place in Dr. Dan's heart. It had been Mr. Anderson's generosity and confidence in Dan that had allowed him to fulfill his dream of becoming a doctor.

(For more information about this individual, see *Black Scientists of America,* National Book, 1990.)

BRIEF BIOGRAPHIES

George Hamilton-Gordon Aberdeen
British Prime Minister

George Hamilton-Gordon, fourth Earl of Aberdeen, was born on January 28, 1784 in Edinburgh. When he was eleven years old he lost both his parents and was brought up by his two guardians: William Pitt the Younger and Henry Dundas (later Viscount Melville.) Both men were politicians. In 1814 Aberdeen signed the Treaty of Paris for his king and was then made a viscount. As foreign secretary Aberdeen ended old eastern and western boundary disputes between the United States and Canada through the Webster-Ashburton Treaty of 1842 and the Oregon Treaty of 1846. Aberdeen served as prime minister from 1852-55, during which time his government involved Great Britain in the Crimean War against Russia.

Aberdeen, who added his first wife's last name to his own in 1818, died in London on December 14, 1860.

Jean Le Rond d'Alembert
French Mathematician and Philosopher

The shrill cries of a baby who had been abandoned on the steps of a Parisian church named Saint-Jean-le-Rond pierced the cold air and the warm hearts of some pedestrians. He had been born on November 17, 1717, the illegitimate son of the famous salon hostess Mme. de Tencin and chevalier Destouches-Canon, an artillery officer. Destouches finally found the child and put him in the care of a glazier's wife named Rousseau. D'Alembert would always regard this special woman — whom he loved dearly and with whom he lived until age fifty — as his mother. His first and middle names are derived from Saint-Jean-le-Rond, the church where he had been abandoned. Later he added the name d'Alembert.

Although Destouches never revealed his identity as the boy's father, he left his son an annuity of 1,200 livres. After studying law, and then, briefly, medicine, d'Alembert — who had become fascinated by mathematics — decided to devote his life to the subject. Except for a few lessons, he was mostly self-taught. D'Alembert's essays on integral calculus and the motion of solid bodies in a liquid earned him a place in the Paris Academy of Sciences. In 1746 d'Alembert was selected as editor of the mathematical and scientific articles to be included in Diderot's famous Encyclopedie. D'Alembert, who was very generous by nature, gave much of what he earned to charity. He died in Paris in 1783.

Josephine Antoine
Opera Singer

On October 27, 1908 a baby girl was born in Colorado. But only months after her birth, she was left an orphan.

She then became the chosen daughter of a loving couple named Arthur and Bertha Antoine. Josephine Antoine always insisted that she had no interest in learning more about her biological ancestors because her adoptive parents gave her all she could ever want or need. Although Antoine enjoyed school, her true love was music. When she was eight years old her parents bought her a piano and in high school she took voice lessons. At the University of Colorado she majored in English, hoping that she could teach while preparing for a singing career. In 1929 the coloratura soprano entered a national singing competition and after winning the regional contests, she placed third for the final competition, singing *Caro Nome* from *Rigoletto*. Her prize was a year's tuition at any American conservatory and one-thousand five-hundred dollars. Antoine chose the Curtis Institute of Music in Philadelphia and shortly thereafter entered the Juilliard School of Music. So impressed was Artur Bodansky — who heard her sing at Juilliard — that he wanted her to audition with the Metropolitan Opera. Antoine did, and was soon presented with a contract. Those who saw Josephine Antoine perform said she possessed not only a gorgeous voice but extraordinary grace and elegance. She married S. Edwin Hinkle in November, 1948. They had one daughter. Josephine Antoine died on October 30, 1971.

Aristotle
Greek Philosopher

Aristotle was born in Stagira, a town in northern Greece in 384 B.C. Both his parents died when he was quite young. Proxenus, court physician to Amyntus II of Macedonia, raised Aristotle who probably lived at Pella, the royal seat. Here Aristotle may have learned and practiced surgery. Later Proxenus' son Nicanor was himself adopted by Aristotle. At about age eighteen Aristotle was sent to the finest school available, The Academy, run by the philosopher Plato who was greatly impressed by his pupil. In addition to being a philosopher and educator, Aristotle also became one of the first great biologists. It is believed that his childhood environment greatly influenced Aristotle's outlook and his development of the scientific method. Aristotle, tutor of Alexander the Great, founded the Lyceum, containing the first research library. Aristotle ranks as one of the most influential philosophers of Western thought.

Ingrid Bergman
Actress

Ingrid Bergman was born on August 29, 1917 in Stockholm, Sweden, the only child of Justus and Friedel Bergman. When Ingrid was only two years old her mother died and nine years later, with the death of her father, she was left an orphan. Raised by relatives, Bergman often felt lonely and self-conscious because of her height. Bergman, who was not particularly popular in school, would later be called one of the most beautiful women in the world. In spite of ridicule by some of her relatives, Bergman was determined to become an actress and entered the School of the Royal Dramatic Theatre, in Stockholm. Among Bergman's many films are *Casablanca* (1942), *For Whom the Bell Tolls* (1943), and *Spellbound* (1949), an Alfred Hitchcock thriller. Bergman won an Academy Award for best actress in the film *Gaslight* (1944) and another Academy Award for *Anastasia,* (1956). Bergman won her third Oscar for best supporting actress in the film *Murder on the Orient Express* (1974). From her marriages she had four children. Bergman, who was fluent in five languages, died on the same day she was born, August 29, 1982, in London.

John Green Brady
Governor of Alaska

John Green Brady was born into a very poor family in New York City in 1848. He became a street orphan at age eight, and never saw his family again. The Children's Aid Society found Brady and sent him to Tipton, Indiana where he was adopted by Judge John Green. After graduating from Yale University in 1874, Brady then began studies for the ministry at New York's Union Theological Seminary. Brady's first ambition as a new minister was to establish a school for disadvantaged boys. But when this plan did not work out, Brady agreed to teach Christianity to Alaska's Northwest Coast Indians as part of the Presbyterian Board of Home Missions. In 1884 President Chester Arthur appointed Brady United States commissioner and ex-officio registrar of the land office in Sitka, then Alaska's capital. Because of Brady's success in this post, President McKinley appointed him governor of the District of Alaska in 1897. Tirelessly Brady fought to win equal treatment, schooling, and job opportunities for Alaska's native population. He was reappointed governor by President McKinley and again by President Theodore Roosevelt in 1905. Anticipating Alaska's importance in the United States Pacific defense system, Brady pressed for more military bases. Throughout his years as governor, Brady crusaded to make Alaska in the eyes of all Americans a vital part of the Union.

Angie Elizabeth Brooks
Liberian government official, diplomat, lawyer

Born on August 24, 1928 in Virginia, Montserrado County, Liberia, Angie Elizabeth Brooks was one of nine children. Her mother was a descendent of the Mandingo and Vai tribes and her father — a minister of the African Methodist Episcopal Zion Church — of the Grebo people. Unable to care for all their children, Brooks' parents placed her in a foster home. She was brought up by a widowed seamstress who lived in Monrovia, Liberia's capital.

Her foster mother was a very religious woman. Soon Brooks' ambition to better herself and her country became evident; at eleven she taught herself to type and took jobs copying legal documents where she first got the idea of becoming a lawyer. In spite of prejudice against women lawyers Brooks remained determined. Clarence L. Simpson, later Liberia's Foreign Minister agreed to accept Brooks as an apprentice in his law office. Her dream of studying law in the United States seemed bleak without funds, but Brooks learned that Liberia's President Tubman often took early morning strolls and one day she walked right up to him and described her plight. Tubman, impressed by Brooks' earnest appeal agreed to help finance her trip. In 1949 Brooks graduated from Shaw University in North Carolina with a B.A. in social science.

Working in the law library and nights as a nurse's aid in a hospital, in 1952 she graduated from the University of Wisconsin with an LL.B. and M.Sc. in political science and international relations. She continued graduate work in international law at the University College law school of London University. In 1953 Brooks became counsellor-at-law to the Supreme Court of Liberia. She was the first Liberian woman to practice law. From August 1953 to March 1958 she was Assistant Attorney General of Liberia, during which time she helped establish the law school at Liberia University where she also taught part-time. In 1958 President Tubman appointed her Assistant Secretary of State. On September 16, 1969, Brooks was chosen president of the 24th session of the United Nations General Assembly becoming the first African woman to hold this prestigious position. Once divorced and now married to a teacher, Brooks has two biological sons and over the years she has been foster mother to numerous children some of whom would go live on a large rubber plantation she owns. Among her adopted children, one became a teacher and another went to study at Shaw University. Brooks enjoys dancing, reading, and collecting African art.

Rosie Casals
Tennis Star

One of the shortest players in professional tennis at five-feet two and one-fourth inches tall, Rosemary Casals also became one of the fastest. On September 16, 1948 Casals was born in San Francisco to parents who were immigrants from El Salvador. Feeling unable to care for their two children they gave them up for adoption. So at age one, Casals and her older sister Victoria went to live with their great-aunt and uncle whom they would regard as their mother and father. Casals says she feels no resentment toward her biological parents; they could not keep her or her sister so they did what they thought was best.

Casals' adoptive father, Manuel Casals y Bordas taught his daughters how to play tennis. But though Victoria's interest waned, Rosie's grew. Her father, the only coach Casals has ever had, was thrilled at his younger daughter's enthusiasm; sometimes she would practice five hours a day. Money in the Casals household was tight and sometimes Rosie would save lunch money to purchase tennis equipment. Her father was even more pleased when in 1961 Rosie won the hard court singles championship for girls thirteen and under. In 1962 she won the USLTA's (United States Lawn Tennis Association) hard court singles tournament for girls fourteen and under. In 1964 and 1965 she won the hard court singles championship in the eighteen and under category. She won, too, the women's hard court singles and was a semi-finalist at Forest Hills. Her opponent was the number one ranked tennis player in the world, Maria Bueno.

The USLTA ranked Casals at age seventeen the number eleven woman player in the U.S. In 1966, she was ranked number three and in that year she and her doubles partner, Billie Jean King, won the U.S. hard court doubles, the U.S. indoor doubles, and went all the way to the quarterfinals at Wimbledon. Casals, a very outgoing, colorful player has made it to four Wimbledon semifinals, two U.S. semifinals, and won nine Grand Slam doubles titles, five at Wimbledon.

Casals' hobbies include photography, attending rock concerts, the Grand Old Opry, and playing the piano and the guitar.

Catherine I
Empress of Russia

Born Marfa Skavronska on April 15, 1684, a Lithuanian peasant, she was orphaned at age three. She was then raised by Ernst Gluck, a Lutheran pastor in Marienburg (today Aluksne, Latvia) and grew into a beautiful girl with sparkling black eyes and a ready smile. During the Great Northern War when the Russians took over Marienburg in 1702, Skavronska was taken prisoner. She was soon given over to Aleksasha Menshikov, a close adviser to Peter I (also known as Peter the Great.) Skavronska filled wine goblets as a serving wench to Menshikov, and Peter I fell in love with her. Entering the Orthodox Church in 1703, Skavronska was rechristened Catherine (in Russian Yekaterina.) During his travels Peter sent Catherine love letters from all over Russia and although Catherine could not read, she treasured his letters and had her companion Anisia Tolstaia read them over and over to her. On February 9, 1712 Peter publicly declared his love for Catherine and married her, giving her the title of empress. So devoted was Catherine to her husband that she traveled with him everywhere, even to battlefields. In 1725, when Peter died at age fifty-three, Catherine became empress of Russia. She died on May 17, 1727.

Nicolas Sebastien-Roche Chamfort
Playwright and Conversationalist

Nicolas Sebastien-Roche Chamfort was born an illegitimate child in April 1740 or '41 in Clermont France. He was given to a grocer's wife to be raised and was educated as a free scholar. Chamfort took to writing plays and soon gained fame. He later worked with Mirabeau, a French statesman and revolutionary leader on the newspaper *Mercure de France*. Chamfort even became secretary of the powerful Jacobin Club, an organization of French political leaders. Horrified by the actions of the French Revolution's Reign of Terror, Chamfort joined the Moderates. Among Chamfort's famous sayings, "Be my brother or I'll kill you" summed up the Terror's idea of "fraternity," or brotherhood. Chamfort died in Paris on April 13, 1794.

Jean Baptiste Charbonneau
Mountainman, guide

Born on the Lewis and Clark expedition, Jean Baptiste Charbonneau was the son of Toussaint Charbonneau and his Shoshoni wife, Sacagawea, who were serving as the explorer's interpreters. William Clark soon grew enormously attached to the playful, dark-skinned child whom he nicknamed Pomp or Pompey. When the Charbonneaus prepared to continue their own route to upper Missouri, Clark, unable to part with the little boy, implored them to leave Jean Baptiste behind with him. At last the Charbonneaus agreed and the joyous Clark brought the child to St. Louis where he had him educated at a Catholic school. Some years later, when Prince Paul of Wurttemberg came West on a scientific expedition, he was so impressed with Charbonneau's hunting skills and capability with horses that he invited Charbonneau to his castle near Stuttgart. For six years, Charbonneau stayed in Europe studying French, German, and Spanish, went hunting in the Black Forest, and traveled through Europe and North Africa. But Clark had instilled in Charbonneau a deep love for the frontier, and when he returned to the U.S. Charbonneau became employed as a mountainman by the American Fur Company, traveling with Joe Meek and Jim Bridger. In 1839-40 Charbonneau aided Louis Vasquez and Andrew Sublette in establishing Fort Vasquez on the South Platte. While his skill as a guide became widely celebrated he continually impressed people with his broad education. Charbonneau led Lieutenant J.W. Abert on a government-sponsored exploration of the Canadian River and, at the start of the Mexican War, led Colonel Philip St. George Cooke's Mormon Battalion from Santa Fe to San Diego.

Charbonneau became alcalde of the mission of San Luis Rey and died on the Owyhee River of either pneumonia or mountain fever as he headed for the Montana gold strikes.

Edward Day Collins
Educator

Edward Day Collins was creator of the renowned Middlebury College foreign language sessions, where educators, government officials, military personnel, and other language experts are still trained today. He was born on December 17, 1869. He was adopted by I.D.R. and Mary E. Collins who impressed upon him the importance of education. Receiving his B.A. and Ph.D. from Yale University, he taught history there himself. Collins held various important positions in education before serving as president of Middlebury College.

At Middlebury he established the rigorous summer language program where students take the famous pledge to speak only the language they are learning. Collins married Ruth Mary Colby in 1903; they had three children. He died on January 1, 1940.

Countée Porter Cullen
American Poet

Porter Cullen's lifelong wish was to be called simply, a poet instead of a "Negro poet." Little is known about Cullen's parents or exactly where he was born on May 30, 1903. Brought up by his grandmother, he was adopted when she died by a Methodist minister, Frederick Cullen and his wife in 1918. Rev. Cullen, who took his son on a tour of the Holy Land and to the literary shrines of Europe, strongly encouraged him to succeed in school. Vice president of his senior class at the largely white high school of DeWitt Clinton, Cullen maintained a grade average of 92, edited the school newspaper, was associate editor for the literary magazine, and won first prize in a city-wide contest for his poem *I Have a Rendezvous with Life*. Receiving a Regent's scholarship, Cullen entered New York University in 1922 where he won the Witter Bynner Poetry Prize and graduated Phi Beta Kappa. After obtaining a master's degree in English from Harvard, Cullen worked a couple of years as assistant editor of *Opportunity, A Journal of Negro Life*. Later he was awarded a Guggenheim fellowship. In April 1928 he married Nina Du Bois but they were soon divorced. The year 1934 found Cullen teaching English, French, and creative writing at Frederick Douglass Junior High School in New York. He later married Ida Mae Roberson. Considered one of the outstanding poets of the Harlem Renaissance, Cullen died in New York City in 1946.

Dalai-Lama
Spiritual and Temporal Ruler of Tibet

Following the death of the 13th Dalai Lama, according to Tibetan religious belief, begins the life of the 14th Dalai Lama. Believed to be the earthly incarnation of the Bodhisattva Chenrezi — or Avalokitesvara, the Lord of Compassion — when a Dalai Lama dies, his spirit selects another earthly form. It is the task of the hierarchy of Lamaist monks, guided by signs, to seek out the next Dalai Lama. In their search, two monks disguised as merchants entered a peasant home in the Kokonor region of Tsinghai. They were met at the door by a smiling two-year old boy who climbed onto the lap of one of the monks and pulled at the rosary he was wearing which had belonged to the 13th Dalai Lama. After a number of tests, the small boy correctly distinguished between possessions of the late Dalai Lama and false duplicates. The boy, named Lhamo, had been born on June 6, 1935, the fourth of five children to Chokyong Tsering and Sonam Isomo. Concluding that the boy was, beyond a shadow of a doubt, the 14th Dalai Lama, the monks brought the boy with them to the holy city of Lhasa to raise him in the beautiful 1,000 room Potala Palace. On February 22, 1940 the young god-king was officially installed on the Lion Throne. The child was called Gyalwa Rinpoche which means "the Victorious and Precious" as well as Kundun which means "the Presence." The boy soon impressed his teachers with his intelligence and his caring nature. They knew he would make an excellent ruler. But in 1959, the Dalai Lama was forced to flee to India, where he still lives in exile, following the unsuccessful Tibetan revolt against Communist Chinese forces who have occupied Tibet since 1950. The Dalai Lama has tirelessly campaigned to arouse the world's attention in the cause of Tibetan independence.

Alexandra Danilova
Ballerina

After a Christmas show in school, when at age seven she danced the part of a butterfly, Alexandra Danilova has never stopped dancing. Danilova was born in Peterhof, Russia in 1903. When she was only three years old both her parents died. For a time she and her older sister lived with their grandmother and then with their godmother. But eventually they were separately adopted, Alexandra by Lidia Mstislavna and her second husband General Mikhail Batianov. Lidia recognized the little girl's talent and urged her to try out for the Imperial Ballet School located in St. Petersburg. The long hours of practice in front of the mirror at home would pay off; Danilova was one of seventeen chosen from two-hundred and fifty applicants. In 1920 Danilova formed part of the Soviet State (today Kirov) Ballet.

During the summer of 1924 she toured in Europe as part of the Soviet State Dancers. Sergei Diaghilev — founder of the Ballets Russes — hired Danilova and the other Soviet dancers for the 1924-25 season. In 1938 Danilova became a charter member of the Ballet Russe de Monte Carlo. Later she would create her own troupe called Great Moments of Ballet.

Danilova's final appearance on stage was in 1958. Toward the end of that same year Danilova was the choreographer for dances at the Metropolitan Opera House. In 1964 she joined the teaching staff of the School of American Ballet in New York. Danilova, a naturalized American citizen, now lives in Manhattan. She has received many major dance awards, including the first Capezio Award and the 1984 Dance Magazine Award. Yet, she says, without the early encouragement she received as a child, she would only have dreamed of becoming a ballerina.

Peter Duchin
Pianist

It is not unusual for Peter Duchin to receive $15,000 or more for a night's playing of the piano. In fact, Peter Duchin Orchestras, Inc. bring in about a million dollars a year. Peter Oelrichs Duchin was born on July 28, 1937 in New York. His mother, Marjorie Oelrichs, the daughter of one of New York's most prominent families, was shunned after she married Edwin Frank Duchin, a pianist, who was considered socially beneath her. (Their love story was made into a 1956 movie produced by Columbia Pictures.) Six days after Duchin was born, his mother died. Duchin's father, grief-stricken, left his young son in the care of various foster mothers and went to fight in World War II. He stayed mostly with the affluent Averell and Marie Harriman who brought him up with their own children and some young war refugees from England. Young Duchin often rode to dinner on his bicycle through the great halls of the Harriman mansion.

Duchin remembers that as a boy when he wanted to play baseball or go fishing, Mrs. Harriman, whom he called "Ma" or "Mom," insisted that he finish practicing the piano first.

In 1947 Duchin's father remarried and he went to live with him and his stepmother. His father died of leukemia in 1951, however, when Duchin was thirteen years old. Majoring in French and music at Yale University he graduated cum laude in 1958, with the proud Harrimans in the audience.

Stationed in Panama, Duchin served two years in the U.S. Army. In October 1962, Duchin appeared on the Ed Sullivan Show and was asked to play for engagements at the White House.

By 1967 Duchin had produced ten LPs on the Decca label. He married Cheray Zauderer on June 22, 1964 but was divorced in 1982. Three years later he married Brooke Hayward. Duchin was been involved in many important causes including Defenders of Wildlife, Citizens for Clean Air, and he is on the board of directors for such worthwhile projects as Boy's Harbor and the South African Education Program. Duchin has four children.

Peter Francisco
Revolutionary War Hero

One June morning in 1765 Peter Francisco arrived at City Point (today Hopewell), Virginia under very unusual circumstances. A foreign ship had come into the harbor, deposited the five year-old boy ashore and then hurriedly sailed away. The boy spoke a mixture of Spanish, Portuguese, French, and very little English. By his clothing it was obvious that he was not the son of a peasant. Perhaps he had been stolen from his home in Spain or Portugal.

Judge Anthony Winston, Representative for Buckingham County in Virginia's Legislative Assembly, raised the boy abandoned so mysteriously. At fifteen Peter stood six feet six inches tall, and weighed almost two hundred and sixty pounds.

A frequent visitor was Winston's nephew Patrick Henry, whose impassioned speeches aroused in Peter a deep loyalty toward the Patriot cause. Determined to help the Patriots any way he could, Francisco enlisted in the army. At Camden, when the horses pulling an eleven-hundred pound cannon were killed, Francisco, unaided, dragged the heavy cannon into position. At the Battle of Guildford he killed eleven British soldiers. A close friend of General Lafayette, Francisco's remarkable strength and bravery became widely celebrated.

Sir Matthew Hale
Lord Chief Justice of England

Sir Matthew Hale was born on November 1, 1609 at Alderley, Gloucestershire. At age five he was left an orphan and raised by his guardian, who brought him up in the Puritan tradition. In 1628 Hale studied at Lincoln's Inn and some years later opened a very successful law practice.

During the English Civil War (1642-51) Hale, although he supported Parliament, defended many Royalists and even advised Charles I during his trial. In 1649 Hale swore his loyalty to the republican Commonwealth. Under Oliver Cromwell he became a judge and in 1660 Charles II made him chief baron of the Exchequer (treasury) and knighted him.

In 1671 Hale was appointed lord chief justice. Hale was famous for his honesty and fairness. He is considered one of the best scholars on the history of English common law. Hale wrote extensively although his writings — including his well-known Historia Placitorum Coronae (History of the Pleas of the Crown) — were not published until after his death on December 25, 1676.

John Hancock
Signer of the U.S. Declaration of Independence

John Hancock was born in Braintree Massachusetts on January 12, 1737 to John and Mary Hancock. When Hancock was seven, his father — a pastor of the Braintree Congregational Church — died, leaving his wife impoverished, with three children to feed. Hancock's mother gave him up for adoption to his uncle Thomas Hancock and Aunt Lydia. They were childless and delighted to adopt John.

Exchanging his modest home and small town for his wealthy uncle's Beacon Hill mansion in Boston, a whole new world opened up for young Hancock. Never very strong, however, he suffered from severe headaches which plagued him his entire life. At age nine Hancock entered the Boston Public Latin School (also called the South Grammar School). Although not the brightest of students, Hancock's grades were good. After his uncle died in 1764, Hancock inherited his estate and became one of the wealthiest men in the colony of Massachusetts. Well-known for his generosity, Hancock often gave food and firewood to the poor and the sick and was particularly generous to widows and orphans.

Convinced that the colonies must separate from England, Hancock, with his friend Samuel Adams, became part of the "Sons of Liberty." Hancock and Adams, to protest the English tea tax, organized the "Boston Tea Party." Pursued by the troops of British general Thomas Gage, Hancock fled to Philadelphia. He was chosen president of the Continental Congress in 1775. In that year he married Dorothy ("Dolly") Quincey. On August 2, 1776, Hancock became the first signer of the Declaration of Independence. He wrote his name in letters so large that King George would not need his eyeglasses to read it.

Tragically, his son John George Washington was killed at age nine in a skating accident. While serving his ninth term as governor of Massachusetts, he died on October 8, 1793.

Deborah Ann Harry
"Blondie" Singer

Deborah Ann Harry, better known as the lead singer of the pop/rock group Blondie, was born in Miami, Florida in 1945 or '46. At three months she was adopted by Richard and Catherine Harry of New Jersey. Debbie grew up with a sister, Martha, and a brother, William, a nephew of the Harrys. The family, who lived in a middle-class New Jersey neighborhood, attended Sunday services at an Episcopal Church.

While in high school, Harry was a member of the student council, the fencing team, and year book staff, as well as a baton twirler. She also participated in the annual school show. Harry stood out from most of her classmates in her fondness wearing black clothing, trying out new kinds of makeup, and dying her hair.

A few years later Harry formed part of a singing trio known as the Stilettoes. But when the Stilettoes broke up in 1974, Harry and backup guitarist Chris Stein created the rock/pop/dance group that would later become known as Blondie. The group's third album called *Parallel Lines,* released in 1978, sold 7,000,000 copies worldwide in two years.

Harry does not drink or smoke and is, according to people who know her, a warm, caring person — which her Blondie image might not readily suggest. Every Christmas, Harry, who as a little girl used to get homesick at camp, happily returns to her adoptive parents' home.

Joseph Haydn
Austrian Composer

Joseph Haydn was born in the small Austrian village of Rohrau on March 31, 1732 and nicknamed "Sepperl" by his family. His father Matthias was a wheelwright and his mother, before her marriage, a cook.

When Haydn was six years old, his musical ability won the attention of "cousin" Johann Frankh, a schoolmaster, choirmaster, and band director in Hainburg. Cousin Frankh was married to Haydn's father's half-sister Rosina. Cousin Frankh took Haydn to live with him and his family, but his wife was not pleased and Haydn was often dirty, received little food, and was teased by the schoolchildren because they believed he had been thrown out of his house. Even cousin Frankh would beat him for small mistakes.

When Haydn was eight years old, he was put under the care of Georg Reutter, the director of the choir of St. Stephen's Cathedral in Vienna. From Reutter, however, Haydn received few lessons in musical composition. Determined to be a composer, Haydn used his money for clothing to buy books about conducting choirs and orchestras and rules for composing music. When Haydn presented Reutter with his first composition Reutter laughed. Still determined, Haydn studied on his own. In 1749 he was dismissed from the choir because his voice had changed and, supposedly, for cutting another boy's pigtail in one of the jokes he loved.

In 1761, Prince Pal Antal Esterhazy — whose court was in eastern Austria — named Haydn assistant conductor to his aging musical director. Haydn was so loved and admired by the musicians there that they nicknamed him "Papa." By 1766 Haydn was in charge of all music at the Esterhazy court, where he would remain for about thirty years. Haydn met the composer Wolfgang Mozart in 1781 and they soon became friends.

When the woman Haydn loved entered a convent, her parents persuaded Haydn to marry their oldest daughter. Haydn did but the marriage was not a happy one. Haydn's wife, who was argumentative and indifferent to Haydn's work, often used his music sheets to line her pastry pans or as papers for curling her hair. In 1791 Haydn received the honorary degree of Doctor of Music from Oxford University in England. When Napoleon invaded Vienna and a cannonball nearly struck Haydn's house, Napoleon posted a guard of honor outside the musician's residence.

Called the Father of the Symphony, Haydn is considered one of the most important figures in the development of instrumental music. The combination of instruments he used in his symphonies have become the basis for modern symphony orchestras. Haydn composed over one hundred symphonies, and wrote over eighty string quartets as well as operas and works for voices. Haydn died on May 31, 1809 in Vienna.

Lemuel Haynes
Minuteman/Clerqyman

Born in 1753, the son of a white mother and a black father, Lemuel Haynes would soon be abandoned. He was raised by Deacon David Rose of Granville Massachusetts. Extremely intelligent, Haynes astonished the Deacon by writing mature sermons while only a young boy. But as Haynes prepared for the ministry, the Revolutionary War broke out and, interrupting his studies, he went to aid the Patriots.

Haynes fought in the first battle at Lexington on April 19, 1775 and was with Ethan Allen's Green Mountain Boys at the capture of Fort Ticonderoga. Moving to Torrington, Connecticut in 1786, Haynes became the first black minister of a church with a white congregation. Later he served as pastor in Vermont and New York where his fame as a sermon writer spread. He died in 1833.

Herbert Hoover
31st President of the United States

Herbert Hoover, one of three children, was born on August 10, 1874 in West Branch, Iowa. Tragedy soon entered Hoover's life: his father died. Not long after, his mother — returning from a religious meeting — caught a cold. The cold turned into pneumonia, and she, too, died. The children were separated and sent to live with relatives.

At age eleven Hoover travelled on a train to Oregon to his doctor uncle, Henry John Minthorn. In his uncle's home there was not the happy, pleasant atmosphere Hoover once knew in his own, for his uncle was a stern and strict man.

Hoover met his future wife, Lou Henry, whom he would marry in 1899, while studying at Stanford University. They had two sons. Graduating during the Depression, the only job Hoover could find was pushing a car in the tunnels of a California mine.

At age twenty-three, however, Hoover was recommended to an English mining company which sent him to their gold mines in Australia . . . where he even had to learn to ride camels! When the company needed a manager for its mines in China, they choose Hoover. Other westerners wanted to exploit the Chinese resources with as little cost to themselves as possible, but Hoover proposed a mining law to protect Chinese interests. When the mining company was bought by Belgians who wanted to cancel the agreement to protect Chinese interests, Hoover returned to England. At twenty-seven, as a partner in the firm, Hoover traveled to Burma to assess the possibilities of an old silver mine, which was eventually to make him a very rich man.

When the Germans invaded Belgium during World War I, the people of that small neutral country were soon on the verge of starvation. A group of highly placed Belgian and American diplomats approached Hoover and asked him to organize a relief effort of such magnitude as to feed an entire nation. Hoover accepted but insisted on working without pay. Acting quickly, he bought wheat and all other needed supplies in the United States, averting possible disaster. When the U.S. entered the war on the side of the Allies, President Woodrow Wilson chose Hoover to handle U.S. food supplies during the war. Hoover insisted again on working without pay. After the war, Hoover was asked to organize the relief of Europe. Hoover made a special effort on behalf of orphaned and hungry children, and in Poland 50,000 children expressed their thanks by marching for him while singing the American national anthem. In 1928 he was elected President.

Many years later, President Truman sought Hoover out, and — although Hoover was seventy-three years old — asked him to organize European relief after World War II. Then in 1947 Truman appointed Hoover chairman of the Commission on Organization of the Executive Branch of the Government. Hoover's suggestions saved the U.S. billions of dollars. Hoover died on October 20, 1964.

Langston Hughes
Poet

Langston Hughes was born on February 1, 1902 in Joplin, Missouri. His parents had never been happy together and after his birth, his father left the family to practice law in Mexico because he was not allowed to practice in Kansas. Working hard, his mother tried to support her son, but sometimes they did not have enough to eat.

When Hughes was five years old he attended Harrison Street, previously an all-white school. All the teachers were nice except one who made comments about him in front of the class because he was black. Soon his classmates, because of these comments, were throwing rocks at him after school. One boy, however, always stood up for Hughes, until the other children eventually learned to accept him. But as a black in Kansas in the early 1900s, Hughes could not even buy an ice cream soda or a ticket to see a movie.

When Hughes was eight his mother sent him to live with her seventy-year-old mother in Lawrence, Kansas. Hughes was very lonely and soon turned to books for companionship. After his grandmother died, he went to live with family friends, the Reeds, who had no children of their own. They were wonderful people whom Hughes remembered with love. When his mother later sent for him, he moved to Lincoln, Nebraska to live with her and his new stepfather, Homer Clark.

Elected class poet and yearbook editor in his senior year, Hughes graduated from high school in Cleveland, Ohio in 1920. His poem *The Negro Speaks of Rivers* was published in *Crisis* and brought him much attention. For one year (1921-22) Hughes attended Columbia University, but left because he was made to feel unwelcome.

His first book of poems, *The Weary Blues,* was published in 1926. His first novel, *Not Without Laughter,* was published in 1930. Some of his other books were *The Ways of White Folks,* a collection of short stories, *Shakespeare in Harlem,* a book of poems, and the autobiographical *The Big Sea,* and *I Wonder As I Wander.* The last book published before his death was an anthology, *Best Short Stories By Negro Writers.* One of his best-known characters was Jesse B. Simple, who appeared in newspaper columns and three of Hughes' books. Simple also became the hero of a 1957 Broadway musical.

Langston Hughes incorporated elements of jazz and blues music with black speech patterns to create a new form of poetry. Today his poetry is considered a national treasure. In 1960 Hughes received the Spingarn medal for his contribution to a better understanding of the Afro-American experience. He died in New York City on May 22, 1967. Hughes' great uncle was the famous Congressman from Virginia, John Langston. (See profile on page __.)

Thomas "Stonewall" Jackson
Confederate General

Thomas Jackson was born in Clarksburg, Virginia (today West Virginia) on January 21, 1824. He had two sisters and a brother, but soon his father and older sister died of an unknown fever. When his mother died too, Thomas was six years old. People always said that his father had been a failure, gambling his way to ruin. It hurt Thomas to hear his father criticized this way. Ears and cheeks burning, as a young boy he resolved to bring glory back to the Jackson name. He went to live with his Uncle Cummins, a big, strong man with a hearty laugh. For a time he was sent to live with a cousin, the stern William Brake who was considered a better influence, but Thomas ran back to Uncle Cummins.

Jackson entered West Point in 1842. Although a slow learner, he was so determined to remain at West Point that after lights were out at night, he would study by the light of the glowing coals in the fire. During his senior year in 1846, the U.S. declared war on Mexico and Jackson served bravely. Probably because he witnessed so much death — as a child and in his chosen career — Jackson was a hypochondriac. Often he sucked on lemons, which he thought were good for his health. In October 1850 he was sent to Forte Meade, Florida to fight the Seminole Indians. Later he was asked to teach science at the Virginia Military Institute at Lexington.

In August, 1853 Thomas Jackson married Elinor Junkin, who died a year later, after giving birth to a baby who also died. In 1857 he married Mary Anna Morrison.

Politically, Jackson was a moderate and with Civil war brewing he supported the Union, but when his beloved Virginia seceded, he decided to stand by her.

On July 21, 1861 the Battle of Bull Run (known also as the Battle of Manassas) exploded as South met North. As always, Thomas Jackson's brigade responded by fighting courageously. Meanwhile West Point classmate General Bee, trying to prevent his men from retreating, pointed and shouted, "There is Jackson standing like a stone wall!" Shot to death only seconds after uttering those words, General Bee could not know that he had christened Jackson with the nickname he would bear in history's pages. Forever after Thomas Jackson was called "Stonewall Jackson" and the brigade he led, the "Stonewall Brigade." Striking terror in their enemies' hearts, Stonewall's soldiers would often charge into battle collectively shouting in a deafening roar, "Stonewall Jackson, Stonewall Jackson!"

Jackson won international fame in the Shenandoah Valley in 1862, when — with but 17,000 men, employing brilliant strategy — he defeated 60,000 Union troops.

On May 1, 1863 as the North and South clashed, Stonewall fought his greatest battle. But then, on a scouting mission, a frightened North Carolina unit rained bullets at Stonewall and his men in the darkness of the night, believing they were being set up for a Yankee trap. One bullet caught Stonewall in his right hand while another two penetrated his left arm. The Confederate Army won the battle in which Stonewall fell, the Battle of Chancellorsville. Doctors amputated his arm two inches below the shoulder. Lee, learning what had happened to Stonewall said, "He has lost his left arm, but I have lost my right arm." Developing pneumonia, Stonewall Jackson died on May 10, 1863.

In 1955 Stonewall Jackson was elected to the Hall of Fame. He possessed a military genius and a peculiar charisma that brought the best out of his men.

Steven Paul Jobs
Co-founder, Apple Computers

Steven Jobs was born in 1955 and adopted the same year by Paul and Clara Jobs of Mountain View, California. Jobs is the self-taught businessman who, with electronic expert Stephen Wozniak, founded Apple Computers. While Wozniak delighted in the engineering aspects, Jobs concentrated on promoting sales and marketability. When Wozniak and the other personnel could not think of a name for their computer company, Jobs suggested Apple because it reminded him of an enjoyable summer he had spent working in an Oregon orchard. The company was immediately successful with its first crude computer because it incorporated several concepts not found in earlier personal computers. But the Apple II series was *hugely* successful, and the innovations of the MacIntosh user interface irreversibly influenced the direction of the computer industry.

But as Apple grew to become a truly big business, the corporate bureaucracy clashed with Jobs' free-spirited management style. In an effort to recover the atmosphere more favorable to innovation, Jobs left Apple in 1985 to start a new business — NeXT Computer — designing hardware and software for universities.

Frederick McKinley Jones
Inventor

Frederick McKinley Jones was born in Cincinnati, Ohio in 1892. As a little boy he was left an orphan when his mother died. Jones then moved to Covington, Kentucky where a priest took him in and raised him until he was sixteen. After Jones left the rectory, he searched for a job and obtained work as a pinsetter in a bowling alley. Moving on he became a mechanic's helper and later chief mechanic on a Minnesota farm. But in 1917, Jones — like many other black Americans — left his job to serve his country in World War I.

After the war, Jones started to gain fame for his mechanical abilities. He invented a series of devices for adapting silent movie projectors to talkies, developed an air conditioning unit for military field hospitals, a refrigerator for military field kitchens, and a portable x-ray machine. Jones' most impressive technical breakthrough, however, was his application in 1935 of refrigeration techniques to railroad cars and trucks. In this way perishable foods grown in one part of the country could be transported great distances in trucks and trains without spoiling. Prior to Jones' invention, foods traveling long distances had to be packed in ice. He became the first black member of the American Society of Refrigeration Engineers. During his lifetime, sixty-one patents were issued in Jones' name, including forty for refrigeration processes. He died in 1961.

(For more information about this individual, see *Black Inventors of America,* National Book, 1989. For related information, see *Black Americans in Defense of Their Country,* National Book, 1992.)

Benito Juárez
President of Mexico, National Hero

A full-blooded Zapotec Indian, Benito Juárez was born in San Pablo Guelatao, Mexico, on March 21, 1806. He never knew his parents, who died when he was a very young child. Juárez and his two sisters were placed first in the care of their paternal grandparents and then of their bachelor uncle, Bernardino.

When some muleteers distracted the young Juárez and stole one of his sheep, afraid of what his uncle might do to him, coupled with a burning desire to obtain an education and be someone, Benito, then twelve years old, left, and walked forty miles to Oaxaca. There his sister Josefa was working as a cook for the family of don Antonio Maza. The Mazas treated Juárez kindly and Mr. Maza found young Juárez a home with an elderly lay brother, don Antonio Salanueva, who worked as a bookbinder.

Don Antonio grew to love his foster son and did everything in his power to help him obtain an education. In 1821, Juárez entered the Oaxaca Seminary and in 1828 transferred to the Institute of Arts and Sciences. Majoring in law and minoring in science Juárez would occasionally substitute for the physics professor. Juárez eventually married Margarita Maza.

Ambitious and honest, Juárez ran and was elected municipal alderman. Intensely interested in politics, some years later he became a member of the state and national legislatures, a judge in 1841, and then governor of his state.

Because of his liberal ideas, Juárez was exiled when the conservatives came to power and lived in New Orleans for two years. When the liberals were restored in 1855, Juárez returned to his country and became minister of justice and public instruction. In 1857 Juárez was chosen to preside over the Supreme Court and, according to the constitution, was also vice-president of the country. Through Juárez, the government enacted the law of separation of church and state, guaranteeing religious freedom to all Mexicans.

In 1861 Juárez was elected president. Because of mounting economic problems, Juárez suspended payment on foreign debts and in 1862 England, Spain, and France sent troops to Mexico to protect their investments. Realizing, however, that Napoleon III had installed Archduke Maximilian as Emperor of Mexico, they withdrew their forces. With U.S. diplomatic support Juárez and his supporters waged a guerrilla war against the French, and in 1867 Napoleon withdrew his troops. Juárez was re-elected president in 1871 but died a year later.

Edmund Kean
English Actor

Born in 1789, Edmund Kean was the son of a travelling actress and street peddler named Ann Carey and Edmund Kean a deranged youth who took his own life at the age of twenty-two. During his early years Kean was brought up by his paternal uncle's mistress, Charlotte Tidswell who was a member of the Drury Lane Theatre Company. Tidswell provided Kean with a basic education as well as some stage training.

Tidswell was ambitious for her adopted son but wanted to provide him with an orderly home life. However, Kean resisted and on several occasions returned to his biological mother, who only exploited his talents. Later he was adopted by a well-to-do middle class couple and again Kean ran away, this time because he felt they regarded him as socially inferior. When he was fifteen Kean joined an acting company and in 1808 married Mary Chambers who was part of the same company. They had two sons.

Kean projected his intense personality into the roles he played, making him one of the greatest English tragedians of all time. Kean collapsed on stage during a performance of Othello and died shortly thereafter on May 15, 1833.

Rudyard Kiplinq
English Author

In 1907 Rudyard Kipling was awarded the Nobel Prize for Literature. His foster mother would have doubled over laughing had someone predicted such an absurd turn of events.

Born on December 30, 1865, Kipling had an unhappy childhood. His parents, who were living in India, sent him (then age six) and his sister to a foster home in England where they stayed for five years. Kipling's parents left them one day at the strange house without giving them any previous warning. Kipling's foster experience with the Holloways was a nightmare. Although Captain Holloway showed Kipling some kindness he died not long after the childrens' arrival, and "Aunty Rosa" Holloway beat him. Aided by her teenage son she terrorized young Kipling to the point that he would cower when anyone came near him. Trix, Kipling's sister, however, was openly favored and treated with utmost kindness.

In 1888 Kipling published the story *Baa, Baa Black Sheep,* detailing the horrors of his foster experience. Kipling's parents then sent him to an inexpensive boarding school called the United Services College at Westward Ho which also proved to be a harrowing experience for the sensitive Kipling. These school days were immortalized in his book *Stalky and Co.*

In 1882 Kipling returned to India to work as a journalist. He married Caroline Balestier in 1892. Together they travelled to the United States and settled for a time in Vermont where Caroline owned some property. They would return to England, however, unable to adjust to life in America. In 1894 and '95 he published *The Jungle Books,* and in 1901 his most famous novel *Kim.* Kipling died in London in January, 1936.

John Mercer Langston
Black Leader, Educator, Diplomat

John Mercer Langston is believed to have been the first black ever elected to public office in the United States.

He was born on December 14, 1829 in Virginia and was of black, Indian, and English ancestry. When his father, Ralph Quarles, an estate owner, died, Langston was raised by a friend of his father's in Ohio. Langston attended private schools and graduated from Oberlin College in 1849. He then studied law and was admitted to the Ohio bar in 1854.

Opening up his practice in Brownhelm, Ohio, Langston was elected by the Liberty Party in 1855 to serve as clerk of Brownhelm. Becoming a recruiting agent for blacks during the Civil War, Langston helped form such famous regiments as the 54th and 55th Massachusetts, and the 5th Ohio. (For more information, see *Black Americans in Defense of Their Country,* National Book, 1992.)

In 1864 he helped establish the National Equal Rights League and served as its first president. Following the war, Langston became inspector-general of the Freedmen's Bureau and dean and vice-president of Howard University. In 1877 he served as U.S. Minister to Haiti and charge d'affaires to Santo Domingo. Later he was named president of the Virginia Normal and Collegiate Institute. A Republican, Langston served in Congress from September 1890 to March 1891. Langston's publications include *Freedom and Citizenship* and *From the Virginia Plantation to the National Capital.* He died on November 15, 1897.

(For more information about this individual, see *Black Americans in Congress,* National Book, 1992.)

Robert Laurent
Sculptor

Robert Laurent was born on June 29, 1890 in Concarneau, a fishing village on France's Britanny Coast, to Louis and Yvonne (Fravaal) Laurent. One day the twelve-year old Laurent stopped to watch, fascinated, as Hamilton Easter Field, a visiting American artist, put the finishing touches on a painting. Field was so moved by the boy's interest in art that he talked with Laurent's parents and it was decided that Robert would go to Field's home in the United States where Field provided him with an excellent art education.

In 1908 and 1909 Laurent travelled with Field and Maurice Sterne to Rome and took lessons at the British Academy. After an apprenticeship to the wood carver and framemaker Giuseppe Doratori, Laurent knew what most interested him. In his first exhibits at the Daniel Gallery in 1915 and 1916 and at the Whitney Studio Gallery in 1917, he displayed his wood sculpture. During World War I Laurent served in the United States Naval Aviation Corps at Pensacola, Florida.

Following the Armistice, he returned to France and while visiting Britanny in 1919, met and married Marie Caraes, with whom he later had two sons. Laurent exhibited his work in cities throughout the United States and soon critics began to note a distinctly American style to his sculpture. Laurent taught in various institutions including Vassar College, the Corcoran Gallery in Washington, D.C., the Brooklyn Museum of Art, and at Indiana University. In Paris he exhibited with such important artists as Matisse and Maillol. Laurent was president of the Hamilton Easter Field Art Foundation, a member of the National Sculpture Society, and received many honors and awards including election to the National Institute of Arts and Letters.

Laurent lived with his family in Brooklyn, in the same house where he was raised . . . which Hamilton Field left him upon his death. Laurent enjoyed golf, bowling, and, of course, art collecting. He died on April 20, 1970.

Malcolm X
Militant Black Leader

Malcolm X was born Malcolm Little on May 19, 1925.

Growing up in Lansing Michigan, he watched the Ku Klux Klan set his house on fire and burn it to the ground. Two years later, when Malcolm was six years old, his father, Reverend Earl Little, a fighter for black rights, was murdered.

Following her husband's death, Malcolm's mother was placed in a mental institution and Malcolm and his brothers and sisters were sent to foster homes. Malcolm liked his foster family; but one day, after putting a thumbtack on his teacher's chair, Malcolm was expelled from school and sent to a detention home. Again, Malcolm liked the couple who ran the home and they liked him, but when he was fourteen he went to live in Boston with Ella, his father's daughter from a previous marriage. At sixteen Malcolm went to New York but in 1946 he was put in jail for stealing. It was while in jail that he converted to the Black Muslim faith (Nation of Islam.)

After his release from prison, Malcolm changed his last name to "X" which many Black Muslims did, believing their own last names came originally from white slave masters. Soon Malcolm X became an influential speaker for the Black Muslims. In 1964, however, he formed his own religious organization. After a pilgrimage to Mecca Malcolm concluded that blacks and whites could indeed live together as brothers and sisters.

Tragically, as tensions increased between Malcolm's followers and those of the Black Muslims, Malcolm X was shot to death on February 21, 1965. Three Black Muslims were found guilty of the murder. After his death, in addition to three other daughters, twin daughters were born to his wife, Sister Betty X whom he had married in 1958.

Nelson Mandela
South African Political Leader

On July 18, 1918 Nelson Mandela was born in South Africa, to Chief Henry Gadla and Nonqaphi Mandela, members of the royal family of the Thembu people. In 1930, Mandela's father, who was very ill, realized that he would soon die, and therefore took his son to the Paramount Chief and asked that the boy be given a good education. Mandela thus became the ward of David Dalindyebo and went to live in a hut at the Great Palace, Mqekezweni. The chief provided Mandela with new clothes and sent him to a Methodist boarding school, and later began studies at University College at Fort Hare. As a young man, Mandela was an amateur heavyweight boxer and long-distance runner.

In 1940 Mandela was expelled for participating in a student protest. His guardian, the Paramount Chief, insisted that he give up the protest. Deciding, too, that it was time for Mandela to take a wife, the Chief selected a girl and began the wedding arrangements. Mandela knew that the Paramount Chief loved him very much and wanted him to be his successor as Chief, but Mandela had other ideas. He was going to lead all of his people — all blacks — in the struggle for racial equality in South Africa. Mandela obtained a law degree from the University of South Africa in 1942 and two years later joined the African National Congress. In 1944 Mandela and others formed the Congress Youth League.

Mandela was soon recognized as an outspoken, and, to some, dangerous leader of black rights. In 1964 the South African Supreme Court sentenced Mandela and seven others to life in prison on charges of sabotage and plans to overthrow the government by violent means. On February 11, 1990 Mandela, who had been imprisoned for over twenty-seven years was, at last, released from a maximum security prison. Symbolizing to many the struggle that blacks have endured, Mandela, while visiting the U.S., was hailed with a ticker-tape parade in New York. Mandela's first marriage ended in divorce in 1957. He is married to Winnie Mandela and from both marriages, has four living children.

Harry Martinson
Nobel Prize for Literature

When Harry Martinson — born on May 6, 1904 in the Swedish province of Blekinge — was six years old, his father, a retired sea captain, died. Abandoning her son and six daughters, Martinson's mother left for the United States.

Most of Martinson's childhood was spent in a series of foster homes from which he often ran away. When World War I ended, the teenage Martinson became a ship's cabin boy and between 1920 and 1927 he worked on board fourteen ships. Frequently, Martinson would jump ship at the different ports such as China and South America; his experiences during this time would serve as material for later books. A bout of tuberculosis forced Martinson to leave the sea and soon after he began writing poetry. In 1929 Martinson married the writer Moa Swartz. Publishing *Nomad,* a book of poems, in 1931, Martinson began to establish a reputation for himself as an up-and-coming writer. Later, in 1935 and 1936, Martinson published the novels *Nasslorna blomma* (Flowering Nettle) and *Vaqen ut* (The Way Out) which were based on his childhood.

When the Soviets invaded Finland in 1939, Martinson enlisted in the Swedish Volunteer Corps to aid in the liberation of Finland. However, his health deteriorated and he was forced to leave the military. In 1940 he published *Verklighet till dods* (Realism Unto Death) which is about Europe's struggle against dictatorial forces. He was divorced in 1940.

In 1949 Martinson was elected to the Swedish Academy and in 1959 received an honorary doctorate from the University of Goteborg. These honors are especially amazing in view of the fact that Martinson had no formal schooling. In 1974, along with fellow Swede Eyvind Johnson, Martinson was awarded the 1974 Nobel Prize for Literature. He died in Stockholm at age 73, on February 11, 1978.

Stan Mikita
Hockey Player

The former Chicago Black Hawks Superstar, Stan Mikita, was born Stanislav Gvoth in Sokolce, Czechoslovakia on May 20, 1940 to George and Emelia Gvoth. In 1948, when Czechoslovakia became Communist, Mikita's childless aunt and uncle from Canada, Joe and Anna Mikita, came to visit Sokolce and begged the Gvoths to let them adopt their eight-year-old son. Finally convinced that many more opportunities were available for their son in Canada, the Gvoths agreed and the Mikitas left Czechoslovakia with young Stan and a niece, Irene Gonda whom Mikita regards as his sister. The hockey great says he vividly recalls, as the train pulled away from the station, the terror-filled moment when he first realized that his parents were to be left behind. Only as an adult, with children of his own, does Mikita say he fully appreciates the agonizing decision his parents were forced to make as they struggled to think not of themselves but of his best interest.

Mikita grew up in Southwestern Ontario, finally winning his schoolmates' acceptance by becoming a winner in sports. Signing up with the Black Hawks in 1959, during his first ten seasons Mikita made the first All-Star team six times and the second team once. In the 1966-67 season Mikita made NHL history when he became the first player to win hockey's "Triple Crown," an achievement he repeated the following season. It was Stan Mikita who along with Bobby Hull developed a hockey stick with a curved blade that has been adopted by many NHL players. Mikita has also designed a light weight helmet to reduce serious injuries.

Mikita married Jill Cerny on April 27, 1963 and lives in Elmhurst, a Chicago suburb. Since leaving professional hockey Mikita, who, to develop his powerful arms and wrists would do one hundred push-ups a day, now enjoys another sport — golf.

Marilyn Monroe
Actress

Marilyn Monroe — the world famous beauty and motion picture actress — was born on June 1, 1926 in Los Angeles.

Marilyn Monroe was her stage name; her real name was either Norma Jean Baker or Norma Jean Mortenson. After her mother suffered a mental breakdown and was hospitalized, Monroe spent her childhood in twelve foster homes and stayed at least once in a Los Angeles orphanage. Her education was continuously interrupted as she moved from house to house and she became increasingly confused by the different moral standards she encountered. In order to avoid returning to an orphanage or another foster family, Monroe, at age sixteen, married James Dougherty. During World War II she worked as a parachute inspector and paint sprayer in an aircraft factory.

When her marriage ended in divorce after the war, Monroe turned to modelling to support herself. She made her movie debut in 1948 in *Dangerous Years,* and in 1950 she played a small role in the movie *Asphalt Jungle.* That role was so small that she was not even mentioned in the screen credits, but Twentieth Century Fox received such a deluge of fan mail for Monroe that they gave her a part in the movie *All About Eve* that same year and offered her a seven-year contract.

In 1953 she appeared in the comedy *Gentlemen Prefer Blondes,* and toward the end of 1953 Monroe was bringing in more money for her studio than any other star in Hollywood. Another comedy, *The Seven-Year Itch,* came out in 1954, and she received dramatic success in the 1956 *Bus Stop.* In 1959 she starred with Tony Curtis and Jack Lemmon in the now classic comedy *Some Like It Hot.* In 1961 she again demonstrated her dramatic ability in *The Misfits.*

But in spite of her popularity as a sex symbol, and growing success as a film actress, Marilyn Monroe's personal life was unhappy. Two more failed marriages — to the famous baseball player, Joe DiMaggio (married and divorced in 1954), and writer Arthur Miller (1956 to 1961) — did little to reassure her. She died tragically in 1962 at the age of thirty-six, of an overdose of sleeping pills.

Anthony Newley
Actor, Director, Writer, Singer, Composer

When German bombers pounded London during World War II air raids, many city children were sent to live with foster parents in the British countryside where it was safer. Anthony George Newley, born on September 24, 1931, was among these children. His parents, George Anthony and Frances Grace, who separated when Newley was younger, sent him, and two of his friends to live in Brighton with George Pescud, who had once been a music hall performer.

According to Newley, his stay with Pescud opened up a whole new world for him and influenced the path his future would take. Pascud encouraged Newley to use his imagination and soon Newley had joined the local choir, was acting out plays, and putting out a magazine. When World War II ended, Newley worked for a short time in an insurance office but when he saw an advertisement for a London acting school, he applied. Unable to afford the tuition, he worked his way as an office boy. Newley's big break came after only three weeks, when English film director Geoffrey de Barkus walked in, spotted him, and asked if he would like to play the title role in *The Adventures of Dusty Bates.*

Newley appeared in various other films, but the one which brought him the most acclaim was in his role as the Artful Dodger in *Oliver Twist,* produced in 1951 by United Artists. Then, in 1959, he played a rock n' roll singer in *Idle on Parade* and one of his songs *I've Waited So Long* went to the top of the British charts. From 1960 to 1961 Newley had his own television show. Playing the part of "Littlechap" Newley directed the popular play *Stop the World — I Want to Get Off* which opened both in London and New York, for which Newley and Leslie Bricusse co-authored the book, lyrics, and music. One of the songs from the play, *What Kind of a Fool Am I?,* was recorded in over seventy versions and would allow Newley and Bricusse to live in ease the rest of their lives.

Newley has appeared in forty motion pictures, including *Dr. Doolittle.* He wrote, with Bricusse, the title song for the James Bond movie *Goldfinger,* composed

Candy Man, and the music for *Willie Wonka and the Chocolate Factory.* In 1962 he received a Grammy award, and was named the Male Music Star of the Year in 1972 at the Las Vegas Awards. Twice divorced, Newley is married to Dareth Rich. He has four children.

Gabriel Pascal
Film Director

Born in Transylvania, Hungary, on June 4, 1894, Gabriel Pascal was cared for by Jesuits. But when he was four years old he ran away and joined a band of gypsies. The authorities found him two years later, when he was six. Soon adopted by a wealthy, educated Viennese family, Pascal's life took a sudden turn for the better; he was surrounded by opportunities which would influence his choice of career, such as travels to Italy for summer vacations, where he met the actress Eleanora Duse. At first Pascal was not sure what he wanted to be and his parents enrolled him in the prestigious Military Academy of Vienna. Pascal, however, finally decided he wanted to be a farmer so he went to Berlin to study agriculture. But at age eighteen he joined a stock company in Hamburg. Aided by the well-known tragedienne, Baroness Nordhoff, he later joined the Imperial Theatre Company of Vienna. After a part in the movie *Midnight,* directed by Robert Wiene, Pascal decided to go to New Zealand and try his hand at producing his own documentary film. When World War I broke out, Pascal returned to Hungary and enlisted in the army, fighting on the Eastern Front for four years. After the war Pascal travelled to different countries and finally found backers for his films.

Success was immediate. Two of his movies were sold at three times production costs in Berlin. In 1932 Pascal travelled to the United States with John Sinclair, a member of the Paramount staff. With Sinclair, Pascal formed P. and S. Films, in conjunction with both Paramount and Columbia Pictures. Toward the mid-1930s Pascal decided to realize his dream of making George Bernard Shaw's plays into movies.

Overcoming Shaw's hesitancy, Pascal produced *Pygmalion* in 1938 and shortly thereafter — amid interruptions by Nazi bombers — *Major Barbara* and still other plays by Shaw which were hugely successful. Pascal, who became a British citizen, died on July 6, 1954.

Pierre Esprit Radisson
French Explorer and Fur Trader

Arriving from France in 1651, Pierre Esprit Radisson and his family settled in the little village of Trois-Rivieres (Three Rivers), situated between Montreal and Quebec.

Deciding to go hunting one day, sixteen-year old Radisson and two friends secretly left the safe confines of their village. Radisson's companions were soon ready to return home, but not Radisson. Waving goodbye, he followed the shore of Lake St. Peter. Hours later, he came upon the scalped and bloodied bodies of his friends. Aghast, Radisson watched as suddenly twenty to thirty Mohawk Indians rose from the tall grasses, their faces smeared with war paint. Seizing Radisson's guns, they stripped him naked. Reaching the Indian camp, a woman who had lost three sons on the warpath ran to the warriors, pleading with them to spare young Radisson's life. The elders at last relented and Radisson's overjoyed Indian mother and father prepared a fabulous feast for the adoption ceremony, inviting three hundred Mohawks.

Radisson, who thus acquired a brother and two sisters, was so utterly happy in his new life that he nearly forgot his old one on the St. Lawrence. In spite of opportunities to escape, Radisson stayed with his Indian family. Still, he later travelled to France, returning to Canada with his brother-in-law, Medard Chouart des Grosseilliers. Together they became the first men to explore Lake Superior (near which they discovered copper deposits) to its western boundaries, the first to enter the villages of the fearsome Dakota Sioux, and the first to realize the importance of the beaver trade which led to establishment of the Hudson's Bay Company in 1670.

Radisson had learned much about woodcraft and survival from the Indians and, according to some historians, Radisson and Groseilliers saw the Mississippi River more than ten years before Marquette and Joliet. Both Radisson and Groseilliers served in the French fleet in Guinea and Tobago.

Harold Robbins
Bestselling Novelist

Harold Robbins' *The Carpetbaggers* (1961) is the fourth-most-read book in history. It is estimated that total sales for his books, which have been translated into thirty-nine languages, is over 250,000,000 copies worldwide

Abandoned as a child, Robbins, whose original name was Francis Kane, was born on May 21, 1916 in the Hell's Kitchen area of Manhattan. He never knew his natural parents. Brought up in a Roman Catholic orphanage in New York, Robbins was placed in a number of foster homes until he was adopted in 1927 by a Manhattan pharmacist and his family. Taking the name Harold Rubin, he later legally changed his name to Harold Robbins when he started writing.

Harold dropped out of high school at age fifteen and became an inventory clerk in a grocery store. There he realized that while people were going hungry in some parts of the country, in others crops were rotting. Borrowing $800 he took flying lessons and rented a Waco biplane in which he travelled all over the south buying options on crops which he sold to canning companies and wholesale grocers. At age twenty, Robbins was a millionaire.

But in 1939, figuring that a war would make sugar prices go up, Robbins invested his money in sugar. The Roosevelt administration, however, froze food prices and Robbins went bankrupt.

Determined as ever, Robbins took a job as a shipping clerk with the Universal Pictures Warehouse in New York City. He discovered that the company had been overcharged on different occasions by $30,000. Eventually he became the executive director of budget and financing.

In answer to a challenge, Robbins published his first and favorite book *Never Love a Stranger* in 1948. His most critically acclaimed novel, *A Stone for Danny Fisher* (1952) was made into the 1958 movie *King Creole,* starring Elvis Presley.

Robbins, who has been divorced, is now married to Grace Palermo. He has two children. Robbins owns an 85-foot yacht, a home in Beverly Hills, and a villa on the Riviera.

John Baptist Rossi
Saint

John Baptist Rossi was born in 1698 in the village of Voltaggio, Italy. From their window, a nobleman and his wife spending the summer months in Voltaggio could often see the ten-year-old John Baptist playing and laughing. They became so attached to the boy that they pleaded with John Baptist's parents to allow them to take him with them to their house in Genoa. John Baptist's parents finally agreed. His foster parents were very kind to him and very impressed with John Baptist; so were two Capuchin priests who came to visit his foster parents' home in Genoa. In fact they brought such high praise of the boy's character to his uncle that a cousin, Lorenzo Rossi, a canon of Santa Maria in Cosmedin — asked John Baptist to come to Rome. His foster parents were very sad, but his foster parents knew that there were wonderful opportunities in Rome, and that John Baptist would receive an excellent education at the Roman College. As a student John Baptist frequently went to visit hospitals. He wondered, though, what he could do to help these people more. On March 8, 1721 he was ordained a priest. For forty years he worked in the hospice of St. Galla, providing comfort and advice for all patients.

John Baptist also became very concerned about homeless girls and women, so he opened a house behind the hospice where these women could go. When his cousin, the Canon Lorenzo Rossi died in 1736, his canonry and house went to John Baptist. But he insisted upon giving up the house for those who might need it more and he went to live in an attic. He also taught classes for prison personnel and other state officials. Among the penitents who came to see him was the public hangman. On May 23, 1764 John Baptist Rossi died at the age of sixty-six. He had done so much for others that at his funeral hundreds of people attended. His beatification process was completed by the bull of canonization in 1881.

Jean Jacques Rousseau
French Writer and Philosopher

Jean Jacques Rousseau was born on June 28, 1712 in Geneva, Switzerland. A few days after his birth, his mother — Susanne Bernard Rousseau — died. His father — who alternated between affection and rejection toward the young Jean — made his son feel guilty about his beautiful wife's death and, when Rousseau was ten, his father finally abandoned him. Throughout his life Rousseau suffered from feelings of inferiority and guilt. In 1722 Rousseau, along with his cousin Abraham

Bernard, was sent to live with a minister and his wife named Lambercier. Rousseau's first experience of country living at so young an age probably influenced some of his later theories, including that of the noble savage.

When he returned to Geneva, Rousseau stayed briefly with an uncle before being apprenticed to a lawyer. Deciding Rousseau was not intelligent enough, the lawyer sent him away and he was then apprenticed to Abdel Du Commun, an engraver. Du Commun, however, turned out to be a brutal master, from whom Rousseau fled in 1728. Rousseau then held a variety of jobs in which he either failed or quit.

The turning point for Rousseau came in 1749 when he read about an essay contest sponsored by the Academy of Dijon. He entered and won the prize. Rousseau eventually became one of the most important writers of the Age of Reason. His ideas also influenced the development of the French Revolution and of education and literature. He died on July 2, 1778.

William Tecumseh Sherman
Civil War General

William Tecumseh's father died when Sherman was only nine years old. One of eight children, he was chosen for adoption after his father's death in 1829 by a family friend Thomas Ewing.

Sherman was named after the famous Shawnee Indian chief who, ironically, had also been left fatherless at a young age. The Indian Tecumseh too was adopted — by a Shawnee chief, Blackfish — and grew up with several white foster brothers who had been kidnapped, including, for a brief time, Daniel Boone. Worried that no priest would baptize her adopted son without a Christian name, Mrs. Ewing added the name William

When Sherman turned sixteen, Ewing secured an appointment for him at the West Point Military Academy. After graduating, Sherman went to Florida to fight the Seminole Indians, and in 1850 he married Ellen Ewing, his adoptive father's daughter. Living in Louisiana, when the Civil War began and that state seceded, Sherman went back north. In 1861 he was made a colonel in the U.S. Army and promoted that same year — after the Battle of Bull Run — to the rank of brigadier general. He fought with General Grant at the Battle of Shiloh and, as a major general, in the capture of Vicksburg. In 1864 Sherman was put in command of 100,000 Union soldiers.

Because he engaged in economic warfare as he marched his troops through the south, Sherman is considered the first modern general. Sherman died in February, 1891 in New York City. He was elected to the Hall of Fame in 1905.

Vishwanath Pratap Singh
Prime Minister of India

On December 2, 1989 Vishwanath Pratap Singh was sworn in as India's eighth prime minister. Singh was born on June 25, 1931 in the kingdom of Daiya, a large northern Indian feudal estate, son of the king's second wife. In 1936 his father asked his friend — the childless ruler of the nearby kingdom of Manda — if he would like to adopt one of his five sons. Eagerly, the king, Ram Gopal Singh, adopted the five-year-old boy who was thereafter prohibited all contact with his natural family.

The king provided his adoptive son with an excellent education but suffered from tuberculosis and the boy was largely brought up by a Scottish couple who had been hired to care for him. In 1941 or '42 the king of Manda died and Singh became heir to the throne. But some members of the king's family disputed the boy's right to the estate and throne, while other members battled Singh's natural family for custody. As a result, during the next few years Singh was protected by armed bodyguards, and a judge managed his estate until he came of age. After finishing secondary school, Singh obtained a law degree from Allahabad University.

Becoming involved in the reform movements of the 1950s and '60s, he generously gave much money to the poor. Succeeding his mother as prime minister after her assassination in 1984, Rajiv Gandhi appointed Singh minister of finance. Singh became increasingly concerned over corruption in government posts, and Gandhi eventually transferred the controversial Singh to the Defense Ministry. When he continued his corruption investigations there, Singh was pressured to resign his post on April 11, 1987 and, three months later, he was also expelled from the Congress (I) Party. In answer, Singh established the "People's Movement." Following the 1989 elections, as Singh's popularity grew, Gandhi acknowledged his party's defeat on November 29, and resigned the prime ministership.

Singh has been married to Sita Kumari since 1955. They have two sons, one a banker in New York and the other a doctor residing in England. In his spare time, Prime Minister Singh likes to paint and write poetry.

Robyn Smith
Jockey

Not much is known about Robyn Smith's past or about her natural parents. She spent most of her childhood and all of her high school years in a foster home. Smith was always an excellent athlete despite suffering from asthma. Never failing to believe in her abilities she became one of the first women to break into the traditionally male world of horse racing. Since her debut race in 1969, she was the first woman jockey to win a major stakes race when on March 1, 1973 she rode the horse North Sea to win the $27,450 Paumanok Stakes Race at Aqueduct. Smith has encountered prejudice in her career but she has persevered and proven time and again her physical and mental toughness.

Dame Kiri (Janette) Te Kanawa
Opera Singer

When Charles, Prince of Wales, chose Dame Kiri Te Kanawa to sing at his royal wedding in 1981, over 600,000,000 people watched on television around the world as she sang Handel's *Let the Bright Seraphim*. In 1982 she was made a Dame Commander of the Order of the British Empire.

Born on March 6, 1944 in Gisborne, New Zealand's North Island, the lyric soprano was adopted when she was five weeks old by Tom and Nell Te Kanawa. Like her biological parents, her adoptive father was a Maori and her adoptive mother was of British ancestry. Te Kanawa attended a Roman Catholic girl's college in Auckland. Her first singing teacher was a nun named Sister Mary Leo who was amazed by Te Kanawa's talent.

After leaving school, she won several singing competitions in New Zealand and Australia and in 1966, with the prize money, went to study at the London Opera Center. At first she was unhappy there but later met the Hungarian Vera Rosza who helped shape her singing career and remains a strong influence in Te Kanawa's professional life today. After various appearances at the Royal Opera House in London, in 1971 she sang at Covent Garden where she enjoyed her first major success as the Countess in Mozart's *Le Nozze di Figaro*. Today the critically acclaimed Te Kanawa is in demand all over the world. In her spare time, she likes to play golf. Married, she has two adopted children.

Giovanni Battista Tiepolo
Italian Painter

Modern critics of art place Giovanni Battista Tiepolo along side the greatest painters of all time. Tiepolo was born on March 5, 1696 in Venice. When he was but a year old his father died and his mother entrusted him to the painter Gregorio Lazzarini who taught young Tiepolo all he knew about painting.

Tiepolo's first public work was "The Sacrifice of Isaac" for the church of Sta. Maria dei Derelitti in 1716. Soon after, he married Cecilia Guardi who bore him nine children. By the 1730s, Tiepolo's fame as an artist had spread outside of Venice. He was asked, in 1731, to decorate the Palazzo Archinto in Milan. Tragically, bombers destroyed the Palazzo during World War II. In 1750 Tiepolo and his two sons Giovanni Domenico and Lorenzo — who were also painters — decorated several rooms of the Residenz in Wurzburg. Some of Tiepolo's masterpieces include *The Crucifixation, Adoration of the Magi,* and *Apotheosis of the Pisani Family.*

Tiepolo died in Madrid on March 27, 1770, just a few years after the king of Spain, Carlos III, had asked him to decorate the royal palace.

Leo Tolstoy
Russian Novelist

Leo Tolstoy was born the fourth of five children on September 9, 1828 (or August 28, by the calendar used then) to Nikolai and Marya Tolstoy, on the family estate called Yasnaya Polyana. When he was two years old, his mother died. His father's second cousin, Aunt Tatyana came to take care of the children, becoming a positive influence in Tolstoy's childhood. The second most important influence in his life was his older brother Nikolai. When he was nine years old, their father died suddenly and the children were sent to live with their grandmother and then with an aunt, Alexandra Osten-Saken who became their legal guardian. When she too died, the Tolstoy children were sent to live with yet another aunt, Pelageya Yushkov.

Unsurprisingly, an awareness of death dominates much of Tolstoy's writing. In 1843 Tolstoy entered Kazan University but left in 1847 without graduating. Accompanying his brother Nikolai, Tolstoy joined the 4th Battery of the 20th

Artillery Brigade serving on the Terek River and later in the Crimean War. In 1852 Tolstoy submitted his first work, *Childhood,* which was very well received. In 1856 Tolstoy left the military as a lieutenant and returned to Yasnaya Polyana where he established a school for peasant children. In 1862 he married Sofya Andreyevna Behrs and they had thirteen children. According to their son Ilya, his mother copied out the complete text of *War and Peace* seven times for her husband. Other well-known classics by Tolstoy include *Anna Karenina* and *The Death of Ivan Ilyich.* On November 9, 1910, while on a trip with his daughter Alexandra, Tolstoy died in the home of the stationmaster of a small depot at Astapovo.

Francois Truffaut
French Film Critic and Director

Francois Truffaut was born on February 6, 1932, the son of a Parisian architect and his wife Janine de Monferrand, both of whom were sports enthusiasts.

Disappointed in their frail child, they shunted him aside, and he went to live with his grandmother until he was eight years old. Neglected by his parents, Francois was extremely lonely until he turned eleven — and discovered the world of movies.

When he was fourteen, Francois left school and held a variety of menial jobs. He also operated his own movie club, stealing copper doorknobs and reselling then in order to keep his club going. When he was sent to a reformatory, journalist and critic Andre Bazin entered his life. Bazin took him to live with him and his wife and ultimately straightened him out. When Truffaut, as a conscientious objector, was imprisoned by the military in 1953, it was again Bazin who came to the rescue. Bazin found the young Truffaut a job as a film critic for the magazine *Cahiers du Cinema* and later for *Arts.*

Truffaut's first feature-length movie *The 400 Blows* grew out of a challenge issued by his father-in-law, successful movie producer Ignace Morgenstern. For years, even after his marriage to Morgenstern's daughter, film critic Truffaut severely criticized Morgenstern's movies. Exasperated, Morgenstern finally told Truffaut that he would financially back him if he thought he could make a better film.

Largely autobiographical, *The 400 Blows,* was a resounding success receiving twelve international awards. Francois Truffaut is considered one of the most brilliant of French film directors. He died on October 21, 1984 in Neuilly-Sur-Seine.

Maxime Weygand
Commander-in-chief of Allied Armies

Maxime Weygand was born in Brussels, Belgium on January 21, 1867 above Waterloo Tavern. There is some mystery concerning Weygand's parentage. Brought up by the childless Empress Charlotte on her Belgian estate, it is believed that his natural mother was a German from the Saar district. Later it was rumored that Weygand was perhaps of royal or Napoleonic descent.

He was sent to Lycee Louis-le-Grand, a preparatory school, and then by Leopold II of Belgium to St. Cyr, a French training school for officers, where Weygand demonstrated outstanding ability in mathematics. Graduating in 1888 with high honors, Weygand studied and then taught at the Cavalry School at Saumur.

During World War I he was chief of staff under General Foch. Between World War I and II, Weygand, who was made a lieutenant general in 1918, held many important posts including vice-president of the Superior War Council of France and Inspector General of the Army (1931-35).

In 1935 he retired at the age of sixty-eight. On May 20, 1940, however, Weygand was reactivated to replace General Gamelin as commander-in-chief of the Allied Armies . . . but France was already overrun by German troops. Thus Weygand again retired in December 1941. But after the Allied invasion of North Africa in 1942, he flew to Algiers, where he was captured by the Germans and imprisoned in an Austrian castle. Weygand was freed by U.S. troops on May 5, 1945. Weygand married Renee de Forsanz in 1900. They used to enjoy, from time to time, feasts of his favorite food, corn on the cob. He died on January 28, 1965, in Paris.

Flip Wilson
Comedian

When he was five years old Flip Wilson's mother deserted her family, leaving her janitor husband to care for their numerous children. Born Clerow Wilson, on December 8, 1933, he changed his name to Flip when a fellow cook in the Air Force told Wilson, as he entertained the men in the mess hall, that he had "flipped his lid."

Growing up, Wilson lived in a poor Jersey City neighborhood. His father, unable to keep the family together, placed his children in foster homes. Repeatedly running away from his foster family — in the hope of joining his brother who had been sent to reform school at Whitesboro, New Jersey — the seven-year-old Wilson finally got his wish.

At Whitesboro, Wilson was given clean clothes and ate so much he was nicknamed "Tin Can." One of the guards would save his dessert each night to give to Wilson, and one of the teachers, Mrs. Jones, made him feel intelligent and special. Wilson actually enjoyed reform school and made phony escape attempts to prolong his stay. When he did leave, Wilson was again placed in Jersey City foster homes. Often he snuck into the Mosque Theatre to watch the vaudeville stars perform, becoming fascinated by the comedians. Skinny as a child, Wilson learned to use his sense of humor rather than his fists against bullies.

Dropping out of high school at sixteen, Wilson joined the Air Force in 1949 by convincing the recruiter that he was eighteen. Soon Wilson was ordered to travel from base to base and lift morale with his comic routines. After leaving the Air Force in 1954, Wilson became a bellhop and part-time comedian. But in 1959, a man named Herbie Shul offered him $50 a week for a year so that he could improve his style. Wilson began performing regularly at the Apollo in Harlem and by 1965 was making appearances on the *Tonight Show*. In the early 70s he had his own television show and fast became one of the most popular comedians of the decade.

Wilson has served as national president of the American Cancer Society. Divorced, with four children, Wilson's favorite pastimes include golf and going for long rides in the California desert in his blue Rolls Royce.

FOSTER & ADOPTED CHILDREN IN FICTION

There have also been many occurrences of foster or adopted children in fiction, often in books, sometimes in movies. Below are a few of these, listed by author and title

Louisa May Alcott
Little Men

Life in that delightfully different school, Plumfield, and the joys and tears of the family of boys who live there with Mr. and Mrs. Bhaer, Daisy and Nan.

Mildred Ames
Foster Home

When his father dies and his mother cannot keep him, an eleven-year-old boy is placed in a foster home. The book tells the story of the boy's loneliness, his slow acceptance of the new situation, and the happiness he finds with his new family.

Frank Baum
The Wizard Of Oz

The magical adventures of a girl who lives with her aunt and uncle in Kansas. Dorothy enters Oz, a land of make-believe, with witches and wizards, where scarecrows and tin men come alive and where a cowardly lion looks for courage. (Also made into a wonderful movie classic starring Judy Garland.)

Anne Bernays
Growing Up Rich

Sally, fourteen, is placed in the house of her guardian when her mother and stepfather are killed in a plane crash. Used to luxury and elegance, she must now live in a completely different environment, but Sally and her guardian grow to respect and love one another.

Rose Blue
Seven Years From Home

Eleven-year-old Mark Cranston feels loved and wanted by his adoptive parents, but his dream is to search for his biological parents. Mark must learn to accept the love of his adoptive parents and to forget an impossible dream.

David Budbill
Bones On Black Spruce Mountain

Daniel, an adopted orphan, and his friend Seth spend five days in the mountains looking for clues about a boy who ran away from a foster home seventy-five years before. The two friends are determined to solve the mystery. While doing so, Daniel realizes that not only adopted boys feel lonely and unwanted at times.

Frances Hodgson Burnett
The Secret Garden

When orphaned Mary Lennox must go to live with her uncle she is furious. In Misselthwaite Manor Mary discovers mysterious secrets, and a cousin who believes himself an invalid. Mary knows that she can help him . . . or can she?

Betsy Cromer Byars
The Pinballs

Three lonely and unrelated children come to live in the home of Mr. and Mrs. Mason. With the love and support of their new parents, the children realize that they are valued for themselves and that they can have good lives no matter what their origins were.

Helen Fern Daringer
Adopted Jane

Jane Douglas lives in the Ballard Memorial Home. She feels unwanted until one summer when not one but *two* families invite her to their homes and then want her to become part of their families. Jane must decide which family *she* will adopt.

Charles Dickens
David Copperfield

David is orphaned early in life. When his stepfather sends him to work in London, little David finds the situation unbearable and runs away to his great-aunt Betsy, whom he has never seen. Aunt Betsy turns out to be quite a character; she faces up to David's stepfather and decides to adopt the boy. This is only the beginning of the many happenings in this classic novel.

Judith Guest
Second Heaven

Gale, a teenager, runs away to the home of Cat Holtzman, a divorced woman who shelters her. This book shows good people who care and help each other.

Nan Hayden
Joe Bean

Joe Bean is an eleven-year-old boy who gets into scrape after scrape. Then Mr. Tipper takes the boy for the summer and Joe finds a friend and a home.

Roberta Hughey
Radio City

When the aunt and uncle with whom she lives adopt two babies, fourteen-year-old Casey decides to go to New York City to find her own father. Although she does find him — and he is as she had pictured him in her dreams — her father does not want to keep her permanently. Casey discovers the meaning of love as she returns to her one true family.

Louis L'Amour
Reilly's Luck

Reilly, a tough gambler with a big heart finds a six-year-old boy abandoned by an uncaring mother, saves his life, and takes care of him. Travelling throughout the West, Val learns to deal with crooked gamblers, Indians, people, and life. They even travel to Europe, where they escape from people who don't wish Reilly to marry the woman he loves. Later, when his foster father is killed by those people, Val must make it alone. He helps a family start a cattle ranch, travels East, where he studies law, and returns West to find love and a family for himself, all the time trying to find the people who killed his foster father.

Rutgers Van der Loeff
Children On The Oregon Trail

The adventures of thirteen-year-old John Sager, who loses his parents while travelling to Oregon. When the rest of the wagon train decides to take the easier route — to California — John and his six brothers and sisters strike out alone for Oregon, to fulfill their father's dream. In Oregon they are adopted by Dr. Whitman and his wife.

George Eliot
Silas Marner

The tale of a disillusioned recluse who is brought back to the society of his fellow men by a little baby girl who one day appeared at his hearth and whom be adopts as his very own.

Lucy Maud Montgomery
Anne Of Green Gables

An eleven-year-old girl is sent to live with a foster family, a middle-aged brother and sister. Anne must win a place in their hearts. Her many adventures and misadventures and the warm ending make delightful reading. (Also the basis for a movie and Disney Channel series.)

Thomas Meehan
Annie

A heart-warming tale of the little orphan girl adopted by a millionaire. (Also the basis for a musical movie.)

Eleanor Porter
Pollyanna

A little orphan girl with a big heart conquers her cold aunt and a whole town in spite of the great odds against her.

Jim Razzi (adapter)
Pinoccio

The delightful story of a puppet who wins the right to be a real boy and of the father who carves him out of wood and adopts him forever.

Ovida Sebestyen
Far From Home

Now that his mother is dead, a boy needs a home and must search for the father who never acknowledged him. Will the boy find his father and will both of them find the meaning of love?

Roberta Silman
Somebody Else's Child

Peter, a fourth grader, is a happy adopted child. One day a bus driver mentions that he would not want somebody else's child. Peter eventually understands that caring and loving a child is what makes him the parents' very own.

Mark Twain
Tom Sawyer

The unforgettable and hilarious adventures of a boy growing up along the Mississippi River in the South, with his Aunt Polly and best friend Huckleberry Finn.

Jean Webster
Daddy Long Legs

An orphan girl is sent to college by a rich, anonymous benefactor, to whom she must write letters periodically.

The book relates Judy's adventures in the asylum and in college, and has a charming twist at the end. (Also the basis for a charming musical movie starring Fred Astaire and Leslie Caron.)

T. H. White
The Once And Future King

The story of Arthur, given to Merlin the magician upon his birth and brought up by Sir Ector, far away from his father's court. His adventures transport the reader to a magical time in England and to places where dreams come true.

AFTERWORD

Did we say it is best not to look back too much? We have to confess that in compiling this book it has been difficult *not* to look back . . . at all the other adopted or foster people — including other leaders such as Bo Diddley, Art Linkletter, Harold Brodkey, J.R.R. Tolkien, Christoph Eschenback, and so many others — crowding around the computer to have their life stories recounted once again. We hope in this book it has become evident what caring for others more than for ourselves can accomplish. The message these famous people have sent to the world is clear and simple: believe in yourself, work hard, and remember you *are someone's* dream. The future is yours, but only if you take it and *make* it yours.

BIBLIOGRAPHY

Amacher, Richard E. *Edward Albee.* New York: Twayne Publishers Inc., 1969.

Beacham, Walton, Ed. *Research Guide to Biography and Criticism,* v. 1. Washington D.C.: Research Publishing Co., 1985.

Benson, Mary. *Nelson Mandela.* Vermont: David and Charles Inc. 1986.

Bigsby, C. W. E. *Edward Albee.* Englewood Cliffs, New Jersey: Prentice Hall, Inc., 1975.

Blancke, W. Wendell. *Juárez of Mexico.* New York: Praeger Publishers, 1971.

Block, Maxine. *Current Biography.* New York: The H.W. Wilson Co., 1940.

Block, Maxine. *Current Biography.* New York: The H.W. Wilson Co., 1942.

Borland, Kathryn and Helen Speicher. *Phillis Wheatley.* New York: Bobbs-Merril, 1968.

Braun, Thomas. *On Stage Flip Wilson.* Minnesota: Creative Educational Society, Inc., 1976.

Burner, David. *Herbert Hoover, A Public Life.* New York: Alfred A. Knopf, 1979.

Camar, Howard,. Ed. *The American West.* New York: Thomas Y. Crowell, Co., 1977.

Carmer, Carl, Ed. *A Cavalcade of Young Americans.* New York: Lothrop, Lee and Shepard Co. Inc., 1958.

Cayne, Bernard, Churchill, James, et al. *The Americana Annual.* Danbury, Conn.: Grolier Inc., 1989.

Cayne, Bernard, Churchill, James, et al. *The Americana Annual.* Danbury, Conn.: Grolier Inc., 1990.

Christiansen, Rupert. *Prima Donna.* New York: Viking Penguin Inc., 1985.

Clarke, Mary and Clement Crisp. *Ballet.* New York: Universe Books, 1973.

Cochran, Jacqueline. *The Stars at Noon.* Boston: Little Brown and Co., 1954.

Cohen, Daniel. *Sir Henry Morton Stanley and the Quest for the Source of the Nile.* New York Evans/Dutton, 1985.

Coleman, Ray. *Lennon.* New York: McGraw-Hill Book Co., 1984.

Davis, Burke. *They Called Him Stonewall.* New York: Holt Rinehart and Winston, 1954.

Day, Grove. *James Albert Michener.* New York: Twayne Publishers, 1964.

Dukore, Bernard, Ed. *Encyclopedia of World Drama,* v. 1. New York: McGraw-Hill Inc., 1972.

Eggenberger, David, Ed. *The McGraw-Hill Encyclopedia of World Biography*, vols. 1, 10. New York: McGraw-Hill Book Co., 1973.

Faber, Doris. *I Will Be Heard, The Life of William Lloyd Garrison*. New York: Lothrop, Lee, and Shepard Co., 1970.

Field Enterprises, Inc. *The World Book Encyclopedia*, v. 16. Chicago: Field Enterprises Educational Corporation, 1977.

Flexner, James Thomas. *The Young Hamilton*. Boston: Little Brown and Co., 1978.

Flink, Steve. *World Tennis*. "Goolagong Stands Alone." July, 1988.

Fritz, Jean. *Stonewall*. New York: G. P. Putnam's Sons, 1979.

Garraty, John, A. and Edward James, Eds. *Dictionary of American Biography*, Supplement four, 1946-50. New York: Charles Scribner's Sons, 1974.

Goetz, Philip, Ed. *The New Encyclopedia Britannica*, v. 9, Chicago: Encyclopedia Britannica Inc., 1986.

Goetz, Philip, Ed. *The New Encyclopedias Britannica*. Chicago, Illinois: Encyclopedia Britannica Inc., 1990.

Goodman, Michael Harris. *The Last Dalai Lama*. Boston: Shambhala Publications Inc., 1986.

Goolagong, Evonne. *Evonne! On the Move*. New York: E. P. Dutton, 1975.

Graham, Shirley. *The Story of Phillis Wheatley*. New York: Julian Messner, 1949.

Graves, Charles, P. *Eleanor Roosevelt First Lady of the World*. Champaign, Illinois: Ganard Publishing Co., 1966.

Guiles, Fred. *Legend: The Life and Death of Marilyn Monroe*. New York: Stein and Day Publishers, 1980.

Hammond, J. R. *An Edgar Allan Poe Companion*. New Jersey: Barnes and Mobile Books, 1981.

Harte, Barbara and Carolyn Riley. *Contemporary Authors*, vols 5-8. Detroit, Michigan: Gale Research Co., 1969.

Haskins, James, S. *Malcolm X*. New York: Franklin Watts Inc., 1975.

Hayes, John P. *James Michener, A Biography*. New York: The Bobbs-Merrill Company, 1984.

Haylett, John and Richard Evans. *The Illustrated Encyclopedia of world Tennis*. New York: Exeter Books, 1989.

Herda, D.J. *Free Spirit: Evonne Goolagong*. Milwaukee, Wisconsin: Raintree Editions, 1976.

Holt, Rackham. *George Washington Carver*. New York: Doubleday and Co., 1963.

Jacobs, William Jay. *Eleanor Roosevelt, A Life of Happiness and Tears*. New York: Coward-McCann, Inc., 1983.

Jeal, Tim. *Livingstone*. New York: G.P. Putnam's Sons, 1973.

Jones, Roger. *The Rescue of Emin Pasha*. New York: St. Martin's Press, 1972.

Kaufmann, Helen. *The Story of Haydn*. New York: Grosset and Dunlap, 1962.

Klein, Leonard, Ed. *Encyclopedia of World Literature in the Twentieth Century*, v. 1. New York: Frederick Ungar Publishing Co., 1981.

Larson, Norita. *Langston Hughes, Poet of Harlem.* Minnesota: Creative Education, Inc., 1981.

Lee, John and Susan. *John Hancock.* Chicago: Children's Press, 1974.

Leonard, Hugh. *Da.* New York: Atheneum, 1973.

Leonard, Hugh. *Home Before Night.* New York: Atheneum, 1980.

Lichtenstein, Grace. *A Long Way Baby.* New York: William Morrow and Co. Inc., 1974.

Lincoln, W., Bruce. *The Romanovs.* New York: The Dial Press, 1967.

Lynn, Carole. *John Lennon.* Corbin, New York: Franklin Watts, 1982.

Magill, Frank N., Ed. *Cyclopedia of World Authors.* Englewood Cliffs, New Jersey: Salem Press Inc., 1974.

Magill, Frank N., Ed. *Great Lives from History,* v. 1. Pasadena, California: Salem Press, 1988.

Marquis Who's Who, *Who's Who in America,* v. 1, 1988-89. Illinois: MacMillan Inc., 1989.

Marquis Who's Who, Inc. *Who Was Who,* v. 5, 1969-73. Chicago: Illinois: Marquis Who's Who, 1973.

May, Hal and James Lesniak, Eds. *Contemporary Authors.* Detroit, Michigan: Gale Research Inc., 1989.

McKeon, Richard, Ed. *Introduction to Aristotle.* New York: Random House, 1947.

McMurry, Linda. *George Washington Carver: Scientist and Symbol.* Oxford: Oxford University Press, 1981.

Mason, Philip. *Kipling, The Glass, The Shadow.* New York: Harper and Row Publishers, 1975.

Milton, Joyce. *Greg Louganis: Diving for Gold.* New York: Random House, 1988.

Moritz, Charles, Ed. *Current Biography.* New York: The H.W. Wilson Co., 1959.

Moritz, Charles, Ed. *Current Biography.* New York: The H.W. Wilson Co., 1965.

Moritz, Charles, Ed. *Current Biography.* New York: The H.W. Wilson Co., 1969.

Moritz, Charles, Ed. *Current Biography.* New York: The H.W. Wilson Co., 1970.

Moritz, Charles, Ed. *Current Biography.* New York: The H.W. Wilson Co., 1980.

Moritz, Charles, Ed. *Current Biography.* New York: The H.W. Wilson Co., 1981.

Moritz, Charles, Ed. *Current Biography.* New York: The H.W. Wilson Co., 1983.

Moritz, Charles, Ed. *Current Biography.* New York: The H.W. Wilson Co., 1984.

Moritz, Charles, Ed. *Current Biography.* New York: The H.W. Wilson Co., 1985.

Moritz, Charles, Ed. *Current Biography.* New York: The H.W. Wilson Co., 1987.

Moritz, Charles, Ed. *Current Biography.* New York: The H.W. Wilson Co., 1990.

Murray, Marian. *Plant Wizard: The Life of Lue Gim Gong.* London Collier-Macmillan, 1970.

Morse, Charles and Ann. *Evonne Goolagong.* Mankato, Minnesota: Minecus Street, 1974.

Nolan, Jeannette C. *John Hancock Friend of Freedom.* Boston: Houghton Mifflin, Co., 1966.

North, Sterling. *Captured by the Mohawks*. Massachusetts: The Riverside Press, 1960.

Palmer, Alan. *Who's Who in Modern History, 1860-1980*. New York: Holt, Rinehart and Winston, 1980.

Palmer, Jim. *Jim Palmer's Way to Fitness*. New York: Harper and Row Publishers, 1985.

Patterson, Lillie. *Sure Hands, Strong Heart*. Nashville: Abingdon, 1981.

Pearlman, Moshe. *Moses*. New York: Abelard-Schuman, 1973.

Perry, Margaret. *A Bio-Bibliography of Countée Cullen. 1903-1946*. Westport, Conn.: Greenwood Publishing Co., 1971.

Ploski, Harry, and James Williams, Eds. *The Afro-American*. New York: John Wiley and Sons, 1983.

Rachleff, Owen, S. *Bible Stories*, v. 1. New York Abradle Press, 1971.

Randall, John Herman. *The Career of Philosophy*, v. 1. New York Columbia University Press, 1962.

Reichler, Joseph. *The Great All-Time Baseball Record Book*. New York: Macmillan Publishing Co. Inc., 1981.

Richmond, Merle. *Phillis Wheatley*. New York: Chelsea House, 1988.

Rollins, Charlemae. *Black Troubadour*. Chicago: Rand McNally and Co., 1970.

Roosevelt, Eleanor. *On My Own The Years Since the White House*. New York: Harper and Brothers Publishers, 1958.

Rosen, Elliot A. *Hoover, Roosevelt and the Brains Trust*. New York: Columbia University Press, 1977.

Rothe, Anna, Ed. *Current Biography*. New York: The H.W. Wilson Co., 1945.

Roudane, Matthew. *Understanding Edward Albee*. South Carolina: University of South Carolina Press, 1987.

Seaver, Tom. *The Art of Pitching*. New York: Hearst Books, 1984.

Solt, Andrew and Sam Egan. *Imagine John Lennon*. New York: Macmillan Publishing Co., 1988.

Stanley, Henry, M. *In Darkest Africa*, vols 1, 2. New York: Charles Scribner's Sons, 1890.

Steere, Michael. *Scott Hamilton*. New York: St. Martin's Press, 1985.

Steinem, Gloria. *Marilyn*. New York: Henry Holt and Co., 1986.

Stern, Van Doren Phillip. *Edgar Allan Poe: Visitor from the Night of Time*. New York: Thomas Y. Crowell Co., 1973.

Symons, Julian. *The Tell-Tale Heart*. New York: Harper and Row Publishers, 1978.

Thacher, Alida M. *Raising a Racket: Rosie Casals*. Milwaukee, Wisconsin: Raintree Publishers, 1976.

Therese, Marie, Sister. R.S.M. *Catherine McCauley Foundress of the Sisters of Mercy*. New York: The Declan X. McMulle Co., 1947.

Thomas, John L. *The Liberator: William Lloyd Garrison*. Boston: Little Brown and Co., 1963.

Thomas, R. David. *Dave's Way*. New York: G. P. Putnam's Sons, 1991.

Towne, Peter, *George Washington Carver.* New York: Thomas Y. Crowell Co., 1975.

Trapp, Maria August. *Around the Year with the Trapp Family.* New York: Pantheon Books, Inc., 1955.

Trapp, Maria, von. *Maria.* Carol Stream, Illinois Creation House, 1972.

Trapp, Maria Augusta. *The Story of the Trapp Family Singers.* New York: Dell Publishing Co., 1949.

Wallace, Edgar. *Novelas de Acción.* Madrid: Aguilar S.A., 1968.

Walsh, Michael. *Butler's Lives of the Saints.* San Francisco: Harper and Row. 1985.

Wasson, Tyler. *Nobel Prize Winners.* New York: The H.W. Wilson Co., 1987.

Webb, Robert N. *Jean Jacques Rousseau.* New York: Franklin Watts, Inc. 1970.

Wheeler, Richard. *We Knew Stonewall Jackson.* New York: Thomas Y. Crowell Co., 1977.

Wise, William. *Alexander Hamilton.* New York: G.P. Putnam's Sons, 1963.

Wootton, Richard. *John Lennon.* New York: Random House, 1984.

United States History Society, Inc. *People Who Made America,* vols. 1, 4, 12. Skokie: Illinois, 1973.

Yost, Edna. *Modern Americans in Science and Technology.* New York: Dodd, Mead, and Co., 1962.

To order additional copies of this book, or the others below

Black Inventors of America, McKinley Burt Jr., copyright 1969,1989, ISBN 0-89420-095-X, stock # 296959, $11.95

Black Scientists of America, Richard X. Donovan, copyright 1990, ISBN 0-89420-265-0, stock # 297000, $10.95

Black Musicians of America, Richard X. Donovan, copyright 1991, ISBN 0-89420-271-5, stock # 297059, $13.95

Black Americans in Defense of their Nation, Mark R. Salser, copyright 1991, ISBN 0-89420-272-3, stock # 297130, $15.95

Black Americans in Congress, Mark R. Salser, copyright 1991, ISBN 0-89420-273-1, stock # 297150, $14.95

House for Sale!, M. Luisa Michael, copyright 1992, ISBN 0-89420-282-0, stock #344044, $17.95. A Halcyon House book. Mismanagement, special privileges, and other misdeeds in the U.S. House of Representatives.

Check or Money Order:
Include $2 for postage ($3 for UPS delivery, no PO Boxes)

VISA, MasterCard, American Express, or Discover:
Call (800) 827-2499 to order

Purchase orders:
accepted from Libraries, other Educational Institutions, and qualified re-sellers

available from:

National Book Company
PO Box 8795
Portland OR 97207-8795